Library of
Davidson College

Chicago School Architects
and Their Critics

Studies in the Fine Arts: Architecture, No. 1

Stephen C. Foster, Series Editor
Associate Professor of Art History
University of Iowa

Other Titles in This Series

No. 2	*The Concept of Function in Twentieth-Century Architectural Criticism*	Larry L. Ligo
No. 3	*French Iron Architecture*	Frances H. Steiner
No. 4	*Michel de Klerk, 1884–1923: An Architect of the Amsterdam School*	Suzanne S. Frank
No. 6	*Architectural Competitions in Nineteenth-Century England*	Joan Bassin
No. 7	*Science Plus Sentiment: César Daly's Formula for Modern Architecture*	Richard Bechcrer
No. 8	*The Development of the American Modern Style*	Deborah Frances Pokinski
No. 10	*Business Architectural Imagery in America, 1870–1930*	Kenneth Gibbs

Chicago School Architects and Their Critics

by
Wichit Charernbhak

UMI RESEARCH PRESS
Ann Arbor, Michigan

Copyright © 1981, 1978
Wichit Charernbhak
All rights reserved

Produced and distributed by
UMI Research Press
an imprint of
University Microfilms International
Ann Arbor, Michigan 48106

Library of Congress Cataloging in Publication Data

Wichit Charernbhak.
  Chicago school architects and their critics.

  (Studies in the fine arts. Architecture ; no. 1)
  Revision of thesis (Ph.D.)–University of Michigan, 1978, published under title: Architectural criticism as reflected in publication on Chicago commercial architecture in the 1880s and 1890s.
  Bibliography: p.
  Includes index.
  1. Chicago school of architecture (Movement) 2. Architecture, Modern–19th century–Middle West. I. Wichit Charernbhak. Architectural criticism as reflected in publication on Chicago commercial architecture in the 1880s and 1890s. II. Title. III. Series.

NA722.W53 1984   725'.2'0977311   83-24299
ISBN 0-8357-1537-X

To my mother, Siri, whose sacrifices since my birth have helped to make me who I am today; and to Poranie, my wife, whose patience and understanding during our long years of being apart while I was pursuing my study in this country have given me courage and will to go on to get the job done.

Every problem of whatsoever name or nature contains and suggests its own solution; and the solution reached is invariably found to be simple in nature, basic and clearly allied to common sense.

Louis Henry Sullivan

Contents

List of Illustrations   *xi*

Preface   *xiii*

1   Introduction   *1*

2   Architectural Criticism   *9*

3   The Critics and the Publication   *25*

4   Chicago   *47*

5   Chicago Commercial Architecture   *61*

6   Adler and Sullivan   *87*

7   Burnham and Root   *121*

8   Conclusion   *149*

Illustrations   *171*

Notes   *185*

Bibliography   *199*

Index   *211*

List of Illustrations

Following page 168

1. Home Insurance Building, 1884-85, by William Le Baron Jenney
2. First Leiter Building, 1879, by William Le Baron Jenney
3. Marshall Field Wholesale Store, 1887, by Henry Hobson Richardson
4. Auditorium Building, 1887-89, by Adler and Sullivan
5. Garrick (originally Schiller) Theater, 1891-92, by Adler and Sullivan
6. Stock Exchange Building, 1893-94, by Adler and Sullivan
7. Wainwright Building, 1890-91, by Adler and Sullivan
8. Guaranty (now Prudential) Building, 1894-95, by Adler and Sullivan
9. Carson, Pirie and Scott (originally Schlesinger and Mayor) Store, 1899, 1903-4, by Sullivan and Company
10. Montauk Building, 1881-82, by Burnham and Root
11. The Rookery, 1884-86, by Burnham and Root
12. Monadnock Building, 1889-91, by Burnham and Root
13. Reliance Building, 1894-95, by D.H. Burnham and Company
14. Railways Exchange Building, 1903-4, by D.H. Burnham and Company

Preface

The title of this book is "Chicago School Architects and Their Critics." Therefore, the main sources of information are architectural writings from various forms of publications particularly from periodicals, journals, and magazines, architectural or otherwise. It has been the intention of the writer from the beginning, in keeping in line with the object of the study, that each source of information quoted be identified immediately before or after the quotation, even though as a common practice its identification also appears in the footnote. While mention of the "who," the "where," the "when," and the "which" that accompany the quoted passage at times may seem to encumber the text, such references are indispensable to discussion. The reader is asked to indulge this practice as a peculiarity intrinsic to this study.

Equally peculiar to this study is the fact that quoted passages from the writings and critiques of various architectural writers and critics are more numerous and, in most cases, longer than is normally deemed judicious. The writer feels that in order both to avoid fragmenting the quoted sources and preserve the context, the continuity and the impact of each quotation, long citations are necessary. My principal object has been, through words uttered in the period itself, to recapture the substance and spirit of a unique yet germinal moment in the history of architectural thinking. From beginning to end, great effort has been expended to relate the sentences, the paragraphs, and the chapters so as to constitute an organic whole. If this is mostly successful, long quoted passages are, in part, responsible.

It was several years ago when I was a young student studying for a Bachelor of Architecture degree at Chulalongkorn University in Bangkok, Thailand that I first became aware of the architecture of the late nineteenth century in Chicago. Louis Sullivan and Frank Lloyd Wright were then everybody's heroes. Through a few courses in the history of Western architecture, I was awakened to an appreciation of the concept and philosophy of the Chicago School. Yet, it was not until my inital sojourn in the United States when I came here to pursue graduate studies in architecture and fine arts first, from 1962 to 1964 at the University of Illinois and then, from 1965 to 1967 at Michigan State University that I became fascinated with the School, its architects and its ideals. When the opportunity presented itself for me to return to the United States in 1973 for further study in the field of the history of art, I was determined to make the Chicago School of Architecture my special object of investigation. Throughout this study my fascination with the subject has remained unabated. It is a study that represents the culmination of my intense and enduring interest in the theory, concept and philosophy of the Chicago School. Ever since I was a young architecture student in my native country, I had come to believe that the principles that lay behind those tall commercial buildings in Chicago in the 1880s and 1890s were the important initial steps towards modern architecture not only for this country, but for the world as well. This belief has been firmly reinforced through first-hand experiences gained in the research for and the writing of this study.

In the course of undertaking this study, many people have been helpful and I am grateful to all. Notable among these kind individuals is Mr. Malcolm M. Williams, A.I.A. of Warren Holmes-Kenneth Black, Architects, Lansing, Michigan who has been thoughtful and supportive, both materially and mentally speaking. In addition to Mr. Williams, I extend my thanks to Professor Alan K. Laing, an architectural historian and professor emeritus of the Department of Architecture, the University of Illinois, Urbana, for his prompt and willing response to my requests for information and for his advice from the start. Above all, I am especially indebted to Professor David C. Huntington and Professor R. Ward Bissell of the Department of the History of Art, the University of Michigan, Professor Kingsbury Marzolf of the Department of Architecture, the University of Michigan, and Professor Sadayoshi Omoto, the Department of Art, Michigan State University, East Lansing, Michigan. It was Professor Omoto, my former professor of the history of American art and architecture at Michigan State University, who suggested the topic of this study. Professor Bissell, my academic advisor at the University of Michigan, has been so kind and helpful ever since I returned to study in the United States five and one-half years ago. Had it not been for his kind cooperation in endorsing my requests for extensions of my leave of absence from Chulalongkorn University in Thailand, I would have had to terminate my research prematurely. I am also deeply grateful to Professor Huntington, my professor of American art, not only for guidance beneficial to this study but also for the moral support he has kindly given me.

1
Introduction

The architectural criticism of a layman is very apt to be warped and vitiated by his failure to make allowances for difficulties under which the designer labors. In fact, it is almost sure to be defective on this account. To be sure, the layman may say that he does not get very much light in this respect from professional criticism, and that the architects, who ought to know about the difficulties from their experience of the same or the like, do not as a rule make the allowances when they are indulging in private in frank and free remarks about the performances of one another. It is only in the case of a purely monumental building, where the very site is chosen by the architect and he is limited in cost, that he does not stand in need of allowances, but is privileged "to set his own free thought before us." And of course such an opportunity as that never occurs. The architect's solutions of the ordinary problems of his profession are and must be "modified at every turn by circumstance and concession." Especially, one may say, is the architect of a skyscraper in need of sympathy, having to do a building which must be grimly and strictly utilitarian, to the extent of utilizing every cubic foot of habitable space, by the very same considerations as those which necessitate that it shall be monumental in its magnitude or at least in its altitude and by its necessarily aggressive conspicuousness. What the steel framed construction tends to become, what is the practical basis of such architecture as can be evolved from it, may be seen as one watches the skeleton arising undraped, or, still better, as one looks at the back or side of a towering structure, with its mere veneer of brickwork, the back or side unregarded by the architect, who concentrates his architecture on the street front that is meant to be seen, and leaves the architecture elsewhere to take care of itself, as it of course fails to do. One sees that the ultimate solution of the architecture of the skyscraper must be the recognition that it is a skeleton, and the expression of its articulations, with the protective envelope reduced to its lowest terms in simplest expression. In other words, the skyscraper is a frame building and not a concretion of masonry. There are almost no precedents applicable to the expression of such a structure in the whole of architectural history.[1]

Montgomery Schuyler, one of the most perceptive architectural critics at the turn of the century, wrote the above in his article entitled "The Evolution of a Skyscraper," which was published in *The Architectural Record* in November 1903. In this very same article, Schuyler continued:

But in fact, what the architects of skyscrapers are called upon to do is to create a new architecture, an architecture which in its problems has immensely more affinities with modern engineering than with historical architecture. And this task is sprung upon them at a time when, more than at any previous time in human history, architectural education has to do exclusively with reproduction and imitation, and less than at any with invention. Honor to the very few who have tackled this gigantic task, and every allowance for their shortcomings in the fulfillment of it! Every allowance also for the far more numerous architects who have declined it, and have rested in compromises and conventions, or even have contented themselves with concealing the new construction behind such accents of historical architecture as could be mechanically adjusted to it, without the pretense of architecturally expressing it! "Comprendre tout, c'est a pardonner tout." And one must see and catch the design for a skyscraper in the making really to "comprehend" the peculiar difficulties it involves.[2]

Schuyler visited Chicago in 1891 and wrote several critical articles on the cast-iron fronts that were made to imitate stone. By the time he wrote, these cast-iron fronts were things of the past and already stood in the shadow of the stripped steel-framed skyscrapers as Schuyler himself described in his 1903 essay quoted above which ushered the new commercial era in Chicago. The period between 1875 and 1905 was the time the so-called Chicago School of Architecture flourished. Members of the school were conscious that they had developed new techniques and new forms which radically altered the course of architectural development in America. They described the form of their buildings as the "Commercial Style," and they referred to their innovations in structural techniques as "Chicago Construction." This self-consciousness characterized not only the architects and engineers, but also those enthusiasts in Chicago who publicized their work in the course of advertising the merits of the city which grew miraculously out of the devastation of the disastrous great fire in 1871.

In addition, two most acute and perceptive critics and historians of architecture of the late nineteenth and early twentieth century, Montgomery Schuyler and Russell Sturgis, alone among the savants of the museums and universities of the east, discerned the potentialities if not the intrinsic greatness of the Chicago School. Both were leading exponents of a rational and realistic architecture. Both were among only a few critics and scholars who grasped the importance of the architecture that was growing up in the city of Chicago. Sturgis maintained consistently that works like that of the Chicago School represented the only structural art of the time. He pointed out in numerous articles that no other school of architecture could train men like Sullivan, Root, and the rest. But aside from Schuyler and Sturgis and the citizens of Chicago who were concerned with the matters, the rest of the country remained ignorant of the impressive and influential achievements of the school. By the time of Sullivan's death in 1924, the ideal that he stood for seemed to be a lost cause. As a consequence the Chicago School had to be rediscovered by a later generation.

It was not until 1930 that any interest in and intelligent understanding of the "Commercial Style" spread. Perhaps the first to do so was Lewis Mumford whose discerning chapter on Richardson, Sullivan, and Root in his *The Brown Decades* (1931) drew attention to the excellence of their work and awakened interest in the background of the modern movement in the building arts. In 1932, the Museum of Modern Art in New York showed a small exhibit entitled "Early Modern Architecture in Chicago" and issued a slim catalog on some of the architects and their works. In connection with another exhibit at the Museum of Modern Art, Hugh Morrison's critical and biographical volume on Sullivan followed in 1935. However, Siegfried Giedion's *Space, Time and Architecture,* which was first published in 1941, provided the comprehensive treatment of the Chicago School in its full historical setting. Today, recognition of the school is worldwide, and its once forgotten principles now constitute the basis of architecture as it is practiced on every continent. Even guidebooks and atlases frequently refer the tourists to the "famous architecture of Root and Sullivan."

In the 1930s, as nowadays, the frank and intelligent architectural criticism seemed to disappear. As Talbot Faulkner Hamlin puts it:

> Gone are those bold days of Montgomery Schuyler's "Architectural Aberrations"[3] that enlivened *The Architectural Record* of the nineties—nowadays we can smile at each other like women at a tea party whose external good manners hide a multitude of jealousies. Nor is this attitude confined to the architectural periodicals. Newspapers usually vary between fear of giving free advertisement, willingness to fall into the hands of the most brazen publicity agents, and forgetfulness that architecture exists. Even the better class magazines avoid actual criticism; the ogre of a libel suit not unjustly stares at them continually from afar, and even a witty criticism may bring the architect pouncing down with bared claws, as a New York weekly publication expensively discovered not so many years ago.[4]

Hamlin also pointed out that there never was a time when rigid and relentless architectural criticism was more necessary. There were plenty of books on architecture but proportionally their readers were few, and many were controversial rather than critical. Many were too technical; some too tricky in content and presentation. So the great run of interested people were forced back to newspapers, periodicals, and the architectural press where they usually found arid statistics, sentimental gush in the homemaking and furniture magazines, and critical vapidity in the architectural journals.

Hamlin, himself an architect, also stressed that the confusion between architecture as a profession and architecture as a business was no better illustrated than in the architect's inaction to criticisms of the aesthetic side of his work. The architect who considered his vocation a business necessarily thought in money terms; his job was to sell a commodity at a profit. To him any criticism of his work from an artistic standpoint seemed unjust. Therefore, Hamlin in the 1930 provocative article made an appeal to his fellow architects:

> Let us see ourselves as professional rather than business men, earning our living, not merely getting a profit, creating works of a difficult and noble art for the joy of mankind, not selling goods. Then we will come to welcome criticism, not resent it—at least to tolerate it and the temporary pain it may cost. Are architects smaller minded than authors? More fearful than

musicians? Weaker than actors? The poor things! Servility and arrogance. Servility to the great god Business—arrogance to the critic and criticism. A beautiful attitude—let's change all this. Let some architectural magazines establish a column of sound and careful criticism of current work. Think of the controversies it would start and how vital and stimulating to us all such controversies might be![5]

Amen, Mr. Hamlin!

The remarks of Montgomery Schuyler quoted earlier and those of Talbot Hamlin, in many ways, represent the two sides of the fence—the architect and the critic. Ironically, Schuyler, a critic, seemed to take the side of the architects and Hamlin, an architect, seemed to take the critics' side. Schuyler also mentioned the architectural criticism written by the party in the middle, that is, the layman, the public, the consumer, or whatever the term may be whose criticism, as Schuyler put it, "is very apt to be warped and vitiated by his failure to make allowances for difficulties under which the designer labors. In fact, it is almost sure to be defective on this account." Whether this is true or not, the layman or the public is certainly justified in commenting as consumer upon the architectural wares offered for his consumption. The layman-critic is one who professes to assess the relative merit of such architectural wares from the point of view of the consumer and one who sets about to instruct the lay public how to use these wares in order to obtain the most value from them. It is not only the architect, however, who shows himself touchy about instructions from the nonprofessional about his job. The professional critics, too, are sometimes notoriously impatient of criticism from anyone who is not himself a professional writer of criticism, particularly those of writers who set about to comment upon the work of the critics themselves. They unfortunately sometimes forget that the professional critic, too, is a producer of wares for public consumption and that the public is entitled as consumer to assess the value of wares which the critic makes available to it.

Architecture is a form of art, as Talbot Hamlin put it, "a difficult and noble art for the joy of mankind" and a building may be defined as a shell constructed of building materials according to engineering principles for the express purpose of housing some social activity. An edifice which cannot be entered, or whose interior space cannot be put to a specific practical use, is not a building at all. Then, a building, in turn, can be said to possess architectural quality only in proportion as it expresses its social function. To be architectural, a church must not merely be constructed according to sound engineering principles and capable of housing a religious congregation; it must express its distinctive religious character with respect both to its exterior and to its interior. Therefore, churches which look like barns, factories, or railway stations are not architecturally expressive and do not possess architectural quality. A building cannot express its social function architecturally unless the architect exploits the expressive potentialities of his building materials and his engineering forms in such a manner as visibly to proclaim their physical properties. The expression of these properties alone will not, of course, suffice to make the building expressive of its social function, but unless these properties are architecturally expressed, the building's social function cannot be given architectural expression.

To understand this dependence of truly architectural expressiveness upon the expressive exploitation of building materials and engineering structure is not so easy for the general public or layman. However, as the architect's audience, the architecturally sensitive layman's response to architecture is primarily directed at a building's perceptual appearance, not at its invisible engineering structure. What is important architecturally is its structural appearance. A well-built edifice which looks insecure is architecturally inferior to a badly built edifice which, while it lasts, looks secure. But to be perceptually satisfactory, a building must, in both interior and exterior appearance, satisfy certain requirements dictated by the observer's knowledge of relevant natural phenomena such as weight or gravity, compression, tensile strength, and the like. The observer has spent his life adjusting himself to physical objects and therefore knows from experience that stone is heavier than wood, that a steel girder is more tensile than a wooden beam, and so on. Accordingly, every visible architectural form will arouse in the average observer certain basic reactions which significantly influence his architectural response to the building as a whole. It is true that even an architecturally competent observer is, from the strictly engineering and architectural point of view, a layman, not an expert. Competence in architectural response presupposes architectural sensitivity and training; and this training, in turn, will involve the learning of certain basic engineering principles of which the architecturally naive layman may not be aware. However, a professional critic, to be competent, must possess whatever basic engineering knowledge is requisite to an understanding of the main visible architectural forms. Bearing in mind these factors which condition man's architectural response to architecture—factors which the architect who is properly sensitive to the social function of his creation will consciously or unconsciously take into account—let us consider an observation of a pure layman, in fact a foreign visitor who visited Chicago in the late nineteenth century and recorded his perceptive observation of the Chicago commercial architecture at the time which translates as follows:

> Men! The word is hardly correct applied to this perplexing city. When you study it more in detail, its aspect reveals so little of the personal will, so little caprice and individuality, in its streets and buildings, that it seems like the work of some impersonal power, irresistible, unconscious, like a force of nature, in whose service man was merely a passive instrument.
> This power is nothing else than that business fever which here throbs at will, with an unbridled violence like that of an uncontrollable element. It rushes along these streets, as once before the devouring flame of fire;[6] it quivers, it makes itself visible with an intensity which lends something tragical to the city, and makes it seem like a poem to me.

6 *Introduction*

> When, from this overhanging tower, you have gazed down upon this immense volcano of industry and commerce, you go down to look more closely into the details of this exuberant life, this exhaustless stream of activity. You walk along the sidewalks of streets which bear works of haste—here flagstones, there asphalt, yonder a mere line of planks crossing a miry swamp. This want of continuity in road material is repeated in the buildings. At one moment you have nothing around you but "buildings." They scale the very heavens with their eighteen and twenty stories. The architect who built them, or rather, made them by machinery, gave up all thought of colonnades, mouldings, classical decorations. He ruthlessly accepted the speculator's inspired conditions—to multiply as much as possible the value of the bit of earth at the base by multiplying the superimposed "offices."
>
> One might think that such a problem would interest no one but an engineer. Nothing of the kind! The simple power of necessity is to a certain degree a principle of beauty; and these structures so plainly manifest this necessity that you feel a strange emotion in contemplating them. It is the first draught of a new sort of art—an art of democracy made by the masses and for the masses, an art of science, where the invariability of natural laws gives to the most unbridled daring the calmness of geometrical figures. The portals of the basements, usually arched as if crushed beneath the weight of the mountain which they support, look like dens of a primitive race, continually receiving and pouring forth a stream of people. You lift your eyes and you feel that up there behind the perpendicular walls, with its innumerable windows, is a multitude coming and going—crowding the offices that perforate these cliffs of brick and iron, dizzied with the speed of the elevators. You divine, you feel the hot breath of speculation quivering behind these windows. This is what has fecundated these thousands of square feet of earth, in order that from them may spring up this appalling growth of business palaces, that hide the sun from you and almost shut out the light of day.[7]

The above remark was written by Paul Bourget,[8] a French novelist, who came to the United States to widen his outlook and visited Chicago in 1894. This trip was the source of *Outre-Mer Impressions of America,* in which he describes the American society, American business, including capitalists and laborers, farmers, and cowboys. He surveys American education and recreation. His impressions were based upon visits throughout the North and the South. This particular book was first published by Charles Scribner's Sons in 1895 and his famous observation of the city of Chicago, Chicago business and Chicago commercial architecture quoted above has been translated[9] and quoted time and time again by architectural historians, critics, and students of Chicago architecture. In it, Bourget shows rare ability and strength as a writer, and one of the most vivid and perceptive observations as a layman-architectural critic. Most importantly, he shows his understanding of not only the life and the business of Chicago but also its commercial architecture at the time in which its architects had developed a new form out of new material and new socio-economic requirements. They had effected a synthesis of aesthetic sensibilities and technical capacities, and they were thus able to point a way toward a spiritual integration based on the humanization of modern industrial techniques. It is this ideal which the modern movement in architecture strives to realize. In his observation, Bourget also consciously or unconsciously discovers the truth of Sullivan's two basic assertions: the first aesthetic, that form must grow organically out of function; the second social, that it is the task of the architect to interpret and to express the life of his own people. The architects of the Chicago School certainly did just that in their "Commercial Style" of architecture and no one could have said it better than Montgomery Schuyler:

> Undoubtedly the most remarkable achievement of our architects and the most creditable have been in commercial architecture. But in this respect Chicago is more American than any of the Eastern cities, where there are signs, even in the commercial quarters, of division of interest and infirmity of purpose. In none of them does the building bespeak such a singleness of devotion, or indicate that life means so exclusively a living.[10]

It has always been easier for a critic to analyze the past than the present. When he deals with contemporary events, his task is immediately more difficult, often more hazardous. He is himself involved in the event, and the judgments he makes and positions he takes may effect the outcome. Yet criticism plays a decisive role in the formation of the attitudes and in standards of judgment of society. On the one hand, it introduces the public to the new event, prepares it for the future. At the same time criticism reflects the public's reaction to the new event, and in this sense modifies the event's subsequent evolution. The critical mechanism is the same whether the field be politics or drama or—as in this case—architecture. And it has had a far wider impact on this field than most architects realize. In many ways, criticism can be not only influential but can also educate the public. It teaches, but it does not simply impart knowledge. Directly or indirectly, it instructs perception, thought, feeling, and imagination, so they can all lean toward the work of architecture sympathetically and knowingly. Thus the critic is the seer and guide. He directs perception to the values of new and unfamiliar styles of architecture and thereby encourages its acceptance. The battle of architectural styles can be fought and won as much by the pen as by the drawing board. The polemics must, of course, be documented by pictures which illustrate the main points of the argument. Sometimes these are photographs of actual buildings, more often they are merely the architect's sketches of what he hopes to build. In any case, tens of thousands of people could learn the rationale of the new architecture from the critics where only tens, maybe, would ever be likely to see it in reality. The architectural critics came from disparate backgrounds. Some of the most perceptive and effective were the architects themselves: Sturgis, Sullivan, Wright, and Hamlin in this country, Adolph Loos and Le Corbusier abroad. But many of the protagonists came from other fields—Schuyler, Mumford, Hitchcock, Giedion. And some were even just simply laymen with sharp eyes like Paul Bourget. Whatever their point of departure, these critics eventually convinced the public of the validity of the new architectural style.

The purpose of this study is to present important points of view on architectural criticism; a nucleus of prominent critics who were active before and after the turn of the century, namely Montgomery Schuyler, Russell

8 Introduction

Sturgis, P. B. Wight, Herbert Croly, among others, and the most important media through which these critics expressed their views; and architectural criticisms, mainly of the aforementioned critics, particularly those of Schuyler, on commercial architecture of the so-called Chicago School which two major firms—Adler and Sullivan, and Burnham and Root—are selected to represent. However, early developments of the City of Chicago and its architecture, with the concentration on the period after the great fire of 1871 in which the concepts and techniques of the Chicago School were formed and implemented are unavoidable and are included prior to the discussion of the architecture of the two selected firms.

2
Architectural Criticism

The content as well as the form of architectural criticism has undergone a fundamental change in the past century. This has been largely a matter of vast increase in knowledge, both of the past and of the present-day world around us. As recently as 1896, Sir Banister Fletcher set up a system of categories in which the successive architectural forms of the West appear as the "historical styles" and those of all the rest of the world as "nonhistorical." General advances in the science of history have made the repetition of this sort of error impossible. And this, in turn, affects the critic benignly, giving him a much more accurate perspective of the past than ever before. One has only to compare the Gothic world which Pugin and Ruskin beheld a little more than a century ago with that of Geoffrey Scott in 1914 or Sir Nikolaus Pevsner today, to appreciate how increasingly precise history has tamed the wilder and more lurid aspects of the critic's mind. As I have mentioned earlier, it has always been easier to analyze the past than to criticize the present. When criticism deals with contemporary artistic developments, as opposed to the past, its task becomes more complex, more difficult by definition. First of all, the critic himself is immersed in events, his judgments colored by his own positions and prejudices. Secondly, criticisms of contemporaneous events play an active, functional role in society. It not only introduces the new development to the public and prepares it for the future but also reflects the public reaction to that new event and in this sense modifies the subsequent development of a given style or movement. Criticism, for this reason, has a far wider significance for architecture than most architects are likely to realize. At the turn of the century, for example, it took only two men from the East, Montgomery Schuyler and Russell Sturgis, to revolutionize the commercial architecture in this country both on the theoretical and technical bases and the actual forms of the new commercial style. Or in the twenties while the battle for contemporary architecture was being fought in Europe, Sullivan and Wright's writings helped to pave the way for the so-called "modern movement" in this country. Today, as has always been the case, the reaction of architects to criticism of their works seldom occupies the middle ground. Few terms conjure up as much reaction in professional circles as architectural criticism, particularly the negative ones written by critics who themselves are also architects. Consider, for example, these samplings from three Fellows of the American Institute of Architects:

> It would be a disastrous thing to allow architects to set themselves up in judgment of other architects. Any such criticism should be through official organizations such as the A.I.A.
> Philip Johnson
>
> We must always respect the feeling of another architect and act in good taste.
> Leon Chatelin, Jr., Former Institute President
>
> I don't care about another architect's feelings. If he is a bad architect, I will say so.
> Gordon Bunshaft, member of Washington's Fine Art Commission[1]

The above quotations were taken from a report of the A.I.A. Committee on Esthetics prepared by Arthur Q. Davis, then its chairman. It triggered action by the Board of Directors, who not only commanded the report but later authorized the Committee to develop, in conjunction with the *A.I.A. Journal*, a series of critical analyses. Therefore, articles on architectural criticism and critiques of completed projects by A.I.A. members have appeared intermittently since the first one, "The Philosophy of Architectural Criticism" by Peter Collins,[2] was published in the January 1968 issue of the *Journal*.

According to Collins, verbal criticisms of buildings are presumably as old as architecture itself, and some have survived in documentary form, as for example, Bernini's views on French architecture reported in Freart de Chantelon's diary (published in 1885). However, Collins doubts if the systematic publication of criticisms of buildings by architects, art critics or teachers of architecture antedates 1750, though occasional critical allusions to architecture are to be found in essays and satirical verse. In his book entitled *Changing Ideals in Modern Architecture* (1750-1950),[3] Collins explains further that the whole notion of publishing detailed criticisms of individual paintings, sculpture and works of architecture is relatively recent, and can be traced back only to the beginnings of the modern age: to the duplicated manuscript criticisms circulated by Grimm and Diderot to their aristocratic correspondents in the mid-eighteenth century, and reached its full flowering with such magazines as the *Quarterly Review*, the *Edinburgh Review*, for example, and to J. F. Blondel's *Architecture Françoise*, a four-volumed illustrated folio published in 1752. Blondel's book was primarily intended for students and there is good reason to suspect that his published remarks were simply a transcription of those he voiced as he conducted his groups of students around Paris, declaiming on the merits and defects of each building as he passed.

In the second half of the eighteenth century, the influence of Rationalism was more marked in criticisms of architecture than in critical writings on any of the other arts, and this was to be expected in the age of the "Encyclopedistes," since architecture is a science as well as an art. In this period of time, the few architectural criticisms published had been mainly written by practicing architects.[4] With the nineteenth century came the great era of popular critical literature, especially in periodicals; by the middle of this century, however, historians, art critics and professional journalists were taking over the task of architectural criticism. From then onward, the theory of architecture became bound up more and more with the history of architecture, just as criticism was to become essentially a form of literature. James Ferguson wrote his *Historical Inquiry* (1849) because of "the immense strides that have been made during the last half century in the true principles of architectural criticism." Ferguson was a convinced Rationalist, and was in effect using history as a convenient instrument for justifying Rationalist ideals. These Rationalist writers regarded architectural criticism as an art form in itself. The critic took it upon himself to absorb a work of art into his system in order to create another work of art which was entirely of his own making. The merits of this approach have been most eloquently put forward by Oscar Wilde in his essay, *The Critic as Artist*.

As has already been mentioned, the first art critic was Denis Diderot. Diderot's most distinguished successor was Charles Baudelaire, whose first criticism of a Salon appeared in 1846, and was deliberately modeled on Diderot's method. The importance of Baudelaire in the history of art criticism lies not so much in the fact that he was an important poet, but the fact that he propounded a specific aesthetic doctrine, though he himself did not know how to paint. Baudelaire, like Diderot, seldom mentioned architecture. Perhaps, the only famous art critic of the nineteenth century to occupy himself predominantly with architecture was John Ruskin and his writings are extraordinarily illuminating, in that they show just how tendentious the architectural criticisms of an impassioned amateur can be. Ruskin originally made his reputation in the description he gives in *The Stones of Venice* of the facade of St. Mark's and later perhaps his most famous critical writing on architecture is *Seven Lamps of Architecture*. The book first appeared in 1849.

In America in the nineteenth century, while the ruling taste called for ornamentation and embellishment, a few articulate men, even in the mid-1850s, expressed their enjoyment of the fitness of things in their functional form and the relation of form to function. No one did this with greater force and clarity than Horatio Greenough, whose praise of ship design is well known and was taken into consideration in both architectural design and concept. Ships, trotting wagons and locomotives in the 1850s became models of the nineteenth-century functional design. Greenough declared in his critical writings that the men who had reduced locomotion to its simplest elements were nearer to "Athens" than those who would imitate Greek forms and that the famous American clipper ships represented an extremely appropriate application of forms, being exceedingly sharp, slim and extraordinarily fast. Greenough writes:

> Observe a ship at sea! Mark the majestic form of her hull as she rushes through the water, observe the graceful bend of her body, the gentle transition from round to flat, the grasp of her keep, the leap of her bows, the symmetry and rich tracery of her spars and rigging, and those grand wind muscles, her sails.[5]

The finest clipper ships that were built in America in the 1850s led Greenough to suggest in his theory of functionalism that architects should take hints from shipbuilders in order to design buildings that would be expressive of their function, structure, and materials. He declares:

> Instead of forcing the functions of every sort of building into one general form, adopting an outward shape for the sake of the eye or of association, without reference to the inner distribution, let us begin from the heart as the nucleus, and work outward. The most convenient size and arrangement of the rooms that are to constitute the building being fixed, the access of the light that may, of the air that must be wanted, being provided for, we have the skeleton of our building.[6]

Greenough pressed his ideas concerning architectural design more than any other American of his generation. He, along with ideas from earlier farsighted men of the period, anticipated Louis Sullivan's ideas, though the line of descent from Greenough to Sullivan cannot be determined with finality.

To Diderot, Ruskin, Greenough, and other such critics of art and architecture, criticism may mean something very different from what it may mean to philosophers, historians and architects. A critic in search of criteria may be guided by other theoretical needs more than an architect in search of a valid solution at the end of his design process, and an architect's theoretical assumptions in turn may be of little relevance to an outside observer such as a critic who tries to respond to a finished work of architecture. Even the critics themselves are always in dispute not only about the meaning of criticism but also the methods which are legitimate to the conduct of their craft and the very roles or functions which criticism exists to fulfill. However, due to the fact that criticism is differentiated from a number of kindred studies which it partially incorporates into itself not by a difference of subject matter but by a difference of interest and purpose, there is agreement among most critics that criticism can only be defined in terms of function. Harold Osborne puts it thus: "We can only agree about a definition which would discriminate criticism from, say, the history of art when we can agree about the true nature and function of criticism."[7] Jeffrey Gutchen in his article "Proposals for Architectural Criticism," published in *Connection* (a Harvard periodical) in March 1965, quotes a passage from T. S. Eliot's "The Function of Criticism" (1923), as follows:

> Criticism by definition is about something other than itself.... At one time I was inclined to take the extreme position that the only critics worth reading were the critics who practiced

and practiced well the art of which they wrote. But I had to stretch this frame to make some important inclusions; and I have since been in search of a formula which should cover everything I wished to include, even if it included more than I wanted. And the most important qualification which I have been able to find is that a critic must have a very highly developed sense of fact... at every level of criticism I find the same necessity regnant. There is a large part of critical writing which consists in "interpreting" an author, a work... but it is fairly certain that "interpretation" is only legitimate when it is not interpretation at all, but merely putting the reader in possession of facts he would otherwise have missed.

And elsewhere in the same essay, Eliot says that criticism is the "commutation and exposition of works of art by means of written words"[8] which Harold Osborne argues that Eliot's definition of criticism is attached only to "commutation" and "exposition" and has nothing to do with "interpretation" at all. This, Osborne says, is contrary to the opinion of another prominent writer, Donald A. Stauffer, who holds that interpretation is one of the critic's main functions. He says: "Every critic is an individual who proposes to act as an interpreter and a systematizer."[9] If we are to understand the critic's views of the function of criticism, such differences of opinion between prominent writers on the subject are clearly important and are genuinely about the function for which criticism exists. To turn to still another critic, Jeffrey Gutchen, writing in the article mentioned earlier, expresses his disenchantment with a few critics who produce "groundless criticism," as he terms it, and who see themselves in one way another as spiritual adjuncts of the architect or his apologists rather than analysts and critics of the architect's work. Gutchen observes:

> The critic must be an identifier—a man engaged in naming architecture and defining its excellences and weaknesses as expression. In a broader view, the critic is the one who says what architecture is, in realistic terms and this including building technology, activity places, elements of abstract composition, nature of the site and so forth. But it would be a mistake to stop here, because criticism is different from art in that it has much less license. The critic has graver responsibilities, and by this I mean several things. For he is necessarily a man with his ear to the wind. In architecture, this means a keen interest in all intellectual and artistic disciplines and current habits of thought not, as the sociologist, for the purposes of making an extravagant generalization, but one who, as the voice of educated, non-professional public, also says what the architecture might be, to the best of his ability, and what it ought not be, to the most sensible of his perceptions. I should be clearer, though, that the critic's responsibilities are not primarily to the architect, but to the public and to architecture—and it is here that the matter of identification, of "putting the reader in the possession of the facts,"comes in.[10]

Criticism is always one strong structural link between the individual and his peer group and, beyond it, society. Architectural criticism is no exception; together with the experiences of works of architecture it is one of the most important factors in an architect's continuous frame of reference for his work. There was a time when the production of verdicts, the sitting in judgment, appeared as the most important and almost only function of the critic. Today his task is much larger and at the same time more complex. Though there might seem to be some differences of opinion as to what the functions of criticism are as I have mentioned earlier, there is consensus amongst the majority of architectural critics that a critic's task is a threefold activity of description, interpretation and evaluation. The workings might be somewhat different from one critic to another but the contents are essentially the same.[11]

Description

If it is the critic's task to "make visible," it is the critic's task to help people to see what was made possible. To this end he has to control carefully all the media of communication at his disposal; he has to be aware of all his possibilities for making visual documentation meaningful beyond its documentary character through an advised choice of telling images and comparison, and he has to watch continuously how his chief instrument, language, and more specifically, his special language, relates to the phenomenon he is describing. He may have to develop, within limits, new terminology or clarify an existing one in order to refine description to such a degree that it can record all levels of architectural reality and experience, not only those acessible to superficial methods of reporting.

Interpretation

If accurate description in a clear language is the first task of the critic, he really comes into his own when he turns from pure description to interpretation. Interpretation demands a great deal of self-discipline on the part of the critic, lest he get carried away by his own imagination or by an excess of sentiment. Especially the interpretation of contemporary phenomena in the light of historical parallel is fraught with pitfalls, as is amply demonstrated in the history of architectural criticism. It may be permissible for the critic to use historic material in support of his interpretation of a contemporary piece of architecture, provided he does not falsify or misuse his historic evidence in the process. The historian at all times has to make a very conscious effort to keep "historical time" separate from "personal time" even though a perfect separation is impossible. A particular danger exists when terms used in interpretation are treated as if they were descriptions of actual properties residing in works and when, moreover, it is imputed to the creators of works from the past to have acted as if they had been aware of such properties.

Evaluation

If interpretation demands rigorously conscientious effort to preserve clarity and to eliminate irrelevant intrusions from sources that have nothing to do with the matter in hand, evaluation, as we all know, requires even greater exertion in order to be authentic. Evaluation is still the function of the critic which is most properly his own and here again it is important to recognize that evaluative utterances, as far as the use of language and its logic is concerned, differ fundamentally from interpretations and descriptions. Evaluations are not descriptive reports and in the present state of our knowledge it is, furthermore, impossible to reduce them to descriptions by restricting what they are based on to those phenomena which can be accurately measured and accounted for in the operation of the human psychophysical systems. However, this does not make them meaningless "merely emotive utterances" unless one is willing to acknowledge no other uses of language than the descriptive and emotive. Evaluations are based on choices for which reason can be given. In this sense they can be validated; the application of criteria can be spelled out. But finally a moment comes when, as both experience and logical analysis tell us, criteria may be brought into play which cannot be challenged reasonably, where in aesthetic validation we must stop for there is no further place to go. This is the moment of "sheer choice" when the critic can rely on nothing except the total sum of his awareness, the quality of his sensitivity or intuition and the depth of his sincerity and commitment. The parallelism to the situation of the artist during the process of artistic creation has often been remarked: "For both, in addition to what is uncontrollable gift or talent and stored awareness, sincerity is the decisive condition."

These are the three functions of architectural criticism and the tasks of architectural critics that most critical writers assent to. They are the tasks that a critic must perform and perform well. If we are to have architectural criticism, the quality of the criticism becomes of vital importance and it must be founded on the "bedrock of what architecture is; it must get down to brass tacks. Only so can criticism guide, chasten, encourage, and at the same time grow with the growth of the artist's creative power."[12] I have quoted Jeffrey Gutchen earlier in this chapter as saying that a critic must be able both to identify a work of architecture and to define its excellences and weaknesses. He must understand the nature of architecture and must possess a keen interest in all intellectual and artistic disciplines. Architecture, unlike any other form of art, is the combination of art and science. It combines both structural and decorative elements. It is not like engineering, which approaches a problem solely from the point of view of structure and efficiency; nor yet is it like painting or sculpture whose value is based solely on the direct impression upon the sight.

This double nature of architecture, which is part of its special essence, its peculiar value, exacts the greatest care in attempting any formulae for the possible basis of a sound criticism. Admiration for clever structures must not blind the critic to obvious failures in handling that structure creatively; admiration for decorative facility, richness, and invention must not be allowed to hide structural or planning falsities or slovenliness. With this in mind, a basis for architectural criticism is presented as follows.[13]

Planning, Structure, Material Consideration

Efficiency

A building's plan should be so designed as to allow the simplest and most direct carrying on of those functions of individual and communal humanity for which it is intended. Comfort, science, air and light, privacy or the reverse are all included in this category.

Economy

This does not mean cheapness, nor necessarily any quality connected with the amount of money expenditure. But it means the quality which avoids vulgar, ostentatious waste; a sort of good manner that results from the use of the right materials in the right places.

Consistency

Plan, structure, effect are obviously independent. The plan, types of buildings, and the structural systems used should be related; effect should grow naturally from both.

Artistic Achievement

Emotional Effect

This is at once the vaguest and most important criterion of all. A work of architecture, as a creative art, stands or falls by it. Emotional effect here does not mean specific emotions of aspiration, wonder, or bewilderment but rather some deeper, vaguer end, that instinctive catch of the breath or opening of the eyes, which it seems the peculiar genius of beauty to produce.

Honesty

A building should not apparently falsify its structure or its function.

Expressiveness

Every new modern problem—factory, apartment house, department store, whatever—is an opportunity for the creation of new creative forms, and yet so developed from the program that the function is immediately apprehended. The same is true of structure; new structural methods offer a thousand new opportunities for beautiful forms. Yet the expression of both function and structure is not a matter which automatically follows an engineering solution; it is a creative quality, art quality, the result of choice, arrangement, emphasis, much study of non-engineering qualities. It is the result of creative play with thoroughly understood and digested forms.

Artistic Method

General Form

Compositional values, relations of void and solid, emphasis, proportion, mass and its handling; these all may be examined in any building; their correct treatment should be insisted on relentlessly. Many buildings are bad because proportions are basically wrong; economic use of space, building to the limits of the zoning law; these are explanations, but never excuses, for ugly masses or silhouette. Economic considerations are inevitably conditions of the program, but when they are allowed exclusively to dictate forms, the result is by that much not architecture at all.

Decorative Detail

Ornament will continue to be used in architecture, despite various attempts to prove its unsuitability to the twentieth-century building. Mankind has decorated its artifacts for too many thousands of years for a dogma to break the habit. The kind of ornament changes with the continuous flux of taste and fashion; yet through the change there emerge certain qualifications of good ornament so constant that they may deserve a place in this canon. Ornament, then, must fulfill the following requirements: it must be suited to its place on the building, and its distance from the average observer's eyes. It must clarify and not confuse design emphasis and not hide structure. In subject matter and treatment it must aid the building's functional expression. It must be suited in its material and the technique that produces it.

Scale

In how many houses may one see the small striving to appear great; how many commercial buildings seem to lack this compelling quality by which things appear their true size! The question of scale underlies every element of a building from the smallest leaf or zigzag of its ornament and the size of window panes to the bulk of mass—and it is in matters of scale that the greatest care, the most searching criticism, is requisite today, for in the styles of the past, the "just scale" of element after element had come to be accepted: It was part alike of the cultivated observer's innate sense, and of every draftsman's training. Now, on the contrary, thousands of forms are used both structurally and decoratively which are new, which have no such accepted scale, and it requires the clearest eyes and the sharpest discrimination to use them in a scale that shall convince, that shall set and enhance, the scale of the whole. Here especially criticism is necessary: Already mere scratchings of the surface utterly ineffective, decorative forms mounting hundreds of feet into the air, or great sprawling beams several feet across equally in the opposite direction.

This list comprises the categories which seem most important in architectural criticism, and furnishes a canon that proves stimulating and helpful to the architectural critic, for these qualities, at least, "we may demand good architecture"[14] as Talbot Hamlin puts it. Otherwise, critics must always demand good architecture and discourage the bad. It is part of their job, or at least most think so. Criticisms of buildings are as old as architecture itself, and as long as there is architecture there will be critics. Therefore, this phenomenon will always remain—the architects on one side, the critics on the other, and sometimes as history indicates, the separation is farther than most people realize. The separation itself is not the deplorable aspect of the situation. The dark side of the opposition is the indifference, the real indifference, of the critic to all the architect does, or tries to do. On the other hand, there is, sometimes, a complete apathy of the architect toward everything the critic can conceivably say—except praise. So far, I have brought up various different points of view from the critic's side as far as architectural criticism is concerned. It is quite stimulating, intellectually, to hear what the architect has to say.

In 1906, Harry Desmond, a noted architectural writer of the day, wrote an essay entitled "The Architect and the Critic" in the April issue of *The Architectural Record* expressing frankly his displeasure of the relationship between the architects and the critics at the time. Right at the beginning of his statement, Desmond declared:

> I have been troubled always by the utter lack of rational explanation as to why, today, so great a distance separates the artist from the critic in matters architectural. Certainly we expect difference wherever taste is concerned. Who is not ready to meet, even to welcome, in all artistical discussions the charming obliquities of the Personal Equation and the infinite variety of the kaleidoscopic Point of View?[15] But the "artistic variable" in any one of its multitudinous manifestations should not legitimately account in our judgments for more than for distinctions, discriminations, modifications—divergencies which, no matter how extreme they may be, still stop this side of fundamental differences. All that falls further over, as it were, on the other side of this line, and therefore really is contradictory or antithetical surely should not be regarded as coming fairly within the operation of the rule of DeGustibus or anything of the kin. Rather should too wide a divergence of opinion create instantly a fair need, not of further argumentation, but of a searching examination of their fundamental principles. So I take it, there must be somewhere a false amount or (to switch the simile) an

undigested particle in the complete opposition that exists between contemporary architectural practice and contemporary architectural criticism."[16]

Desmond continues in his essay quoting a critic as saying:

> Architecture is dead. It is not any more a living art. It is a sort of mass millinery—little better. *The Ladies' Home Journal* tells my women-folk that skirts will be cut full this spring, or after the pompadour manner, and can I not see by the common practice that cornices are heavier this year and worn lower; the colossal order is in vogue and so forth. Do not tell me that the modiste and the architect do not meet on a common ground. Architecture is defunct."[17]

Desmond offers a sharp reply as follows:

> This may be so. On consideration, however, I ask how can I be sure of it, for the practice of architecture or the attempt to practice it continues. Indeed, with critic's speech, and the tone of it singing in my ears, I can almost with greater certainty bring myself to the belief that the defunct one is criticism. Yet, I know that conclusion is not true either. The very bitterness of the reproach against modern architecture indicates reaction. The dead do not indict the dead... Of course, the present condition of the architect's mind is disclosed best by his building. Very few members of the profession are at all able to "explain themselves." If any individual succeeds in formulating himself, or even some of his factors, the resultant theory, description or explanation is wonderfully vague, and usually is so tenuous that it cannot be resolved into useful concrete terms that may be passed, like a working tool, from hand to hand. Yes! If we would know the architect we must confine ourselves strictly to building. But the critic! He is harder to get at. He may be a "terror for his size", but the race is numerous. Are there a score of competent exponents of the theoretical side of architecture in this country? I don't know why I put the number at a "score" instead of a dozen or less, unless it be that one would be careful to eject the element of the ungracious from even a rough calculation. But, really, apart from a few names that we all know, who are our critics? No doubt much writing is done for architectural journals. There are also "papers" delivered before Society[18] meetings. But, I think, all agree these utterances are, in the mass, pretty poor stuff—straw with little grain. Perhaps we find an explanation for this barren state of affairs in the statement recently made to the head of a publishing firm by one of our busiest (should I not say, therefore, one of our greatest?) architects: "We've no time to read. All we need is pictures just to see what the other fellow is up to." The man who spoke thus was not entirely fair, even to himself, but the fact remains that the critical body with us is so small, so withdrawn, so utterly "in opposition", it is impossible to produce sufficient testimony from American sources to establish indubitably the exact whereabouts of the "critical position" in regard to the maze of contemporary architecture."[19]

Deprecatory as the statements of their disagreement are, one must realize that the quarrel between the architect and the critic is a family quarrel, for the two are mutually interdependent. Though, it might be admitted by some that the critic cannot get along without the architect any more than fiction can get along without fact, the architect will not readily admit that he cannot get along without the critic. The truth is that the nature of criticism is often misunderstood, because attention has been fixed too much upon its formal, not to say formidable, expressions. Professional criticism has been and is all very well, but sometimes it suffers under the disadvantages of any such exclusive interest. It takes itself somewhat too seriously. But such criticism is, of course, only the organized and educated product of the simplest and commonest fact of social intercourse. When two people derive different impressions of the same object, or entertain to bear different ideas upon it, they sit down to talk it over, and the result is criticism. As long as there are two people in the world, criticism is inevitable. Criticism originates then, in the ordinary communicative impulse, which all men share to a certain extent, but which is most highly developed among an expansive imaginative and articulate people. Therefore, there is nothing wrong with disagreement and exchanging points of view between the critic and the architect as long as the intention is constructive and might lead to a fruitful result; in this matter, good architecture and good architectural criticism. Therefore, let us heed what Herbert D. Croly has to say as far as "criticism that counts" is concerned.

Exactly at the turn of the century, Croly wrote an essay entitled "Criticism that Counts" in the April 1901 issue of *The Architectural Record* of which he was editor at the time. It was primarily intended as a reply (a counterattack might be a more appropriate term) to P. B. Wight's article [20] published earlier in Scribner's "Field of Art". Right at the beginning of his essay, Croly was quick to announce:

> Artists are as a rule impatient of criticism, and no wonder. It is so hard to achieve; it is so easy to criticise. Even a very shabby bit of work actually anchored to the earth or plastered upon a wall may well cost persistent labor, nice ingenuity, and varied experience; even the most thorough training and finest talent rarely if ever attains the virtue of impeccability: and granted that if it did, what resolute critic would be thereby disarmed? On the other hand, it seems as if anybody with some clean white paper, a scrawling pen, and a bottle of dirty black ink can sit down and write a criticism. So it seems and so to a certain extent it is. No doubt a critic really needs an intellectual discipline quite as exacting as the technical discipline of the artist, but he can much more easily evade the necessity. Using as he does words and ideas which are common properties and writing for people to whom an art is almost an alien thing, he can go through all the motions of criticism and even obtain its compensations, whatever they are, without very much more preparation than a good batch of stationer's stock. It is not merely, however, the incompetent criticism of popular sheets of which artists are impatient. They dislike and suspect, perhaps, even more, the criticism of the intellectual doctors: and here again their suspicions are only too well founded. The critics have seldom dealt with the artists in a becoming spirit of disinterestedness and humility. They have often been arrogant, unsympathetic and biased. They have presumed first of all to dictate, when it was their business first of all to interpret. They have been prone to assume that the arts were primarily a matter of mere ideas. They have failed to put themselves in the sensuous point of view of the artist, and to acquaint themselves with the necessities and limitations of his material and technical resources. It is true that for many years past the critics have been less apt to commit these faults; but they are still very much under the illusion of their own importance, and the complaint is still repeated that the history of criticism is the history of an elaborate and pretentious misunderstanding. The difference of point of view runs so deep that it will probably continue to be repeated until the day comes when the Body of Art and the Body of Criticism are laid together in a common grave. On that day, which is the Day of Judgement,

the Spirit of Criticism may, according to the popular legend, have the last word; but if so, the Spirit of Art will, we are sure, remain rebelliously sceptical of the authority of the Word.[21]

Croly continues in his essay concerning criticisms among artists or architects themselves that they have always talked over each other's work with an intense interest and for a very practical purpose since ancient time, and this very informal and largely technical criticism has been in the long run the criticism that counted. However, Croly also cautions that criticisms among architects themselves are sometimes based too much on the small personal prejudices which professional ambitions and rivalries are likely to engender. It should be added, however, that such personal prejudices and rivalries are merely the measure of the very living interest which architects take in each other's work, and the criticism which issues has the prime value of being chiefly technical. It helps just because it is technical; because it is passed by a man dealing with certain problems upon another man who is dealing with very much the same problems. If both these men are thorough craftsmen, devotedly trying to make their work as good as possible, the effect of this mutual comment is helpful in a peculiarly pervasive and insidious way. An architect, no matter how great, when working alone or in surroundings which offer him no acceptable suggestions, and leave his best designs unappreciated, is almost sure to make an excessively conscious approach to his work, and to have it issue in something fantastic and outlandish. He needs an atmosphere of technical comment which is at once a stimulus and a check, and which can exist only in a group of sincere, enthusiastic, talented and well-trained craftsmen.

As to exactly on what basis the criticism that counts most should be squarely placed, Croly concludes:

> It is not too much to say consequently that a certain kind of criticism has a most important part to play in the development, whatever it may amount to, of American architecture. The purpose of such criticism is to maintain a communicating current of ideas and visible experiments and suggestions throughout the whole body of American architectural practice. Its chief effort should be not so much to praise and to condemn, as to select and to popularize. Obviously the selection implies a standard and the popularization, a general desire for excellence; but both the standard and increasing desire for excellence are yearly becoming better established and more assertive. The general application of such a standard on the part of architects themselves, or of people in touch with them, is, as we have said, the criticism that counts. Of course, there is another kind of criticism, which counts for comparatively little, at all events, in architectural practice. As ordinarily applied this kind of criticism consists in putting together a standard of architectural achievement, made up qualities, mostly moral and intellectual, derived from the best periods of architectural practice, and then condemning contemporary work because it fails to reach this standard. It is something of this kind which artists generally have in mind, when they declare that all criticism is an elaborate and pretentious misunderstanding. We cannot agree with them in turning such criticism down entirely. Ordinarily it is of little or no practical value; but it represents, nevertheless, an interest which cannot be lightly set aside. It endeavors to apply to any particular art, general ideas, which stand for the artistic conscience of the community,

and embody the integrity of its artistic life. Such ideas are, of course, to a very great extent, moral, human, perhaps religious; and when the practice of any particular art is working harmoniously with his general moral conscience, it undoubtedly means that the product gains in spontaneity, vitality and power. But it so happens that our modern conscience speaks with no certain voice, that an artist, in the face of such dubious and conflicting messages, is thrown rather too consciously back upon his technical ideas, and the consequence is that the criticism which we have described in this article is the criticism which counts more than ever nowadays; and unless we are very much mistaken, it counts for a great deal."[22]

Since this study will deal exclusively with criticism on commercial architecture which in some respects is different from any other type of architecture, it is quite appropriate that a discussion on the matter be included here. As reflected in the discussion published recently in some architectural periodicals, it has been revealed that criticism in the field of commercial architecture has reached a lamentably low level, at least in some quarters. In doing so, the need has been underscored for more constructive thinking about the subject. When one looks into the matter, the reason for the present state of affairs becomes understandable. The fact is that very little has been done to establish a set of valid criteria by which business buildings might be judged. Generally speaking, critics of the past and even many today apply standards to commercial structures that are entirely foreign to the buildings. The chief fault seems to lie in the failure to recognize the actualities which govern that branch of architecture. The inference is that there is little profound understanding of the nature of commercial architecture. To judge from much that is written, for example, one gains the impression that office buildings are designed according to the canons that have applied to other types of public buildings such as libraries, city halls, courthouses, and the like. There is a constant carping on proportion and concern about whether the various parts of a skyscraper are harmoniously related. So marked is the emphasis on these points that one is led to believe that proportion is the architect's principle problem. Some architectural writers and editors suggest that, judging by the amount of attention devoted to the subject, "monumentality" is a prime quality. The fact is that some critics always harbor a misconception that commercial buildings are designed by architects who are free of all other responsibilities and have only to concentrate on how to create monumental and well-proportioned structures. Of course, nothing could be farther from the truth. Obviously, criticism based upon such criteria has little validity because it does not deal with the factors with which commercial architecture really is concerned. Oddly enough, very few critics have made an effort to discover the basic concepts underlying commercial design; or have probed deeply into the complex problems which confront the architect. Rarely, for example, does one find mention of "cost and return" planning, the bedrock of all commercial design. Even more rarely does one find the kind of comment which demonstrates in what way the shape of skyscrapers are as expressive of certain aspects of America's own culture.

The basic fact about an office building is that it differs from any other type of public buildings, as, say a courthouse, not only in function but also in a still more significant aspect. It is not only the residence of business: it is a business itself. It is more or less merchandise having commercial value and building space is a product to be sold or rented at so many dollars per square foot for a profit. When this fundamental fact is comprehended, it becomes apparent that architectural standards which have been drawn up for a courthouse are not applicable to the Sears Tower in Chicago. This does not mean that standards of beauty in the classic sense do not apply. It means that classic standards are of secondary importance. A more significant consideration is the way in which the shape of the building fulfills the economic and functional aspects of the problem at hand. It means one must not only ask if the building is attractive; but also if it works in terms of the people who inhabit the space and to the benefit of the people who built it. In a sense, the most beautiful building is the one that maximizes attractiveness, function, and economy. Such a building would fit ideally into the American social environment. It would be an integral and expressive feature of American culture and characteristic of the time. Therefore, architectural criticism on commercial buildings based on criteria of economy, function, and attractiveness, though not necessarily in this order, would have real value since these are the problems with which the architect struggles. He does not strive primarily for "proportion," despite the fact that the best buildings possess that quality. He does not strive for "monumentality" although he often achieves it. The prime consideration is how to design a building so as to make it a going concern and a financial success. To do this the architect uses a system of planning known in the building trade as "cost and return." Its main objective is to create a design in which the return from the space produced is greater than the cost of constructing it. All business buildings from a lowly one story supermarket to the gigantic Sears Tower are planned on the basis of "cost and return." In view of the importance of "cost and return" planning to commercial architecture, it would seem necessary to base standards of judgment on that system of design. A knowledge of the history of "cost and return" planning, the nature of its evolution and the present point of its development is essential to constructive criticism.

3

The Critics and the Publications

In his *Hypocrisy About Art* (1962), Theodore L. Shaw writes in the chapter entitled "The Critic's Job" as follows:

> Critics have been deeply hurt in their souls, I believe, by the well-known saying "Those who can, do; those who can't, teach." That's why they like to emphasize so strongly that criticism is itself an art—thus establishing themselves as artists in their own right, and controverting the accusation that they took up criticism out of disappointment. In spite of my rather low opinion of critics I hesitate a bit at depriving them of this psychological life-belt—to which they have no doubt been clinging during those long hours of the night when their minds hark back over the inanities they have written during the day. I am encouraged to reveal the bad news to them, however, because—as I shall explain in a moment—I plan to make it up to them in another way. No; criticism is not an art. On the contrary it is a "service," like medicine, which means that it is tied down by certain duties and obligations. And for art, of course, that wouldn't do. Any obligation would destroy it. Art demands complete freedom."[1]

Shaw goes on to say that criticism is not that way. Fantasy, extravaganza, exhibitionism are out of place in it. Its practitioners must be guided by the principles of the physician who declines to tell his patient that he might have only six months to live and critics must similarly control their propensities "to be merry-andrews, romancers, harlequins, acrobats and prestidigitators,"[2] at least while they are writing their comments. Elsewhere in this very same chapter, Shaw declares:

> If critics will promise to renounce this selfish, anti-social and even inhuman mode of thought, if they will agree hereafter to look on art as being for people rather than on people as being for art I would be willing to take a chance and allow them not only to express their opinions on art but also to have a voice as to what that art should be—have a voice, that is, in putting on the show. This doesn't mean that they would actually "create" art, which job belongs elsewhere, of course. No; their job would be to acquire a more thorough knowledge than anybody else of the world's available art works; to become better judges than anybody else of what art works would best please what kinds of people under what circumstances; to bring people into contact with those special art works they would enjoy, and to keep them away from those art works they wouldn't enjoy. You might visualize them as aesthetic physicians, running a "giant drug store" of art recipies; organizing a research laboratory to discover new

art recipies; and operating an efficient delivery service. Which—as I think you must admit—offers very interesting possibilities. Critics could make a notable contribution to mankind in thus developing their capacities and ambitions.[3]

Actually, an attack on critics as snide and petulant as this is included here only to demonstrate the fact that ignorant and professionally insecure commentators like Mr. Shaw do regrettably exist even today, particularly when it comes to criticism that is not complimentary to their works. It is true that most artists and architects are impatient and uncomfortable with each criticism but such a response as Mr. Shaw's is patently absurd and vicious, and cannot be taken seriously. It helps one to appreciate what some critics must have been through in contending with such illogical attacks and leads one to be all the more sympathetic. I have mentioned earlier that critics whose architectural writings have been and will be included and discussed in this study represent a variety of backgrounds. Most of them indeed have been distinguished and successful "practicioners" in their lines of profession during their time. In the field of architecture, Sturgis, P. B. Wight, Van Brunt, or, come down to the present, Philip Johnson, are good examples, let alone those world-wide renowned architects such as Adler, Root, Sullivan, and Wright, for instance, who also wrote extensively. These men "can and do" as well as "teach or write."

In September, 1914, Edward R. Smith wrote an article in that month's issue of *The Architectural Record* commemorating the death of Montgomery Schuyler:

> Modern civilization may be said to lack quality. Many of the broad and generous convictions which characterized the generations immediately preceding our own have been abandoned, and the rich culture of other days seems to be passing. Perhaps this lack of quality is creeping into architecture. In the rush of modern competition the architect is more or less at the mercy of the financier, and is yielding pre-eminence to the engineer of construction. He finds it difficult to maintain his standing as a scholar and an artist. The professor of an art so broad as architecture, so fundamental to human society, so necessary to the expression of the larger qualities of human nature, should himself be broad, many sided and sympathetic. The large and genial atmosphere of the older time has persisted in the personality of several men who are in the field of our friendly recollection.[4]

One of these men was Montgomery Schuyler and another one was Russell Sturgis. They were of the same generation and were intimate friends and associates. Schuyler and Sturgis, along with Barr Ferree and Herbert Croly, were among the founders of *The Architectural Record,* who published its first issue in 1891, and were always in the background in the management of the journal, which has stood especially for scholarship in American architecture. Sturgis was a master of literary style such as were few in his day and fewer still are in our generation. He was a distinguished architect but it was not his architecture that made him famous. It was his writing as a master critic of sculpture, painting, and especially architecture. Schuyler had the same large sympathies and the same breadth of knowledge though he was not a trained architect as was Sturgis. But by much study and constant associations with active men like Sturgis, P. B. Wight, and the painter John LaFarge and the like, he became sufficiently conversant with detail. Perhaps the lack of more definite equipment made possible the broad and human point of view which he maintained better than any American writer on architecture. After his death in 1914 and particularly after Sullivan's ten years later, the names of these two most perceptive American architectural critics along with the ideals of the Chicago School of Architecture for which they had fought for so long and of which they had been among their most persuasive advocates, seemed to disappear from the American architectural scene. It was not until 1934 that Lewis Mumford's *The Brown Decades* brought their forgotten turn-of-the-century reputation back to memory. Of Schuyler, Mumford (writing in 1952) says:

> Montgomery Schuyler whose architectural criticism continued to appear in *The Architectural Record* (until 1914), never hauled down the flag: he, who had been such an eager and searching exponent of the new architecture when he did a classic monograph on the works of Adler and Sullivan, almost at the end of his career in 1912, published an article on Frank Lloyd Wright—"an architectural pioneer."[5]

Mumford was discussing the crushing assault of Beaux Arts academicism on the remnants of progressive architecture during the early twentieth century. This assault overwhelmed Louis Sullivan and eventually the entire Chicago School, as well as the second phase of the school working around Wright after 1900, except for Wright himself. And all through the "battle," as Mumford puts it, Schuyler "never hauled down the flag." Following Mumford's lead, architectural writers and historians unearthed Schuyler's critical writings, as well as Sturgis' and others, from those early issues of periodicals, architectural or otherwise. Thus, their works and the merits of the Chicago School of Architecture have gradually become familiar to students of American culture and architecture. To be fair, the fact must be noted here that while one is studying the critical writings of these prominent architectural critics of the turn of the century, namely Schuyler, Sturgis and P. B. Wight, he must realize that these men were not critics without prejudices for they were brought up in the mid-nineteenth century and were familiar with the writings of John Ruskin. Their vision of a "real architecture" depended on the Ruskinean ethic of morality in architecture, the Richardsonian disciplining of picturesque irregularities in forcefully simple compositions, and the structural and functional rationalism of Leopold Eidlitz and Viollet-le-Duc. Ruskin fostered an awareness of the "honest" use of materials so as to display their inherent characteristics of color, texture, and function within the fabric of the wall. From Ruskin, too, ultimately stemmed the idealistic concept of a "real" architecture, not only in material terms, but in a social sense as well. Having called for an end to the classicistic formalism which had dominated eighteenth- and early nineteenth-century architecture. Ruskin demanded that an architecture be sufficiently flexible to grasp the "life" of the men and the world producing it.

These precepts of Ruskin colored the views of Schuyler, Sturgis, and Wight for the rest of their entire lives. Thus they could only view with disgust the overwhelming swing of popular taste towards Beaux Arts and academicism and classic eclecticism which characterized the end of the nineteenth century. Perhaps, it was this hatred of the classic phase which made them so prophetically alert to rebellions against it. To them, Louis Sullivan seemed the bearer of a new light, and again and again they pointed to Sullivan's work along with the work of the rest of the Chicago School, as the most significant that was being done in America. The writings of these critics were perhaps the most important single factor in the artistic reawakening of the American people that characterized the early years of the twentieth century.

In his *Roots of Contemporary American Architecture,* Lewis Mumford proclaims: "Montgomery Schuyler (1843-1914) was the first full-fledged critic of architecture in America, and for his soundness, if not his originality, he must still be counted the best."[6] Whether this statement of Mumford is acceptable to all or not is still a question. However, it can be said for certain that Montgomery Schuyler was, in point of content, the first architectural critic of *The Architectural Record* of which he was one of the founders. His piece on the Romanesque Revival in New York was the first article in Volume 1, 1891, following immediately Harry W. Desmond's introductory note. He had the honor of being the first to enter this periodical which, in subsequent years, depended on him for much of its best material. In his own time, he was not, perhaps, regarded as the first critic in point of rank, nor, as another American architectural critic has regarded him, as the only architectural critic America has produced.

Schuyler was born in Ithaca, New York, August 16, 1843, and died in New Rochelle, July 6, 1914. His father was the Rev. Dr. Anthony Schuyler of Ithaca. He belonged to the Arent Schuyler branch of this New York family, which produced several men of much importance in the Colonial and Revolutionary periods. Schuyler entered Hobart College in 1858, but left without graduating. At the close of the Civil War in 1865, he went to New York City and entered the profession of journalism, serving on the *New York World* and became a member of a brilliant group of young writers gathered around Manton Marble, then editor and owner of the *World*. Schuyler coupled his work on the news desk with literary reviewing, activities he continued throughout his life. Although Schuyler remained on the staff of the *World* until 1883, in 1874 he undertook additional work as a member of editorial staff of the short-lived *New York Sketch-Book of Architecture,* which appeared for three years, through 1876. It was a significant forerunner of the professional journals to follow.[7] The first of consequence, *The American Architect and Building News*, appeared the year the *Sketch-Book* ended. Not until the eighties did the professional journals proliferate so that they replaced books as the principal sources of information about current building.

Schuyler moved from the *World* to a position on the editorial staff of *The New York Times*, where he remained from 1883 until his retirement from active journalism in 1907. Meanwhile, he had been managing editor of *Harper's Weekly* (1886-87) and reader for Harper and Brothers (1887-94). After 1912, he regularly contributed book reviews and articles on literary subjects to the *New York Sun*. Except for an article on the New York State Capitol published in December, 1879, his first magazine article on architecture, it was also during the eighties that the earliest of his major essays on architecture appeared as freelance ventures. Once he had embarked on architectural criticism, this writing virtually amounted to a second career. Although never a member of its editorial staff, Schuyler was a major contributor to the *Architectural Record* since its founding. The *Record* gave him a regular outlet for his architectural essays, often written anonymously and occasionally under the pseudonym of Franz K. Winkler, and this continued until his death in 1914. During those twenty-three years, he contributed more articles to the *Record* than any other writer, possibly with the exception of Russell Sturgis, but no one ranged more widely in the field of American architecture.[8]

While Schuyler was on the *New York World*, his preparation for his future as an architectural critic began. The major elements in his preparation eventually coalesced to create what Schuyler termed his "Point of View." During the sixties Schuyler was undoubtedly caught up in the Ruskinean idealism which pervasively influenced American aesthetic life from the fifties through the Centennial Exposition of 1876. He must have known of the publication here in New York in 1863 and 1864 of the Ruskinean and Pre-Raphaelite journal, the *New Path*. This was not edited by a single individual, but by a group of enthusiasts, including the architect Peter Bonnett Wight and, as its major contributor, Russell Sturgis. By the time he published a preliminary book on *American Architecture* in 1892, Schuyler was mature and had a large store of recollections of the past of American architecture. He was dominated, as Sturgis, Wight, and all serious students of architecture were at the time, by the idea of the civilized world's return to the method, the truth, and the genuineness of medieval work. Everyone read Ruskin's books, which, with all their faults, had the heart of the matter in them; many passed on to the stronger scholarship of Viollet-le-Duc and the medievalists of France and Germany. Ruskinean idealism and the medieval doctrine of the previous period always tempered Schuyler's judgment, and made him antagonistic to the results of the teaching of classic school for the rest of his life.

Being on the editorial staff of the aforementioned *New York Sketch-Book* was also a significant step for Schuyler as a critic, for it furnished him with a platform for his criticism, since he returned repeatedly in his later essays to the buildings, the men, and the implicit ideals illustrated in its pages. The *Sketch-Book* always included the most progressive projects of its day. Victorian Gothic design still predominated, but designs more important for the future challenged this waning style. Prominent were Richardson's early works in a "Romanesque" mode. Schuyler came to know Henry Hobson Richardson, just as he was beginning to evolve a personal style which would shortly mark him as the greatest American architect of his generation. Before his removal from New York to Boston in 1874, Richardson served briefly as the initial editor of the *Sketch-Book* and when Schuyler served a short term as managing editor of *Harper's Weekly* from 1885 to 1887, he took care to publish some of Richardson's works. Later, in 1891, he initiated his long association with *The Architectural Record* with discussions in its first two issues of the influence of Richardsonian Romanesque on American architecture as mentioned earlier. Of all his architect friends, however, it was not Richardson but Leopold Eidlitz, wedded to the cause of structural and functional rationalism, who exerted the most profound influence on Schuyler's thinking. Schuyler's friendship with Eidlitz began with his very first piece of architectural criticism. In the *New York World* for September 2, 1868, he published a critique of Eidlitz's newly completed Emanu-El Synagogue in New York City. And forty years later, he wrote a memorial tribute to Eidlitz in his "A Great American Architect: Leopold Eidlitz" published in Volume 24 (1908) of *The Architectural Record,* in which Schuyler presents Eidlitz not only as a great architect but as a great critic. Throughout his extensive career as an architectural writer, Schuyler also contributed articles on other subjects to various periodicals. Moreover, he wrote one non-architectural book, a short account of the first transcontinental trip of the "Los Angeles Special," entitled *Westward the Course of Empire* (1906). His early criticism on architecture were gathered together in book form in his *American Architecture:* Studies (1892)[9] but apart from his monographs on Chicago architects, the most significant of which is on Adler and Sullivan (first published in *The Architectural Record* and then bound together in a little pamphlet), his later essays are scattered through the file of periodicals, *The Architectural Record* in particular, and had never been collected. It was not until 1961 that William Jordy and Ralph Coe put them together again in *American Architecture and Other Writings* with an expansive bibliography of Schuyler's architectural writings. As the two editors of the book say, this bibliography is primarily based upon three bound volumes of Schuyler's articles collected by him and deposited in the Avery Library at Columbia University. The earliest substantive article on Schuyler is probably the memorial bibliography published in 1914 in *The Architectural Record* immediately following Edward R. Smith's article on Schuyler in which Smith concludes: "How broad Mr. Schuyler's work really was, how keen his interest in the busy men of his time, may be learned from the bibliography, probably imperfect, which we are able to append."[10] Perhaps, Jordy and Coe in the introduction to their book eloquently summarize Schuyler's distinction:

> At his death on July 16, 1914, Schuyler left an extensive body of architectural criticism, which constitutes the most perceptive, most revealing, and most urbane commentary on American architecture to emerge from the critical tenets of progressive nineteenth century theory. Only the collected writing of his prolific contemporary, Russell Sturgis, can offer competition. And it is questionable whether Sturgis was quite Schuyler's equal either in profundity of observation or felicity of expression. In a broader sense, Schuyler not only drew from the tradition of organic functionalism which called forth the most creative architecture in nineteenth century America; but, in the course of his criticism, he helped to define this tradition as well. His contribution thus takes its place beside the formulations of such men as Horatio Greenough, Leopold Eidlitz, and Louis Sullivan. That these three men embodied their theory in three different architectural styles—Greek Revival for Greenough, Victorian Gothic for Eidlitz, and his own protomodern synthesis for Sullivan—indicates the scope and vitality of the architectural idealism embraced by Schuyler."[11]

Recent and present-day architectural writers may not regard Russell Sturgis as of "quite Schuyler's equal either in profundity of observation or felicity of expression" as Jordy and Coe observe, but in their time Sturgis was more prominent and enjoyed higher regard both as a scholar and critic of all branches of the arts, particularly architecture. His contemporaries and friends, Schuyler included, greatly respected his wide range of knowledge and sound judgment. Upon Sturgis' death at the age of seventy-three in 1909, Schuyler wrote:

> The death of Russell Sturgis was by no means premature, according to the ordinary standard of longevity. He had overpassed the scriptural limit, being in his seventy-third year, but to those who knew him, the death was premature. That so eager and omnivorous an intellectual curiosity should have been balked, so avid a capacity of intellectual enjoyment have been nullified, before the curiosity showed any signs of dulling, the enjoyment any signs of slackening, still seems to his friends a cruel and untimely blow... His knowledge was so wide, so "encyclopaediacal," it has been called since his death, his anxiety to be right on any point of fact, and to take nothing for granted without proof, was so keen, that his reader might go along with him on any disputed or disputable point with a singular confidence, even though that reader might differ from artistic judgement that accompanied the erudition."[12]

Although as a critic some recent and present writers might consider Sturgis less profound than provocative and persuasive, this accuracy and sureness, described by Schuyler, were a great source of strength to him. He was animated by a sincere passion for the beauty in the largest sense and had as background an unusually wide knowledge of the history and technique of the arts—the knowledge that was "combined with geniality, with a desire to find out the good rather than the bad in the work he set himself to judge, combined also with perfect and unsuspectible disinterestedness,"[13] so continued Schuyler.

An architect, a critic, and a writer, Russel Sturgis was born in Baltimore, October 16, 1836, while his father, a shipping merchant and a commissioner of pilots in New York, was living there temporarily. He was a descendant of Edward Sturgis who was in Charlestown, Massachusetts in 1643 and was one of the first settlers. Sturgis was educated in the public schools of New York City and in the Free Academy of the City of New York, later called the College of the City of New York, from which he was graduated with the degree of Bachelor of Art in 1856. At the Academy he met Peter B. Wight who later became one of his intimate friends and his business partner when they formed an architectural firm that lasted from 1863 to 1868. After that Sturgis practiced alone until about 1880 when he turned himself to scholarship and freelancing as a critic and writer.

Friendship between Sturgis and Wight began when they were at the Academy together and never ceased until the end as Wight reminisced in 1909:

> My acquaintance with him commenced while in college more than half a century ago; but we have lived nearly a thousand miles apart for thirty-five years since that time.[14] We used to meet after regular hours in the room set apart for the drawing master, for we were not satisfied with the regular work, and put in extra time drawing from the excellent collection of casts from the antique, which the department then contained. On the way homeward we had to pass the All Souls Unitarian Church, then being erected at the southeast corner of Twentieth Street and Fourth Avenue, New York, from the plan of the late Jacob Wray Mould, the first commission of importance which came to him after his arrival in this country, following his apprenticeship with Owen Jones. And such drawings! I have never seen better ones since. Every thing was drawn in ink and colored on fine white drawing paper, backed with muslin. It became our habit every day to study those plans and compare them with the work being executed. We were fascinated, and I may say then and there both were impressed for the first time with the desire to become architects. Our friendship was cemented by the study of Mould's drawings, and then we commenced to read architecture. We read all the books on the subject to be found in the college library, including a set of Ruskin's *Seven Lamps* and *Stones of Venice*, which had just come out, and Sturgis began to buy books, as he had more spare money than I had, and I began to devour them.[15]

Not only their friendship was formed while they were in college, but also their strong belief and conviction in the course of Ruskinean idealism that lasted all through their lives as their friendship did. Soon after leaving the Academy, Sturgis and a few friends, founders of the Society for the Advancement of Truth in Art, published a serious Ruskinean and Pre-Raphaelite little art magazine called *The New Path*. The articles by Sturgis were its backbone, and they revealed his deep critical interest in his profession. Wight recalled this episode of Sturgis' life as follows:

We both were members of the Society for the Advancement of Truth in Art during its existence from January 27, 1863, until February 27, 1865, when it was dissolved. The Society published a monthly journal called the *New Path*, which first appeared in May, 1863, and was discontinued at the end of the second volume, the last number of which was issued December, 1865. Mr. Sturgis was an extensive contributor to its pages. One cause of the discontinuance of the magazine was that its writers attracted attention of publishers of journals of wide circulation. Clarence Cook, who was the editor, went to the New York *Tribune* and was its art editor until his death. Sturgis was afterwards the art critic of *The Nation* from its first appearance, and was art writer for the New York *Evening Post* and other journals, and editor of "The Field of Art" in *Scribner's Magazine* until his death, as well as having been a frequent contributor to the *Achitectural Record*.[16]

Sturgis was also editor-in-chief of *A Dictionary of Architecture and Art* (3 volumes, 1901-1902), editor of *Outlines of the History of Art* (2 volumes, 1904), and author of a series of books (1903-1908) on the appreciation of architecture, sculpture, and painting. In 1904, he gave the Scammon lectures at the Art Institute of Chicago, which later were published as *The Interdependence of the Arts of Design* (1905). The climax of his writing career was the ambitious *A History of Architecture* (1906-1915), on which he was working at the time of his death and of which he completed only two volumes. In his articles on contemporary architects published by *The Architectural Record* in the "Great American Architects Series," he gave vivid expression to the architectural idols of his day, and pointed out with a canny discrimination both their shortcomings and their achievements. But nothing would reveal his thoughts more candidly and sincerely than personal letters he wrote to Wight all through those long years of their lasting friendship as Wight explains:

An author's printed words are the property of his readers, but his private letters are sacred confidences as long as he lives. When he has become famous and has passed to the majority the world has a right to know their content if it can profit by them. They often reveal his inmost thoughts, expressed without the reserve of formality which one has to observe to avoid the antagonism of carping critics and disputants. But they always reveal a personality which is often veiled by the writer's modesty during his life time. That is what the world likes to know, and can only know when they appear as a revelation of candor and character only half suspected. It is with such thought that I have been persuaded to make public a few extracts from letters received from my friend and companion through many years, Russell Sturgis.[17]

Therefore, with the same reason as Wight stated above, some extracts from Sturgis' personal letters to Wight on various important subjects are appropriately presented here, all of which appear in Wight's article entitled "Reminiscences of Russell Sturgis" published in the August 1909 issue of *The Architectural Record*. Sturgis' letter of February 9, 1897 reveals his thought and point of view on the trends of American architecture and the architectural practice of some architects at the time as follows:

Your article in the *Inland Architect* is more to me than a friendly and appreciative review of my book, and more even than a laudatory obituary written before the date. It reminds me of old times, when you and I were beginning our attempts to rectify and magnify, and glorify American architecture—a time when every thing seemed possible. We have had some pretty serious disappointments since then, and we know now that architecture is not going to be revived in its pristine vigor and beauty in our time; nor yet, so far as we can see, in the time of our successors. I have a son in the profession, and he is almost the only one of the young architects here who seem to be trying to design along the designs of intelligent purpose. Apparently there is no one else who, when he has a house front to build, sits down and thinks what that particular series of openings for doors and windows suggests to him in the way of a front. Everybody else is doing the big bow-wow classic, and, generally, in the most unintelligent way. There was a curious instance the other day, showing that some of them, at least, are quite aware of this. At a meeting of the Architectural League one of the more intelligent of the young men was making a vigorous speech about matters connected with the work of men, who, like himself, were trying to work their way up, and he cited the Academy of Design. I was amazed, for I had supposed that no one of these younger men knew that the Academy of Design was an architectural composition at all. He, however, said he was quite aware that their designs amounted to nothing, that they were not really producing designs, but, he said: "Do not you suppose that we know that the men who built the Academy of Design and such like structures had to sweat blood over their work? Do not you suppose that we know that they spent their nights and hard, long days over their designs? We," he concluded, "cannot undertake to do that; we cannot afford to do that. If we are going to make our living we must do our work in simple fashion." The above does not pretend to be in any way a quotation, but a mere recollection of what his speech amounted to. I was glad to know that they were aware, those young fellow who seem to believe in Roman orders and nothing else, that there was something else besides the mere stealing of a page from Vignola.[18]

On this same matter of the American architectural trend, in his letter of December 18, 1886, just approximately two months prior to the above quoted letter, Sturgis wrote:

The Classic revival is having it all its own way here now. It is not the work of highly taught men of the Paris school, but that of fellows who merely take their design ready made from Vignola... If my son should wish to make a design to please the academicians, I should advise him to make a design in the style of the Renaissance. I mean the real Renaissance of the Italian fifteenth century, because he could never endure the hateful restraint of the Roman colonnades, while, at the same time, nothing but classical forms would be expected to go down.[19]

However, the most revealing of his feelings toward the current trend of the Beaux Arts style of architecture in America at the time was his letter of February 16, 1897 in which Sturgis gave his candid opinion of the Beaux Arts Society and the works of some of its most prominent members. In this particular letter, Sturgis was so candid that Wight had to abbreviate names of the firms mentioned in it. Therefore, the abbreviations are Wight's own. However, it takes only a knowledge of the history of American architecture to know the identities. Sturgis says:

There are two things to put on record as regards that society: First, that it is a little more than an alumni association, a gathering of men who came from the Paris school and who want to renew their friendships and recall the good times of their youth; and second, that the leading men of this school are as far as may be from being mere blind classical revivalists. What I mean by a mere blind classical revivalist is precisely anyone of the firm of M—, M—, and W—. That firm is deliberately working—as has been for three years—in the direction of mere bland, bare square, unvaried, unmodified bones with square holes cut in them, except where a Roman colonnade is introduced. They seem to choose deliberately the no-style which consists in following the blankest and least interesting Italian work of the seventeenth century, merely reducing it to a still blanker and bare monotony by leaving out the slight vestiges of sculpture which that late Italian style had preserved. This style they would be wholly unable to recommend but for that good taste which is the unquestionable gift of the designers of the firm. Moreover, they emphatically preach the gospel of this staring revived Roman which is, indeed, a mere continuation of the Lyceum style, the style of the Greek buildings that were going up when you and I were born. Now, in all this, the example of such Beaux Arts men as C— and H— is very different, and their best designs are really of great merit. Their Patterson City Hall seems to me an extaordinary production, one of the best things of our time. If they have sometimes missed their mark and produced such monsters as one or two of their business fronts in New York, that is only one of the incomprehensible vagaries of sensible men. All that I want to insist upon is that, according to my lights, it is not the influence of the Beaux Arts Society or of the Paris school at all, in no matter how remote a degree, which has given us the accursed influence of the Chicago Exposition and the resulting classical revival of our time. You must have observed how uniformly the French visitors to the fair denounced the buildings of the Court of Honor. The only things they had good word for were the Transportation Building and parts of the Fisheries Buildings. As for the Roman colonnades, they sneered at them as being the school work of their authors, revived for the purpose; and they intimated very plainly that this returning to their schoolboy work signified merely the adoption of what was easiest and quickest done. My own belief is that they were right in this. I cannot but suppose that the reason why M—, M—, and W— and other such firms resort to this Roman style is because it must be so very easy to work in. However that may be, it is a most depressing and saddening symptom. Nothing discourages me more than to see the willingness with which our millions here are given to such fatuous designing; but if I go into this subject I will never have done.[20]

Indeed, Sturgis would never have done. His architectural work is entirely different from what he describes above, in terms of styles, concepts, and personal convictions, both during and after those five years of his partnership with Wight in New York (1863-69). His buildings reflect his early study of architecture from Ruskin's books during his college years, his apprenticeship in the office of Leopold Eidlitz after his graduation, and a year and a half of study in Munich. It is true that his technical preparation for practicing architecture had been gained in the office of Eidlitz who was one of the most enthusiastic adherents and promoters of the Gothic revival and who was inspired by either Pugin and eclecticism or Ruskin and Romanticism. Eidlitz was working, in the fifties and sixties, under such inspiration not only in church building, but extending his attempt to all departments of secular work, endeavoring to show that Gothic was good for houses, public buildings, as well as churches. This was what Ruskin was preaching in England and Viollet-le-Duc in France. Owing to

Ruskin's *Seven Lamps* and *Stones of Venice*, and to George Street's *Brick and Marble* in Italy, young American architects of the early sixties were working under the influence of these writings and also were turning more and more toward Italy for the motives and treatment of their secular design in Gothic. The earliest, and perhaps the most successful of these was Wight's competition-winning design for the National Academy of Design in New York in 1862. Towards the end of the decade, the earliest years of which saw the erection of this work, Wight was commissioned to do the Street Art Building for Yale and Sturgis to do two dormitories and a chapel.

The two dormitories are the Farnham Hall (1869) and the Durfee Hall (1870), and the chapel is the Battell Chapel (1876). It is evident that these three buildings were so designed with reference to one another and to the total effect of all three, that they were said to be the most successful buildings that Yale had up to that time produced, and that they had had an excellent influence in the way of moderation, restraint, conformity, and harmony on such of the subsequent architects of the University as would submit themselves to that influence. Other earlier Sturgis' architecural works include several New York townhouses, the Elover Hospital in New York, i.e., that are not as important as the Yale buildings with the exception of the Farmers' and Mechanics' Bank at Albany, New York, with its unusual delicacy of scale. All these buildings are respectable and creditable. But they by no means indicate that their architect forsook his true vocation when he committed himself to discussing architecture instead of creating it. Doubtless he did well in "creating" and could have been as successful as any architect of the time would have wanted to be, though he probably would not have been of the same rank of some architects whose works he discussed in his writings. There are more architects as good as he had been than there are critics as good as he was, and, to the progress of architecture, his critical writings were even more helpful than his architectural work.

Montgomery Schuyler and Russell Sturgis, of course, have been and will be the two critics of greatest interest to this study as a good portion of their architectural writings on the Chicago commercial architecture at the turn of the century will be included and discussed. However, it would be impossible to leave out those who have minor roles to play as their contributions are of no little significance. Foremost among those lesser personalities is Peter Bonnett Wight, already known to the reader. Wight was of the same generation and a close associate and friend of both Sturgis and Schuyler. He was born in New York City, August 1, 1838, and the son of Amherst Wight, a descendant of Thomas Wight who came to Dedham, Massachusetts, in 1635. Wight was educated in New York City public schools and at the Free Academy where he met and became a good friend of Sturgis and from which he was graduated with a Bachelor of Arts degree in 1855. As mentioned earlier, while at the Academy Wight along with Sturgis read works on architecture and the writings of John Ruskin; he also specialized in drawings in which he was always unusually proficient, even for an architect. A post-graduate year spent in drawing and a year as a student draftsman in an architect's office completed his architectural training. In 1858, persuaded by a family friend, he went to Chicago and occupied a position as an independent architect in the office of Carter and Bauer but later when work became scarce, he returned to New York in 1859.

In 1862, Wight, though an unknown youth, won his first and most important competition and was commissioned to prepare the planning and constructing of the building of the National Academy of Design. In 1863 he formed a partnership to practice architecture with Sturgis and shared an office with him in New York City, as Wight recalls:

> A chance loomed up and we both went into a famous competition. After waiting two years it was decided in my favor. Then, in 1863, we decided to hire an office and share the expense between us. It was 98 Broadway, opposite Trinity churchyard. We had a front room on the fourth floor. After a few years we took another adjoining room, also with front windows, the new room being assigned to the writer. There we remained until the fall of 1868. Sturgis never had a draftsman until he engaged George Fletcher Babb, whom I had met in the first office in which I ever worked, in 1857, and who had been in practice for several years with a partner. The tie between Sturgis and Babb became a close one, for they were both sympathetic artists. They worked together several years, until Sturgis decided to take an office alone. It was all very pleasant. We could look over the trees to the architectural "bird nests" in Trinity Building, and sing hymns on red-letter days to the accompaniment of Trinity's chimes. It was while there that we were invited one day to go over to Littell's office and be introduced to the new arrival from abroad, Henry Hobson Richardson. It was in that office also that we first met Larkin G. Mead and his brother William R. Mead.... William R. Mead became a student of Sturgis, and when, in 1868, he moved over to 57 Broadway, Babb and Mead moved with him. This was the beginning of the second "bird's nest" established in New York. Sturgis took other students, there most of his architectural work was done. Charles F. McKim was also a student there for a year before he went to Paris for further studies. When McKim returned from Europe he took Mead in partnership, and they had an office in the same building. That was the beginning of the firm of McKim, Mead, and White, from whose office so many architects graduated.[21]

While sharing an office, Wight and Sturgis erected notable Ruskinean buildings during the following two decades when Sturgis retired from active architectural practice approximately around 1880. Between 1869 and 1886, for example, Sturgis' Farnham, Lawrence, and Durfee dormitories, as well as Battell Chapel, went up on the Old Campus at Yale, a complex of buildings which probably represents the finest existing example of Ruskinean design on a large scale by any American. More precisely, the broad massing, high and angular, with its restrained ornament related to structure, minimized Ruskin's pictorial intricacy of detail and shadow, to reveal the more architectonic inspiration of Ruskin's disciple, George Street, and Street's protege, Phillip Webb. Wight's completed building for the National Academy of Design received wide praise from the public although some critics had some reservation as being a too literalistic or pinched version of the Doge's Palace, which was of course one of Ruskin's principal enthusiasms in his *Stones of Venice*. Its facades, beautifully proportioned and detailed, exemplified the Italian phase of the Gothic revival, so passionately praised by Ruskin. The building stood at Fourth Avenue and Twenty-Third Street, and for many years was one of New York's most conspicuous monuments. Between 1863 and 1866 Wight also completed a building for the Old Campus at Yale. In this School of Fine Arts Building, John Ferguson Weir headed the first professional art department to be established by any institution of higher learning in this country. Wight's Fine Arts Building stands today not far from the dormitories and chapel of his friend Sturgis.

Other interests lured both architects away from design in the seventies and eighties. Sturgis turned to scholarship and freelancing in New York, where he became a fellow contributor with Montgomery Schuyler to *The Architectural Record*. During the sixties Schuyler must have become acquainted with these men, their journal, their buildings, and their ideals—all of which represented the architectural "avant garde" of the decade. The news of the great fire and an invitation from Astor Carter, his old office companion, lured Wight to Chicago in December 1871. The firm of Carter, Drake, and Wight was formed, which became Drake and Wight on the death, two years later, of Carter. A great deal of work was done in this office, commercial and domestic rather than monumental, and it became a training ground for many young architects, among them Daniel H. Burnham and John W. Root. Wight centered his activities on fireproof construction, and for ten years from 1881 to 1891 gave up the practice of architecture to devote himself to the development of terra-cotta structural tile. He claimed to have been the inventor and first user of the "grill foundation," slabs composed of crossed iron rails imbedded in concrete, although Root is generally regarded as its inventor. He resumed practice and did some not very important work in connection with the World's Columbian Exposition of 1893 but after 1895 devoted himself to the passage of a law in the State of Illinois requiring the examination, licensing, and registration of architects. This law, enacted in 1897, was the first of its kind in America. Wight was elected secretary and treasurer of the board of examiners created by this act, and held this position until he retired from professional activity in 1914. All through the years until his death in 1925, Wight contributed numerous articles and critical writings on architecture to several journals, particularly *The Architectural Record* and the *Inland Architect*, some of which will be included and discussed in this study.

Several times earlier, I have mentioned the name of an architect, a critic, and a man who played a very significant role in the lives of Montgomery Schuyler and Russell Sturgis during their formative years, architecturally speaking, of preparation to become an architectural critic and an architect. He was one of the most influential American architects in the mid-nineteenth century in whose office Sturgis received his formal architectural training and idealism and probably from whose advice Sturgis went to study architecture in Munich for a year and a half. Although twenty years older, he was the man who became a good friend and idol of Schuyler and exerted the most profound effect on him. Most importantly, he was among the men whom Schuyler, Sturgis and Wight admired most all through their lives. This architect, critic, and just ordinary man is Leopold Eidlitz.

Eidlitz is said to be a man with a gift of witty expression whose most famous acid remark, much quoted by his friends, was: "American architecture is the art of covering one thing with another thing to imitate a third thing, which if genuine would not be desirable."[22] Schuyler himself quoted this famous significant remark of Eidlitz to open his talk, enunciating his critical position, delivered to the National Association of Builders in New York on February 12, 1891. Eidlitz was born in Prague, Bohemia, March 29, 1823. After his school years in Prague, he entered the Polytechnic at Vienna when he became interested in architecture. Early in 1843 he came to New York and entered the office of Richard Upjohn, at the time the leading exponent of the Gothic revival in American architecture. He was then working on the present building of Trinity Church, New York. After leaving Upjohn's office, Eidlitz formed the firm of Blesch and Eidlitz to design St. George's Episcopal Church in New York. The construction of this church with its successful German Gothic design started young Eidlitz upon a successful career. Much of his best earlier work, therefore, was in church design, However, Eidlitz insisted that Gothic was adequate to every architectural expression, and during his earlier period he designed a number of houses. Among his churches, St. Peter's, Westchester, New York, the Church of the Holy Trinity, New York City, completed in 1853, and the Congregational Church in Greenwich, Connecticut, show his skill, but his most successful church is considered to be Christ Church, St. Louis. Perhaps, the most original ecclesiastical building which Eidlitz designed was the Emanu-El Synagogue on Fifth Avenue. Erected in 1868 and demolished in 1928 to make way for a business skyscraper, it was an extraordinarily successful combination of Gothic structure with Saracenic decoration, including carved and molded as well as colored ornament. Some critics at the time attacked the incongruity of a cruciform interior for a Jewish temple. In secular work, Eidlitz designed a few notable buildings in New York. Among them were the Continental Bank (1856); the American Exchange Bank (1857), the first fireproof commercial building in the city, the Brooklyn Academy of Music (1860). In these, as in other works, he continued with marked success to revert to his favorite German Gothic style. His major monument was the redesign of the New York State Capital at Albany in 1875 in cooperation with Henry H. Richardson. This and his work on the New York Court House were Eidlitz' last significant architectural undertakings.

Eidlitz wrote a number of architectural articles published in professional periodicals and two volumes: *Nature and Function of Art* (1881) and *Big Wages and How to Earn Them* (1887), the latter a criticism of trade unions which was published anonymously. It can justly be said that no American architect of his generation propounded a more thoughtful philosophy of architecture than did Eidlitz. His unduly neglected *Nature of Function of Art* contained the rudiments of much of Montgomery Schuyler's critical theory. He died March 22, 1908. Six months later, Schuyler, as a posthumous tribute to his friend whom he greatly admired, published an essay entitled "A Great American Architect: Leopold Eidlitz," in the September-October, 1908 issue of *The Architectural Record*. In it, Schuyler pronounced Eidlitz not only a great American architect but also a great architectural writer and critic.

Besides Peter Bonnett Wight and Leopold Eidlitz, another critic who was especially prominent as an architectural writer and who played a major role in the turn-of-the-century world of American architectural criticism particularly during his six year "reign" (1900-06) as editor of *The Architectural Record* is Herbert David Croly. Though almost thirty years younger than the others, Croly shared a progressive point of view with a cluster of more or less likeminded commentators, notably his colleagues at *The Architectural Record*, Montgomery Schuyler, Russell Sturgis, P. B. Wight, and Barr Ferree. In critical acumen they ranged from Sturgis, who was perhaps closest to Schuyler in enlightenment and at the time was more prominent, to Croly, whose temporizing as a critic gave evidence more of good will than of keen vision. Croly's social conviction, coupled with his lack of insight as a critic, eventually encouraged his abandonment of architectural criticism, in order to write *The Promise of American Life* (1909) and to edit the *New Republic*. Both the book and his editorship brought him great fame.

A journalist and writer, Croly was born in New York City January 23, 1869. He studied for a year at the City College of New York and for two years at Harvard before becoming secretary to his father, a journalist, in 1888. In the years that followed he edited *The Record and Guide*, a real estate paper, and worked on the staff of *The Architectural Record*. He returned to Harvard in 1892, but suffered a nervous breakdown in 1893 and spent a year abroad to recover from it. He returned again to Harvard in 1895 to study philosophy. Leaving Harvard in 1899, still without a degree, he spent a year in Paris before taking up the editorship of *The Architectural Record* in 1900. He resigned that position in 1906 to write *The Promise of American Life* (1909), which gained him reputation as one of the most perceptive and influential American political writers. Though neither it nor its sequel, *Progressive Democracy* (1914), was a best seller, Theodore Roosevelt's "New Nationalism" policy of reform was influenced by Croly's work. In 1910, Croly was awarded his Harvard Bachelor of Arts degree, credited to the class of 1890. In 1914, when Willard Straight founded the *New Republic*, Croly became its editor. Along with such writers as

Walter Weyl and Walter Lippman, he helped to mold it into a major, nonpartisan, progressive periodical. After World War I, despite having gained a reputation as a spokesman for President Wilson, Croly editorially denounced the Treaty of Versailles, an act that cost the *New Republic* half its circulation. In his final years he moved leftward. He supported Robert LaFollette for president in 1924. Thereafter, he lost interest in political affairs and devoted most of his time to studying religious and metaphysical questions. He died in Santa Barbara, California, May 17, 1930. Despite his shyness, his slight stature, and his quiet voice that often drifted into inaudibility, Herbert Croly led an active social life that brought him into close relations with leading American politicians, intellectuals, artists, architects, and critics. In the days when the Century Club was a center of social and intellectual life in New York City, Schuyler, Sturgis, and Croly were among the wittier conversationalists at its gatherings, where they counted among their intimate friends the painters Homer Martin and John LaFarge, the publisher Henry Holt, the critic and editor William Brownell, and many of the architects whose works they reviewed.

Croly's relationship with other architectural writers, such as Sturgis and Wight, not all pleasant when it came to differences of opinion sometimes. As mentioned earlier, in 1901 during which time Croly was the editor of *The Architectural Record* and Sturgis was editing "The Field of Art" in *Scribner's Magazine*, Croly published an article in acid language in the *Record* as a reply to Wight's earlier article that Sturgis published in *Scribner's* "Field of Art" on the subject of "What is Evolution in Architecture." In it, Wight says of the best periods of architecture:

> There must have been community of interest. Investigation shows that every time a change took place, it was adopted in future work by all, until another step forward could be taken. The old methods were dropped as fast as the new ones were adopted, even in the enlargement of buildings. Where every improvement when tested and approved universally adopted and perpetuated, there was evolution. They did not talk about it or write about it in those days; they were at it all the time unconsciously.[23]

Croly sharply replied:

> Undoubtedly they were at it all the time, with a comparative lack of consciousness, although it is not so certain that they did not write about it as Mr. Wight is obliged to do. But it is absurd to say that such improvements were adopted and perpetuated without being discussed, or that the structural logic of an early Greek temple or an early mediaeval cathedral was not the monumental embodiment of that logic demand in the Greek and French character, the social equivalent of which was the inveterate habit of talking over interesting problems. Be that as it may, however, we may agree with Mr. Wight and Mr. Sturgis that in case the work of modern architects is to be very much improved, there must be an increase of mutual at the expense of individual effort. But how is this mutuality to be brought about?[24]

Croly continues in this same article that he has an answer to the above question but his is quite different from that of Wight in which Wight proposes corporate guilds, organized by a group of architects with much the same point of view, and sufficient in number to form a complete business organization. It is presupposed that such guild would be guided in its work by the principle of intellectual cooperation, that it would acknowledge rules of action, and that it would be a school of mutual instruction within itself, but Wight does not expect that such guilds would be immediately successful; however, he believes them to be entirely practicable, and probably the best hope for the future of American architecture. On this proposal of Wight, Croly comments:

> The proposal smacks decidedly of mediaeval methods, and bears about the same relation to ordinary ideas which one hears advanced upon the same subject as Mr. Wight's old "Academy of Design" building bears to some smart bit of contemporary Parisian architecture. It would, of course, be absurd to suppose that any successful contemporary architect would participate in such a plan any more than a successful American star would join a stock company of Saxe-Meiningen type. At the same time it is by no means impossible that certain groups of competent and enthusiastic young architects might not find that by some such method of cooperation they could both improve their own work and compete most effectively by their combined light with the stars of the architectural firmament.[25]

This is what the nature of architectural criticism is when critics have the opportunity to exchange their points of view on various architectural matters that is not only fascinating but also enlightening to their "audience"—the readers; and nothing could provide a "stage" better for critics to perform their roles than the printed media such as newspapers, magazines, professional periodicals, and other kinds of publications that will be discussed as follows.

"The critic, like the client, can only judge by the final result," declares a British editor in dispelling what he considers myths held by architects. He adds, "It must be emphasized that criticism is not simply fault-finding. It is a poor critic who is concerned only with looking over a building for points of disagreement. Criticism is a matter of discriminating between what is important and what is trivial." It is true that architectural criticism cannot exist unless architectural values are verbalized in some form or another. In this respect, it may therefore be contended that the greatest services have been rendered by the architectural periodicals. As early as 1883, Montgomery Schuyler had criticized a building by McKim, Mead and White as looking "less like a work of architectural art than a magnificent piece of furniture." *The Architectural Record*, with the contributions mainly from Schuyler and his colleagues, was in the habit of publishing "Architectural Aberrations," a series in which one obviously bad building successively was held up to the scorn of the profession. This was shortly after the turn of the century. At the same time, *The Architectural Review* published monthly a department called "Current Periodicals" in which both favorable and unfavorable architectural criticisms appeared. Nevertheless, to come a little nearer to the present, *The New Yorker* was sued for libel by an architect who felt that the periodical's criticism of a building he had designed had effected material damage in loss of possible rentals. Fortunately, the case was settled out of court after a rather abject apology on the part of the paper. Criticism in architecture, therefore, seems to be a somewhat hazardous occupation. Nevertheless, it will exist as long as there are architects and architecture as it has always been.

Interestingly enough, the first architectural magazine to endure for any length of time, namely the *Revue Général de l'Architecture*, began in 1840 with the avowed policy of avoiding architectural criticism, and of confining itself solely to factual information; but this policy was due more to the editor's modesty than to any doubts as to the ultimate efficacy of criticism as a technique of architectural reform. As evident in the past hundred years, the influence of critical writings was proportional to the author's reputation and to that of the periodical in which such views were published; and of the influences brought by literature to bear on architectural developments, that of the architectural magazines has been the most important of all. This has been coupled with the influence of the techniques of reproducing illustrations used in the magazine. There can be little doubt that the coarseness of English detailing in the mid-nineteenth century was very much influenced by the fact that all illustrations in *The Builder* were reproduced from wood engravings, just as the relatively greater delicacy of French detailing of the same period was undoubtedly influenced by the fact that the *Revue Générale de l'Architecture* was illustrated by steel engravings. Similarly, one can hardly overemphasize the importance of the introduction in 1856 of photographic reproductions into architectural periodicals, since not only did this obviate the need for periodicals to rely on architects providing them with perspective which usually were drawn befroe the ground was even broken, but it encouraged their editors to show a preference for photogenic buildings, and a corresponding lack of enthusiasm for buildings which, however excellent, did not provide flattering points of view for the camera. Incidentally, of architectural magazines using photographic reproduction *The New York Sketch-Book* which Schuyler served on its editorial board (1874-76) was the first American periodical to use photography. Its initial photograph was one that recorded the ramshackle condition of Bishop Berkely's house in Newport. Color reproductions, though rare in the earlier issues of periodicals, were provided often enough from 1851 onwards.

It was many years before architectural periodicals began systematically reporting on contemporary buildings, or reproducing illustrations of them. In fact, this practice took hold in the 1860s. After the Art Nouveau fever of the late nineteenth century subsided, the influence of architectural periodicals suffered a temporary eclipse, though they were more numerous than ever. This was partly because of the hesitancy shown by many editors in espousing the more revolutionary trends, but mainly because of the virtual abandonment of architectural criticism altogether. Even the more progressive editors rightly felt that, at this juncture, the new forms then being evolved were so devoid of roots that any adverse criticism might be fatal to their further development. However, the period of uncertainty came to an end in the 1940s. As mentioned earlier, architectural criticism, like all forms of criticism, has always existed, and must always exist, if only in spoken form, where there are men cultivated enough to reflect upon the aesthetic experience architects provide for them.

Speaking of the influence of architectural periodicals upon the developments of architecture, it must by pointed out here that the editor of an architectural magazine must exercise considerable caution so that he will not claim greater influence than he really exerts, for real progress in architecture can be achieved only by architects—by building, not by writing. Basically, architectural magazines have two roles in relation to the architect and in relation to his client. They must help architects to maintain and raise architectural standards, and they must bridge the gap between the architect's and client's viewpoint and thereby create the better informed public opinion which, in turn, encourages good architecture. They must also serve as the architect's newspaper, keeping him up to date with technical and professional developments. Although an influential architectural periodical should be able to appeal to clients as well as architects, most secure virtually all of their support and readership from within the profession. Architecture is unique among the professions in having its ideas and developments normally discussed in such a restricted way. Literary magazines are addressed not only to writers but also to readers; magazines about music are addressed to the people who enjoy listening to music, not only to those who perform or compose it. The same applies to the other arts, except architecture.

Right at the beginning of this study, Montgomery Schuyler was quoted as saying: "The architectural criticism of a layman is very apt to be warped and vitiated by his failure to make allowances for difficulties under which the designer labors. In fact, it is almost sure to be defective on this account." This is a very sympathetic statement from a critic for architects, and reflects general attitude and reaction of the latter toward criticism because it is generally true that architects always claim to be in favor of published criticism of new buildings, as long as, they usually add, it is "informed" criticism. It would be fair enough if by informed they mean that the critic must know something about how buildings are planned and constructed as well as what they look like, and something about the purpose they serve. But often, when architects talked about informed criticism, they really mean that the critic must know about and make "allowances" for, all the difficulties that occurred while the building was being designed and constructed. This is not necessarily correct. The critic, like a client, can only judge by the final result. If the client kept changing his mind, if the local planning regulations prevented the acceptance of the better layout, if the contractor went bankrupt when the job was halfway up—all these are matters of the utmost significance to the architect. But the critic must ignore them and look at the building as it is. The historian is different again. He comes along afterward, and it is his job to discover and explain everything. The architects seem too often to want critics to transform themselves forthwith into historians. Among some architects, there is a degree of resentment at the idea of being criticized at all. This is now less prevalent than it once was. Most architects today accept honest criticism as a healthy thing, and as more magazines become bold enough regularly to print criticism, criticism becomes more widely accepted. Resentment dates from the time when the absence of routine press criticism meant that the few exceptional attempts seemed an invidious attack and created a climate in which reasonable discussion was difficult. Such a climate does not exist in the theatrical, art or literary worlds, in which a critical approach to new work is taken for granted.

I have mentioned earlier that architectural critics come from disparate backgrounds. Some are, or were, architects by profession while some come from other fields. Then there is a problem, for because of the complexity of building and planning techniques in architecture, it is often thought that the only man with the knowledge to criticize architecture is the trained architect. This again turns architecture in upon itself and inhibits the formation of a body of informed public opinion. In addition, to limit the critics to those engaged in the practice of architecture all but stifles criticism, by posing problems of professional ethics. Therefore, it is necessary to repeat that an architectural critc need not, indeed should not, be a practicing architect. Usually, a critic tends to be someone who writes criticism as part of the job of being an editor and architectural writer generally; or else he combines the role of critic with either teacher of architecture or architectural hisrtorian.

If architectural criticism were more widespread, if all newspapers and periodicals had as a matter of course their architectural critics just as they have art and drama critics, this problem would not arise; there would be enough outlet to keep the qualified architectural critic occupied.

Again, it must be emphasized that criticism is not simply fault-finding. It is a poor critic who is concerned only with looking over a building for points of disagreement. Criticism is a matter of evaluating; of discriminating between what is important and what is trivial. Importance should therefore be attached to free and frank criticism especially on the part of architectural periodicals— criticism uninhibited by fear of giving offense to architects and the construction industry or even by fear of being sued for libel. This is second only to the importance of a periodical maintaining its independence from all commercial and other pressure—all hidden motives that might compromise criticism. Intelligent criticism can help to create a climate in which good architecture is possible.

4

Chicago

At the turn of the century, Chicago, the little Indian village on the shores of Lake Michigan, had grown within a generation to be the second largest city in America. New York was already secretly admitting that the future—railroads, the produce of the Great Plains, the business of buying and selling the world's foodstuffs—belonged to Chicago while Boston could only repeat incredulously the Chicagoan's remark that it did not yet have culture in its city but that when it got some it would make its presence felt and known. That was exactly what happened in 1890 when the Congress recognized Chicago as the new world representative of the nineteenth century and granted it exclusive rights to hold the fair that would commemorate the four-hundredth anniversary of the discovery of America. In the spring of that year, President Benjamin Harrison signed the act providing for the World's Columbian Exposition of arts, industries, manufacturers, and the products of the soil, mine, and sea. In those days, Chicago's preeminence in many fields was generally known, but its important contribution to the field of building construction might not have been so widely recognized. Many advancements in building practices originated in Chicago—balloon construction of frame buildings, fireproof construction, the rational proportioning of the areas of isolated footings, the use of steel grillages to secure shallow footings, the Chicago caisson, the evolution of skeleton construction and wind bracing, and the development of reinforced concrete construction. These were outstanding achievements of men in the fields of architecture and engineering in Chicago that at the time no other city could equal.

In the development of the art of building construction, Chicago has consistently led other cities. Only in the height of buildings had it been surpassed in recent years until the Sears Tower was finished in 1974-75. Great credit must be given to the outstanding engineers and architects whose vision, ingenuity, and inventions led to the development of present-day building construction. Except for occasional comparatively dormant periods of economic depression, the city has served as a large-scale research and testing laboratory; the detailed history of its buildings presents a continuous and successful battle for improved construction upon soil that has presented difficult problems. This rapid development has, of course, been aided by an unusual growth in population and increased property values. One of the factors which contributed largely to the remarkable progress of architectural design and subsequent building construction was the great fire of 1871. This fire, in which eighteen thousand buildings were burned, wiped the slate clean, and served as a vivid warning that more permanent construction was required. To date no other city has had such a stimulus to improve building construction, together with the industrial wealth sufficient to finance swift rebuilding.

From the beginning up to the period of World War I and the Depression that followed, the history of Chicago, architecturally speaking, is divided into two phases. The first extended from the founding of the urban community in 1830 to the fire of 1871, a disaster which very nearly required that Chicago begin its material growth all over again. The second began with the reconstruction following the fire and continued until the brief interruption of World War I and the Depression; it was an extremely important phase that saw the emergence of a unique architectural and urban style. An anonymous eyewitness, who had experienced the horrors of the fire in a letter written to the editor of the *American Architect and Building News* in 1876 concerning the rebuilding of Chicago, puts it best:

> The history of Chicago is now distinctly divided into two periods, the division being the great fire. The pre-igneous period concerns us but little now. It seems to have passed out of the memory, except to recall pleasing reminiscences or draw comparison. As fire purifies by its intensity, so may we reasonably look for fresh and vigorous thought and action following in its path. It is safe to say that for this reason the new Chicago is better than the old. The great fire purified our local government for a time, but in this respect its effects have not been lasting. We naturally look for its visible results in the rebuilding, the leviathan task which for two years taxed our capacity to the utmost.[1]

John Wellborn Root also expressed similar opinion in *The Inland Architect and News Record* fifteen years later. He writes: "Some of our older citizens still refer to certain monumental grandeur which existed 'before the fire'—which, in Chicago, means what 'in the beginning' means in the Scriptures."[2] After the great fire, many structures were quickly rebuilt, but the financial panic of 1873 slowed reconstruction for a period of nearly ten years. Then there came a golden decade of building which culminated in the World's Columbian Exposition of 1893. By the turn of the century the most important developments had been realized. Skeleton construction, structural steel, and caissons had been proved and accepted, and reinforced concrete was on its way to acceptance. The materials and methods of construction had been devised, and engineers and architects were in position to meet all demands then current for height of construction.

The city of Chicago[3] owes its existence primarily to the river bearing that name and to the fact that the river emptied into the head of the most southwesterly of the Great Lakes. The history of Chicago, because it is situated at the mouth of one waterway and the head of another, is similar to that of other inland cities. The waterways were the ready-made highways of the interior. Up and down them passed the explorer, the missionary, the trapper, the trader and the pioneer farmer, tracing the way for future lines of commerce. At various locations along these ways, perhaps the head or mouth of a river, a portage, or a natural harbor, the products of adjacent regions were collected, to be forwarded to the Atlantic seaboard. The many manufacturers, which were sent in return, came to these inland points for distribution. Therefore, what had been in turn a little Indian village, a halting place for the explorer or the missionary, a post for the trader, and a rendezvous for the pioneer, became a commercial center which grew to a city. The mouth of the Chicago River was marked by nature to serve such a purpose. The ground upon which the city of Chicago has been built is made up of boulders, sand and clay, a mixture commonly known as "glacial drift." The excavation for a building in any part of the city will show the unstable character of the soil. Beneath it at varying depths lies the solid limestone which may be seen in the stone quarries in many localities just outside the limits of the plain. The bedrock is not level but has many undulations which cause the varying depths shown by borings in different parts of the city. The average depth is estimated to be about fifty feet. Because of the instability of the soil, few localities could have been found more unsuitable for building a city. But demands of commerce have slight regard for topography or for good building sites and the architects and engineers who built the city of Chicago in those days had to find a way to overcome these topographical disadvantages.

In such a soil and on such levels of ground, the river would naturally flow sluggishly and would cut a deep channel, carrying the washings to be deposited in a bar at the mouth. It would in this way form a natural harbor for lake commerce, extended two or three miles inland. However, the recorded history of Chicago dates back to a time when a harbor for vessels of large burden was not dreamed of. It began during the days of the French missionaries when the utility of a river as a highway was the important consideration, especially if there was only a short portage from its head of a stream flowing in the opposite direction. The Chicago River was almost ideal in this respect, since it led by its south branch to the Chicago portage and then into the Des Plaines and the Illinois Rivers being the connecting link between the Great Lakes and the Mississippi. The French explorers and the Jesuit missionaries at first reached the Mississippi by Green Bay and the Wisconsin River. But they soon learned in returning to come up the Illinois to the Kankakee and then to cross the portage to the St. Joseph River. At a later time they found the still shorter way by the Chicago River and portage. Among these Jesuit missionaries was Jacques Marquette, a Jesuit priest from Leon in Picardy. Accompanied by Louis Jolliet, a Quebec fur trader, Marquette embarked on a voyage to explore the great unknown river. In 1673, on their way back to Green Bay following their exploration of the Mississippi, Marquette and Jolliet crossed the Chicago portage. Other Frenchmen came after Marquette: priests, hunters, traders, and trappers. But it is Robert Cavelier, Sieur de LaSalle, who is remembered above all. LaSalle spent a part of the winter in 1682 in the first house built by white men at the portage and it was LaSalle who, sometime around 1681, began using the word Chi-ca-gou to indicate specifically the site of the present city rather than the whole region. It was not until 1779, however, that the first permanent structure on the site of Chicago, a log cabin, was built beside the river near the lake shore by a black man who occupied it until 1803. It was, subsequently, sold in 1804 to John Kinzie, the first permanent white resident of the city. In 1804, Fort Dearborn was built by Captain John Whisler, civil engineer of the U.S. Army, at the location of the southwest corner of North Michigan Avenue and East Wacker Drive. It was of log construction, two stories high. On August 15, 1812, the Fort Dearborn massacre occurred, and on the following day the Fort was burned down by the Indians. It was rebuilt in 1816 by Captain Hezekiah Bradley, also of the U.S. Army, and was torn down about 1875.

The 1830s marked an important phase in the development of Chicago, for in that decade the once-modest village moved swiftly toward cityhood. The first map of the original town of Chicago, by James Thompson, surveyor, is dated August 4, 1830. This date marks the beginning of Chicago as a legally recognized town. The settlement, three-eighths of a square mile in area, was bounded by Madison, State, Kinzie, and Halstead Streets. In 1831, Cook County embracing Chicago was organized. In the spring of 1833, Congress made an appropriation of $30,000 for improving the harbor; and that same year a post office was established. In 1834, the poll list of citizens amounted to one hundred and eleven. In 1837, Chicago became incorporated as a city, and William B. Ogden was chosen as its first mayor.

The lake traffic, which gave the first impetus to modern Chicago, increased enormously between 1830 and 1870. The appearance of steam vessels and the improvements of the harbor were largely responsible for this growth. The exact date of the coming of the first steamer is in dispute, although it must have been near 1830. At the end of 1836, two hundred and twelve vessels were reported to have been able to get inside the river. In 1854, there were forty-six vessels plying regularly between Chicago and other ports. In 1871, more than twelve thousand vessels entered the Chicago harbour. About 1830, railways, instead of canals, were advocated in the United States to connect navigable waterways. Few imagined that the railways could ever supplant the canal. A railway from the head of Lake Michigan to the Mississippi or even to the Rock River was for many years a Chicago vision. By 1848, it had been realized to some extent. The problem of conveying lead from the mine at Galena to the lake caused that city to be made the proposed western terminus. The locomotive "Pioneer," now preserved in the Field Museum, was brought to Chicago by steamer and was put to work on the few miles of strap-iron laid on stringers placed end to end on piling driven into the wet prairie between the Chicago and Des Plains Rivers. This was the Galena and Chicago Railway, whose frame passenger-station stood for many years just west of and across the North Branch from the Northwestern Station on Wells Street.

By the middle of the century, the rival railways between Lake Erie and Lake Michigan, the one constructed through "Central" Michigan and the other through "Southern" Michigan, rounded the head of the lake and came into the city simultaneously. The Michigan Central and the Illinois Central were carried along the lake front as far north as the foot of the present Randolph Street on pilings driven into the water. The railroads soon began to fill the lake front, compelling the public to go beyond them in a park made by artificial means. Michigan Avenue, formerly the beach of the lake, is now far inland, and the mouth of the river at the foot of Madison Street exists only in tradition. Terminal yards and tall buildings occupy that part of the former site of Fort Dearborn. By the middle fifties, nearly three thousand miles of track touched Chicago, and ninety-six trains a day came and went over its ten trunk and eleven branch lines. In these years more miles of railroad were constructed in Illinois than in any other state in the Union, and soon ten thousand miles of track connected Chicago with all the important commercial centers in the country. The Mississippi was bound to it at sixteen points, by the time of the Civil War, the city had eight hundred and twenty locomotives and fifteen hundred cars on its yards, and passenger fares alone were annually bringing sixty-five million dollars. It was the railroad that made Chicago the capital of America's heartland, its attainable metropolis, its possible dream.

Since Chicago's site was low and swampy, the problems of drainage and sewage disposal became more serious as the population grew. The high death rate made a solution of this problem imperative. In line with a comprehensive plan devised by E.S. Chesbrough, the street grades were raised in 1855 and again in 1857. Many buildings were raised correspondingly, one of the first being the block of four-story buildings at the corner of West Lake and North Wells Streets, owned by George Smith. Built in 1850, these structures were considered the finest of their period in the city. The first brick building to be raised to the street grade, in 1857, was the Jennings Building at the northeast corner of Dearborn and Randolph Streets. In 1861 the famous Tremont House, a five-story brick structure, was raised six feet to grade "without a crack in the walls." George M. Pullman was one of the contractors. The filling of the streets to the new grade had not been completed at the time of the great fire of 1871 and was brought to a conclusion largely with debris from the fire.

In 1830 when the city first appeared on the map and recognized as a town, its population totaled one hundred persons. As the city grew, into this busy community poured groups of immigrants and citizens from other parts of the country, all seeking the betterment of their lives. In 1850, Chicago housed 28,269 persons. Ten years later, the foreign group had grown to 54,624 out of a total population of 109,206. The march forward was steady and uninterrupted. When the great fire came, it found a city of 298,997 of which 144,557 were born in foreign countries. The rapid growth of Chicago amazed visitors, not only those who came from various parts of the United States but foreign visitors as well. In common with others, James Stirling, coming from England in 1856, reflected the attitude of many at the time:

> Ever since I came into the States, I have been hearing of Chicago, as the great feature of the new Western World, and was therefore prepared for a wonderful city. But the reality exceeded my expectations. It is a city, not in growth, but in revolution; growth is much too slow a word for the transformation of a hamlet of log-huts into a western New York in the space of a few years.[4]

And at about the same time only a couple of years earlier, Anthony Trollope, an English novelist, came to visit Chicago in 1854 and expressed his opinion upon the true character and spirit of the populace and the city's prospect that is well worth being repeated here. He writes:

> At Chicago the hotel was bigger than other hotels, and grander. There were pipes without end for cold water which ran hot, and for hot water which would not run at all. The post-office also was grander and bigger than other post-offices—though the postmaster confessed to me that the matter of the delivery of letters was one which could not be compassed. Just at that moment it was being done with as a private speculation; but it did not pay, and would be discontinued. The theater too was large, handsome, and convenient; but on the night of my attendance it seemed to lack an audience. Men in those regions do not mind failures, and when they have failed, instantly begin again. They make their plans on a large scale, and they who come after them fill up what has been wanting first. Those taps of hot and cold water will be made to run by the next owner of the hotel, if not by the present owner. In another ten years the letters, I do not doubt, will be delivered. Long before that time the theater will probably be full.[5]

Had Trollope lived long enough and had the opportunity of coming back to see Chicago in the following half of the century, he would have found how amazingly true his prophecy was.

A natural concomitant of an increasing population here was the commensurate construction of dwelling houses and other buildings. Although opinion among visitors was not unanimous, most of them agreed that cheap workmanship and materials and uninteresting design made for unusually uniform buildings, particularly so because they had all been built in the same brief period. On the other hand, some visitors spoke with enthusiasm of "beautiful villa-residences" of great variety which they saw while sight-seeing, and of some of the public edifices and business buildings. The 1830s were a fortuitous moment to begin the construction of a city, for America had embraced a new architecture. If the first few formative years of Chicago's history can be termed the period of the cabin and the fort, the next twenty-five years may be called the period of the Greek temple. After the Federal style with its reflection of the brothers Adam, America had turned to Greece for its inspiration. The aesthetic and political reasons for this change need not be rehearsed here. The Greek Revival tradition in America began with a book, *The Antiquities of Athens*, by two Englishmen, James Stuart and Nicholas Revett, the first volume of which was published in London in 1760. By 1770 a copy had found its way to the Library Company of Philadelphia where it was subsequently studied by Benjamin Latrobe, the second architect of the Capitol, who introduced the Greek Revival style into the United States, and other architects such as William Strickland and Robert Mills. It was not long before illustrated manuals by builders had made it possible for any competent carpenter to produce structures with all the trappings of Greek temples: fluted and plain columns, capitals of every order, pediments, pilasters, for example. And soon the style, in stone or adapted to brick and wood, swept the country. It was an ideal style for a very young city like Chicago at the time because it could be adapted to almost every need. Adapted to domestic architecture, the style could be stretched to any size, from modest story-and-a-half cottages with pilasters at the corners and simple Greek-type moldings, to columned mansions such as one built in 1836 by Archibald Clybourne, Chicago's first constable. The style served just as well for churches and schools, shops and offices, hotels and public buildings. Therefore, it was inevitable that Chicago's first Court House, built in 1835 at the corner of the Public Square at Clark and Randolph Streets, should have been a temple-like rectangular building ennobled by a free-standing portico of four wooden columns. Chicago needed a variety of buildings, for the 1830s were boom times. It was a period of one of the greatest migrations in the history of mankind. At the beginning of the decade the population of Chicago numbered one hundred; by the end it was more than four thousand. This need to erect a house in a few days resulted in the first example of that extraordinary inventiveness which Chicago was to display in various ways for the remainder of the century. It was the "balloon frames" which was invented in 1833 by Augustine D. Taylor.[6] It was an enormously efficient and influential departure from the heavy, New England frame. For the stout girts and ports of the older systems, Taylor substituted a closely ranked series of light studs, joists, roof-rafters, and purlins joined by simple nailing. The resulting structure was usually covered with clapboard siding nailed to the studs.

The earliest non-residential buildings in Chicago were of frame construction. One of these, the Eagle Exchange Tavern, built in 1829 by Mark Beaubein, was enlarged in 1831 to form the Sauganash Hotel, which may be regarded as the first commercial structure in the settlement. At this date, Chicago was a village of only twelve houses. Another early frame building was Hogan's Store at the corner of what are today West Lake Street and North

Wacker Drive. One corner of this store served as headquarters for the first postmaster. In 1834 the post office was moved to another location and subsequently it ended up in the Saloon Building, a three-story structure at the corner of North Clark and West Lake Streets, after which it was located in various buildings until 1855. Around 1833, Lake Street was the main street of town; in this same year the first Tremont House was erected and the first store, building, a two-story frame structure, was built in 1834 by Thomas Church. The first Court House followed in 1835 and the City Hotel, later the Sherman House, in 1837. From 1837 to 1842 the first City Hall was located in the Saloon Building, previously mentioned. All of these early Chicago landmarks were of frame construction. The first brick building in Chicago was built in 1837. After about 1845, brick began to replace wood in the construction of walls, although for many years, even after the great fire, wood continued to be used for floor framing of buildings in the central business district. The dramatic burning of the Grannis Block (1881-85) emphasized the vulnerability of this type of construction, and after that date few such buildings were erected in the business district.

As mentioned earlier, when Chicago was chartered as a city in 1837, William Butler Ogden became its first mayor. He was a businessman of vision—the vision was to make the city the center of the heartland—but that would take time. In the meantime, he was responsible for bringing to Chicago its first architect, John M. Van Osdel. Ogden had met Van Osdel in New York, and after he became mayor he sent for him to build a house worthy of his new civic dignity. Van Osdel arrived, not only with the plans for Chicago's first architect-designed dwelling, but with the necessary windows, stair rails, and all the trimmings as well. The architect of the William Ogden House later became the supreme builder of Greek Revival Chicago. From his office on Clark Street flowed an almost endless stream of designs for houses, hotels, and public buildings. He was also responsible for the new Court House which was built in the fifties in the Greek Revival mode. Peter B. Wight, during his first visit to Chicago in 1858 when he was "only nineteen years of age and fresh from college after a short experience with two of New York's 'old style' architects,"[7] remembered the Court House well. In his article "Reminscences of Chicago in 1859—Architecture and Otherwise," published in the September 1892 issue of *The Inland Architect and News Record,* Wight observed:

> The Court House then standing, the work of J. M. Van Osdel, was the central building, which was afterward enlarged by two wings and destroyed in the great fire. It was a very effective building and was built of blue limestone, which was brought from Lockport, New York. The wings, subsequently built were of white Athens limestone. The courthouse was surrounded by a good lawn ornamented by fountains, and an iron railing. The lawn and railing were at first established city grade, and the streets around it were higher. The courthouse bell, which had such a fine tone, could be heard all over the city, and it sounded the hours of labor and meals. All labor was then suspended at noon, and almost everyone walked home to dinner.[8]

Wight stayed in Chicago for about a year working as an independent architect in the office of Asher Carter but when he had "nothing to do" he went back to New York and subsequently formed a partnership with Russell Sturgis. During his first stay in Chicago Wight had the opportunity to make acquaintance with a number of architects who were active at the time as he recalls:

> The first architect that came to Chicago after Mr. Van Osdel was Asher Carter, brother of T. B. Carter, who still survives him. Mr. Carter was a native of Morristown, New Jersey. There he was a carpenter with a fondness of drawing plans, in which he had no practical experience until he came to Chicago. He was sent by James Renwick of New York to superintend the erection of the second Presbyterian church at the northeast corner of Wabash Avenue and Washington Street... In 1858, Mr. Carter had taken into partnership Augustus Bauer, whom we all know. Mr. Bauer, when he came from Germany, entered the office of John B. Snook, of New York. He then came to Chicago and for a time was the draftsman of Mr. Carter. Carter and Bauer were the first architects whose acquaintance I made. Their office was on LaSalle Street, opposite the Metropolitan Block, which then contained the only music hall in the city. I was introduced to them by one of their clients, who informed them that he was going to employ me on a piece of work which had been promised to them... While first in Chicago I made the acquaintance of Mr. Boyington, Mr. Burling, Mr. Wheelock, and Frederick Baumann. The only other architect practicing here that I now remember was Wadskier. Baumann was then of the firm of Wallbaum and Baumann, mason contractors. It was one of the traditions of Chicago then that he had practiced as an architect several times at earlier dates, and had also amused himself as a boss stonecutter. As to what he really was we all knew then, as we do now, and from my experience I confess to a fellow-feeling when I say that our only motto should be, "once an architect, always an architect."[9]

The 1850s did not only witness the increasing number of architects practicing in Chicago some of whom Wight mentioned above, but also the radical change in architectural taste that altered the way Chicago looked with considerable help, strangely enough, from the railroads. As noted earlier, in those early years, the Greek Revival had been in full bloom in Chicago, but it had its limitations. The style worked perfectly for smaller buildings, but along with the great expansion of railroads, Chicago grew larger and larger and structures that could house hundreds of white-collar workers were needed and in demand. The Greek Revival could not and did not readily expand to this new office-building size. Chicago was no longer a little town on Lake Michigan but the capital of a business empire. The railroads made it possible for a company's central office in Chicago to serve the needs of thousands of scattered small towns. This sudden change in the requirements of American business coincided with a revolutionary shift in taste. The reign of the Greek Revival had not been unchallenged. Americans had long been fascinated by the Gothic Revival structures which were first developed and created in England in the middle of the eighteenth century. In 1838, Alexander Jackson Davis had started constructing a castlelike mansion, Lyndhurst, on the Hudson above New York City; in 1846, Richard Upjohn's Trinity was going up at the head of Wall Street. Along with the Gothic taste came, in America, other revivals—the Egyptian, the Italianate and later the Romanesque. Now, instead of manuals on the Greek style alone, the builder could take his choice from a variety of architectural styles to accord with his client's taste. These were Andrew Jackson Downing's *Cottage Residences* and Calvert Vaux's *Villas and Cottages,* among others. There was one more element in this astonishing change of scene and that was the rapid technological development of the period which readily permitted the construction of buildings of five and six and even seven stories, allowed glass to be made in ever-larger sheets, and facilitated the carving of wood in fantastic shapes. None, though, had a more profound effect than that complete cast-iron front that, again with the helping hand of the railroads, began arriving from New York in the 1840s and were in vogue in the building business in Chicago from 1855 up to the great fire. Painted white in imitation of marble, these precast-iron fronts came in any style the builder wanted: Classical, Gothic, or Italianate. They were evident in the new ofice buildings springing up close to one another on State, Dearborn, Clark, and LaSalle Streets. Among the first buildings of this type was the Lloyd Block at North Wells and West Randolph Streets. A block of buildings with cast-iron fronts was started in 1856 on East Lake Street by Van Osdel. Five stories and one basement in height, this block extended from North State Street eastward toward North Wabash Avenue. Other examples of this type of construction were Frederick Tuttle's building at the northeast corner of North State and East Lake Streets, which with four other buildings had a frontage of 136 feet. On the opposite side of East Lake Street the iron fronts extended eastward approximately 135 feet from the City Hotel. Lining both sides of Lake Street, they gave the appearance of single buildings. A writer of the period declared that this block was the finest in the city with scarcely a rival on the continent at the time. After the great fire, a few more buildings were constructed; one of them was the U.S. Express Company Building on West Washington Street.

Most visitors who came to Chicago in the fifties were greatly impressed not only by its amazingly rapid growth but also by its physical appearance. One of these visitors came from England in 1856 and anonymously wrote an article entitled "Chicago in 1856" which was published in the June 1856 issue of *Putnam's Monthly Magazine.* The following samples the article well:

> Chicago is what Mr. Ralph Waldo Emerson would call a representative town. It is the type of that class of American towns which made themselves conspicuous, and almost ridiculous, by their rapid growth. In 1850, it had a population of twenty-six thousand. In 1856, it claims to be the first grain-market in the world, the first lumber-market in the world, the third city in the Union in post-office revenues. That it has the best back country in the world, the best railroad communication with that back country, that its population is over ninety thousand, that its motto is still "onward," and its destiny among stars... The streets, which are of handsome width, say sixty feet, are laid out at right angles, forming about sixteen blocks to the mile. It will be seen, then, that all the streets, running east and west, cross one of the "Branches," and likewise that each of the Branches, all of the streets running north and south

cross the main Chicago River. The level of the streets is not more than three of four feet above the level of the river; the river being navigable, of course all bridges must be draw-bridges. There is a bridge every third, fourth, or fifth street, more or less... Both carriage-way and sidewalks are planked—stone being as yet too expensive a material, and too slowly laid for this new and fast metropolis. In the spring of the year, the ground asserts its original character of swamp. The planks actually float, and, as the heavy wagons pass along, ornamental jets of muddy water play on every side. The sidewalks of Chicago are remarkable, in their way, as the bridges. With almost every block of buildings there is a change of grade, sometimes of one foot, sometimes of three feet, sometimes of five. These ascents or descents are made by steps, or by short, steep, inclined planes of boards, or without cleats or cross-pieces, to prevent slipping according to the fancy of the adjoining proprietor who erects them.[10]

These remarks and comments of visitors, particularly of those from foreign countries, are interesting and at times enlightening in the way they described what Chicago was like in those days. There is one more that I cannot forego quoting. In the Winter of 1867, F. Barham Zincke, a clergyman and author of several books, came from England to tour the United States. As a result, his *Last Winter in the United States* came out in 1868. In it, he writes:

Chicago well deserves its reputation. Its stores, and private houses and churches, are good, and would be so considered in any city. Its stores are in buildings, two floors higher than the shops of Oxford or Regent Street, as is generally the case in all the large American cities. They have an air of solidity, and are not entirely devoid of external decoration. There are suburbs containing many good private residences, the best of which are to be seen in Michigan Avenue, along the shores of the Lake. These are built of a cream-colored stone, and many of them give one a favorable idea of the architectural taste, as well as of the wealth, of their inhabitants. From the gallery of the City Hall I counted twenty-three towers and spires; but this is very far from giving the number of churches, as perhaps the majority of them still being incomplete, or only temporary structures, are without their embellishments. In the central parts of the city, where all the buildings are good and massive, and the smoke—for here they burn bituminous coal—has put a complexion upon them something like that of London, you could never guess that you were standing in a city so young, that many of its inhabitants, still young themselves, remember the erection of the first brick house in the place; you would be more likely to suppose that you were surrounded by evidences and appliances of the commercial prosperity of many generations. On my mentioning to a "citizen" of Chicago the number of churches I had counted from the top of City Hall, "Yes," he replied, "we are a religious people outwardly."[11]

Most of the buildings the two English gentlemen saw during their visits to Chicago in the late fifties and sixties quoted above suddenly turned into debris and ashes; and at the same time the first historical phase, architecturally and otherwise, of the city of Chicago came to an end when a fire broke out in a barn at the rear of 558 South Dekoven Street at about 8:45 p.m., Sunday, October 8, 1871. This fire had been preceded by a large fire the night before. The earlier conflagration had burned the four blocks east of south Clinton Street. The weather had been extremely dry, giving rise to many earlier fires, and after the

Saturday night encounter the firemen were exhausted from their effort. It would have been difficult to select a worse time to combat the colossal fire in which two hundred million dollars' worth of property were burned—30 percent of the total Chicago property value of that date. The population of the city was then 334,270. This was not Chicago's first great fire, for in October, 1857, one had wrecked a half-million dollars' worth of property and destroyed the lives of twenty-three persons, which led to the creation of a salvage corps by the insurance company, in turn superseded by a paid fire company in 1858.

The exact cause of the great fire of 1871 will probably never be known except for speculations. The blaze spread rapidly: the fire department was not notified for half an hour, and given that start and the high wind, the flames were already out of control before any apparatus arrived on the scene. At the Sherman House, Alexander Frear, a visiting politician from New York, was waiting for friends from Milwaukee when the fire started to spread. He remembered:

> There was a large crowd of strangers and businessmen of the city at the hotel. The corridor and parlors were full of idlers, much as usual. While looking over the register someone said, "There goes the fire-bell again"; the remark was made jocosely, "They'll burn the city down if they keep on." I paid little attention to the conversation... When I came down the wind was blowing fiercely through Clark Street to the river, and I had some difficulty in getting across the Court House square. It could not have been 10 o'clock, for they were singing in the Methodist Chrurch as I passed Follansbe's bank. I noticed the glare of the fire on the west side as I came along, but thought nothing of it... The avenue (Wabash) was a scene of desolation. The storm of falling fire seemed to increase every second, and it was as much as we could do to protect ourselves from the burning rain and guide the horse through the flying people and hurrying vehicles. Looking back through Washington Street, towards the Opera House, I saw the smoke and flames pouring out of State Street, from the very point we had just left, and the intervening space was filled with whirling embers that beat against the houses and covered the roof and window sills. It seemed like a tornado of fire.[12]

The city was indeed in chaos. People staggered in the streets, drunk from the wares of the untended saloons; looting was rampant; children were lost; and

> the thoroughfares filled with half-dressed, frantic women, dazed children, and powerless men, all burdened with dear mementos of the wasted home, and all pushing about in pitiful uncertainty to find the resting place which was not to be found—this was the scene in the West Division as the battalions of fire held on in victorious array.[13]

In the meantime, toward midnight, Dankmar Adler was walking home from his office when he first saw the glare of the fire on the West Side. In his article "Some Notes upon the Earlier Chicago Architects" published in the May 1892 issue of *The Inland Architect and News Record,* Adler recalls:

Chicago

> I went as far as Twelfth Street bridge, did not think it would be much of a fire, turned back, went home and to bed. I was living with my father at No. 41 East Thirteenth Street. He aroused me at two o'clock. It was, even at that distance from the fire, as hot as in an oven. It was almost light enough in the street to read a newspaper. Wabash Avenue was crowded with people rushing southward, carrying books of account, money boxes, clothing, beddings, clocks, furniture, etc. I was stunned and bewildered by the rush of the crowd, and by the roar of the wind and of the flames, which could be heard already at Twelfth Street. But I failed to grasp the situation, or I should have hitched up my horse, driven downtown and saved the many drawings stored in our office, which would have possessed inestimable value in the settlements with insurance companies and the labors of rebuilding on old foundations, which had to be begun so soon after. I sauntered down town as far as the corner of State and Wabash Streets. At that time there was no fire there, and it was thought that the best part of our business district would be saved from destruction. I wandered about at first in an aimless sort of way, and in my wanderings noted the peculiar and insidious manner in which the fire spread from building to building. At that time the North Side was well ablaze, but the South Side, excepting a strip of I think not over two blocks along the river bank, was unscathed, and the main current of the wind, which was blowing almost a hurricane from the Southwest seemed favorable to its preservation. There came, however, here and there, eddies and return currents, which started occasional blazes in the wake of the main fire, and these minor blazes blown to the windward again and again widened the track of fire until it had reached the lake as far south as Congress Street. I engaged several times in efforts to tear down buildings in the track of these minor conflagrations, but in every case the fire overtook us before we had done our work. I also had occasion to help several friends to move their furniture, books, etc., to what were believed to be places of safety. In one instance I carried a great basket containing a set of Encyclopedia Brittanica, to three separate and distinct supposed places of safety. Each finally was reached by the flames, and it, together with everything else I had been trying to save was destroyed.[14]

Indeed, each and everything else was destroyed. The toll: three and a quarter square miles burned, 18,000 buildings destroyed, 100,000 persons homeless, 300 dead, more than $200 million in property lost. Certain irreplaceable things had been swept away; the Academy of Design, filled with paintings for an upcoming exhibition, the Chicago Historical Society, with Lincoln's own copy of the Emancipation Proclamation. Some of those 18,000 buildings destroyed in the fire were the best of their kinds, not only in Chicago but also anywhere on the continent, as Adler reminisces:

> The best work of the architects of early Chicago, and in the enumeration of these Otto Matz and Robert Schmid must not be forgotten, was obliterated in the two great fires.[15] Some of the buildings, such as the old Portland Block, the Marine Bank, the Ogden Building, the Illinois Central Depot, the Masonic Temple, the Rock Island Depot, the Oriental Building, would be considered very creditable productions at this day.[16]

The Great Chicago Fire is history. The year 1871 brought to an end an epoch in which the crudity of a new and growing community was ever evident, although its energy was tireless and its citizens possessed of an unquenchable thirst for the better things of life. The following last quarter of the century would witness the ever-growing city of Chicago[17] at its best.

5

Chicago Commercial Architecture

> Commercial architecture is the just title to be applied to the great airy buildings of the present. They are truly American architecture in conception and utility. The style is a monument to the advance of Chicago in commerce and commercial greatness and to the prevailing penchant for casting out art where it interferes with the useful. It is a commanding style without being venerable... THE COMMERCIAL STYLE, IF STRUCTURALLY ORNAMENTAL, BECOMES ARCHITECTURAL... The requirements of commerce and the business principles of real estate owners called this style into life. Light, space, air, and strength were demanded by such requirements and principles as the first objects and exterior ornamentation as second.[1]

Those are the words of the anonymous authors of *Industrial Chicago*,[2] written in 1891. With characteristic directness they summed up the factors that determined what they called the "commercial style" or what Montgomery Schuyler later termed the "commercial palace." Those recorders of building progress in Chicago were so aware of the unique success of the local architects. With great enthusiasm, they felt that they were witnessing the creation at least of an indigenous American architectural style and that they were recording a great style with great originality of its own. The style was born out of the union of science, technology, and art that reveals itself in the structural-utilitarian-aesthetic unity of the best Chicago building. The capitalization of a sentence in the quoted passage is mine as it is of signal interest. In it resides the basis for any aesthetic analysis of the major stream of the Chicago School. Written at about the same date as the publication of *Industrial Chicago*, the analysis of Montgomery Schuyler in "Glimpses: Chicago,"[3] may seem to illustrate it:

> If beauty be its own excuse for being, this entrance (of the Phoenix Building) needs no other, for assuredly it is one of the most beautiful and artistic works that American architecture has to show, so admirably proportioned it is, so admirably detailed, so clear and emphatic without exaggeration is the expression of the structure, and so rich and refined the ornament. Upon the whole these buildings, by far the most successful and impressive of the business buildings of Chicago, not merely attest the skill of their architects, but reward their self-denial in making the design for a commercial building out of its own elements, however unpromising these may seem; in permitting the building, in a work, to impose its design upon them and in following its indications, rather than in imposing upon the building a design derived from anything but a consideration of its own requirements. Hence, it is that, without

showing anywhere any strain after originality, these structures are more original than structures in which such a strain is evident. "The merit of originality is not novelty; it is sincerity." The designer did not permit himself to be diverted from the problem in hand by a consideration of the irrelevant beauties of Roman theatres, or Florentine palaces, or Flemish townhalls, and accordingly the work is not reminiscent of these nor of any previous architectural types, of which so many contemporary buildings have the air of being adaptations under extreme difficulties. It is the same directness and sincerity in the attempt to solve a novel problem that these buildings owe what is not their least attraction, in the sense they convey a reserved power. The architect of a "commercial palace" seems often to be discharging his architectural vocabulary and wreaking his entire faculty of expression upon that contradiction in terms. Some of the buildings of which we have been speaking exhibit this prodigality. There is something especially grateful and welcome in turning from one of them to a building like one of those now in question, which suggests by comparison that, after he had completed the design of it, the architect might still have something left—in his portfolios and in his intellect.[4]

Elsewhere in this same essay, referrring to Richardson's Marshall Field Warehouse (figure 3), Schuyler writes:

> The great pile is one of the most interesting as it is one of the most individual examples of American commercial building. In it the vulgarity of the "commercial palace" is gratefully conspicuous by its absence, and it is as monumental in its massiveness and durability as it is grimly utilitarian in expression. It is in this observance of the proprieties of commercial architecture, and in this self-denying rejection of an ornateness improper to it, that the best of the commercial architecture of Chicago is a well-come surprise to the tourist from the East.[5]

Indeed, it was a welcome surprise to Eastern tourists who came to Chicago in the last two decades of the nineteenth century. One of them was Julian Ralph, an author and journalist from New York. In 1891-92, and again in 1893, Ralph made an extensive tour of the United States for *Harper's Magazine.* It was on the first tour that he wrote the account of his visit to Chicago. Ralph was deeply interested in the Far and Middle West. Especially did Chicago capture his fancy, for he found the city vigorous and virile. On Chicago architecture, Ralph writes:

> I do not know how many very tall buildings Chicago contains, but they must number nearly two dozen. Some of them are artistically designed, and hide their height in well-balanced proportions. A few are mere boxes punctured with window-holes, and stand above their neighbors like great hitching-posts. The best of them are very elegantly and completely appointed, and the communities of men inside them might almost live their lives within their walls, so multifarious are the occupations and services of the tenants. The best New York office buildings are not injured by comparison with these towering structures, except that they are not so tall as the Chicago Buildings, but there is not in New York any office structure that can be compared with Chicago's so-called Chamber of Commerce office building,[6] so far as are concerned the advantages of light and air and openness and roominess which its tenants enjoy... It is a great mistake to think that we in New York possess all the elegant, rich and ornamental outgrowths of tastes, or that we know better than the West what are the luxuries and comfort of the age. With their floors of deftly-laid mosaic-work, their walls of

marble or onyx, their balustrades of copper worked into arabesquerie, their artistic lanterns, elegant electric fixtures, their costly and luxurious public rooms, these Chicago office buildings force an exclamation of praise, however unwillingly it comes.[7]

Whether willingly or unwillingly always came visitors' praises and expressed astonishments, particularly from those visitors from the East or from abroad when they saw what Chicago was like for the first time. Ralph's comment was a prototype for those from New York. What Ralph probably did not know was the fact that some of the men who created those astonishingly tall "boxes punctured with window-holes" were the products of New York itself while others came from other parts of the country. Few of the leading figures were born or grew up to manhood in Chicago. The architects who came together in Chicago following the fire of 1871 included men of rare creative talent who had no formal education in architecture but who had a remarkable capacity for learning their craft through direct attack on the problems of large-scale commercial building. In a little more than a decade after the great fire they invented and mastered the modern techniques of building construction and were thus able to develop the modern commercial architecture as we know it today as Sullivan in his *The Autobiography of an Idea*, says:

> The construction and mechanical equipment soon developed into engineering triumphs. Architects, with considerable measure of success, undertook to give a commensurate external treatment. The art of design had begun to take on a recognizable character of its own. The future looked bright. The flag was in the breeze...[8]

Before "the future could look bright," however, tremendous effort, and tremendous creativity were demanded of those who were left in haze and shock immediately after the great fire of 1871 if they were to pull themselves together and start all over again. As immediate gloom gave way to hope, reconstruction began and progressed with amazing rapidity. In spite of the losses and hardships, Chicago still possessed a location which could tap the reservoirs of grain, livestock, lumber, coal, copper, iron, and building-stone of Middle and Northwest America. Its lake frontage and eighteen great trunk lines of railway connections remained. Soon the manufacturing establishments which were a natural complement of railway and lake commerce were rebuilt, but only after the immediate and pressing needs of a homeless and destitute hundred thousand souls had been met. Original plans for hasty and cheap rebuilding were replaced by intentions to construct buildings larger and more permanent. Genuine fireproof construction marked nearly every building that was erected in the burned area. In the first year following the fire, 598 permanent buildings were erected. During the seven years from 1872 to 1879 a total of abut 10,200 permits for construction were issued. The average was 1,275 per year, the low being 712 in 1874 and the high 2,698 in 1877. It was this vast program of reconstruction and expansion that gave the architects their immense opportunity and forced upon them the necessity of developing a new form and new technique of building. In a few years following the fire, the scope and scale of building reconstruction, evidence of the expanding life of the community, brought colorful observations from visitors, one of whom was Sir John Leng who came from England to visit Chicago five years after the fire. The fruit of his trip was *America in 1876,* a book he published in 1877. His account on Chicago reads:

> There are miles of streets consisting of blocks five, six, seven, and eight stories high. The thoroughfares are crowded, busy, and bustling; and abounding signs of life and energy in the people and their modes of trading are everywhere apparent. Imagine a city of which all the principal public buildings—the Custom House, Post-Office, Exchange, railway stations, banks, hotels, newspaper offices, warehouses, and shops—were completely burnt down in a conflagration that raged for three days and nights over four square miles of ground, and imagine all these replaced, in the course of five years, by much finer and more costly buildings, and you are enabled to form some idea of the wonderful activity that characterizes the Chicago people.[9]

If we exclude the human loss, the fire proved in one respect to be a blessing. Looking back two decades later, Edwin Erle Sparks in his essay "The Beginning of Chicago" published in the September, 1903 issue of the *American Architect and Building News*[10] could say:

> The beginnings of Chicago may well close with her rebaptism in the fire of 1871. Without this blessing in disguise, it would have taken years to clean out the unsightly buildings due to the growth of the city from a frontier post. The easiest way to be rid of having to wear the clothing which one has outgrown is to burn it. Wooden pavements and frame buildings are stages of development, Chicago was done with both in the business district at one direful stroke. Only those who passed through the experience of the fire know its horrors. Only those who study a map of the "burned district" realize the space which it swept over... No city in the United States can excel Chicago in the picturesqueness of her past. No city has had such a succession of varied and striking types. Above her busy streets and lofty buildings pass in historic shade of the Jesuit, the trapper, the trader, the pioneer, the soldier, the land speculator, and in the appropriations for improvement of the harbor, has never been withdrawn... Some day when all this is materialized on a commemorative column or historic arch, when it stands in enduring pageantry on a memorial bridge, Chicago will mean more to one class of its citizen than a place to make a fortune and to another than a place of securing daily bread. Civic as well as national pride rests most securely on veneration for the past.[11]

The fireproof commercial building that appeared immediately and in enormous numbers during the years following the fire was an evolutionary outgrowth of the more advanced commercial structure that had been developing in the East since the middle of the century. As mentioned earlier, the cast-iron fronts had been very popular in Chicago since 1855 at which time Chicago's pioneer architect, John Mills Van Osdel,[12] introduced cast-iron columns and possibly wrought-iron floor beams into the Court House. During the next four years he designed a number of store buildings on Lake Street immediately east and west of State, so that by 1860 a four-block length of the street was solidly lined on both sides with cast-iron facades. All these buldings were five stories in height and followed the Venetian Renaissance forms so popular in the East which Schuyler called "the American commercial renaissance." Though all of these were very impressive to Chicago's visitors of the time, Schuyler was much less enchanted by them. In this essay "The Chicago Renaissance," he remarks:

> Masonry and metal alike appear to have come from a foundry, rather than from a quarry, and to have been moulded according to the stock patterns of some architectural iron-works. The lifelessness and thoughtlessness of the iron-founders' work predominate in the streets devoted to the retail trade, and the picturesque tourist in Chicago is then compelled to traverse many miles of street fronts quite dismal and as monotonous as the commercial architecture of any other modern town.[13]

Although the cast-iron front was fairly common in Chicago by the time of the Civil War, it began to lose popularity in the late 1860s, when the architects returned to masonry for the street elevations of store and office buildings. No iron fronts survive in Chicago, in spite of the fact that a few were built in the first few years after the fire.

The first impulse of the burned-out merchants of Chicago was not to seize the opportunity the clean sweep of the fire had given them to improve their warehouses and office buildings, but to provide themselves straightway with places in which they could find shelter and do business. The consequence was that the new buildings of the burned district were planned and designed, as well as built, with the utmost possible speed, and the rebuilding was for the most part done by the same architects who had built the old Chicago, and who took even less thought the second time than they had taken the first, by reason of the greater pressure upon them. In his article "Architects of Chicago" published in the January, 1891 issue of the *Inland Architect and News Record*,[14] John Wellborn Root recalls:

> The crudity and self-assertion, the fondness for cheap ornament which always mark the architecture of new and ambitious towns, were characteristic of earlier Chicago work. But we cannot withhold our admiration from the men who, under the tremendous pressure of rebuilding, from October, 1871, to 1873, stood so well between us and architectural abominations. Taken as a whole, Chicago as represented in these structures compares well with cities in which decades were necessary to accomplish what was here done with inconceivable haste in two years. The older men of the profession (W. W.) Boyington, (John M.) Van Osdel, (Otis) Wheelock, will tell you that it was not infrequent that foundations were planned and constructed, even up to the level of the side walk, before the first and other stories were arranged, and one architect is responsible for the statement that in the rush of his work, one building of four stories was under roof before he "got around" to design its facades—the floor being supported at their outer lines by temporary stays. At the time of the fire, the corps of men who had designed the old town were reinforced by the entrance of a

number of men from other cities, especially in the East, who bore no small part of the burden of the day. But the major part was naturally carried by those living here in 1871, and with what steadfastness and enthusiasm no one not then here can ever know.[15]

Immediately after the fire the number of five-story buildings the upper floor of which provided warehouse space for the stores at the ground level soon convinced the owners of the advantages of the power-driven elevator. The first steam-driven elevator in Chicago was installed in the Charles B. Farwell Store on North Wabash Avenue in 1864. This was superseded in 1870 by the hydraulic elevator, the first of which was built and installed by C. W. Baldwin in the store and warehouse of Burley and Company on West Lake Street. At the time of the fire, enthusiasm for the elevator and the increasing number of installations led to the designation "elevator building" for the new multistory commercial structure. The successful application of the elevator made possible in the decade of the 1870s a sudden and marked increase in the number of stories; at the same time the insatiable demands of commerce made the increase a necessity, together with the rise in height went a simplicity of formal treatment and a decreasing dependence on historical styles for the ornamental detail and the overall form of the building. The materials of construction were for the most part brick, dressed stone, plain concrete, cast-iron, small quantities of wrought-iron, and wood. The structural system of the post-fire elevator building was uniform and simple. In considering a building from the ground up, we shall see that the foundations were usually pyramid footing of coursed stone spread widely at the base and contracted upward by steps to receive the lower surface of column or wall. Interior cast-iron columns connected by cast- or wrought-iron floor girders supported iron or timber joists, which in turn carried the loads of floors and roof. The exterior walls were generally of solid masonry divided into piers of brick or dressed stone and strong enough to support themselves, windloads, and the floor and roof loads of the half-bays immediately adjacent to the walls. The building that revealed more fully and with great clarity the characteristics and most advanced work of building techniques of Chicago commercial architecture in the period immediately after the fire and in the 1870s was the Nixon Building. By 1871, ironically enough, the Chicago architects were trying their hands at completely fireproof structures. Designed by Otto H. Matz and erected at LaSalle and Monroe Streets, the Nixon Building revealed the most thorough and costly work of fireproofing, and its fate during the fire justified the care lavished upon it. The iron fronts had by this time become less popular in Chicago, and Matz followed the practice of using stone masonry piers on the facade. The interior frame was composed of cast-iron columns and girders carrying wrought-iron floor joists and roof rafters. The maximum beam span was sixteen feet. The tops of the beams were covered with a one-inch layer of concrete. Brick floor arches spanning between the joists carried marble floors, and a one-inch coat of plaster on the ceiling provided additional fire protection. The elevations of the Nixon, with their subdued classical detail and generous window area, were perfectly appropriate to the functional and structural character of the building. In its great open area and narrow piers, the two-story base of the building clearly foreshadowed some of the advanced designs that were to come in the eighties. The Nixon was nearly complete when the fire struck on October 8, 1871. Except for wood moldings and trim, it survived intact and was opened for use a week after the fire burned itself out. It was demolished in 1889 to make way for the larger LaSalle-Monroe Building of William Le Baron Jenney.

The Nixon building was the first notable example of masonry bearing wall and interior iron frame. Though it was common enough at the time in the East, it was a new construction technique in Chicago that led to further experiments later. In order to achieve what the first generation of architects after the fire did in the 1880s in terms of building techniques for tall commercial structures, Chicago desperately needed men who had extremely thorough engineering backgrounds as Schuyler observes:

> Even if the old-fashioned architects who rebuilt Chicago had been anxious to reconstruct it according to the best and newest lights, it would have been quite out of their power to do so unaided. The erection of a twelve-story building anywhere involves an amount of mechanical consideration and a degree of engineering skill that are quite beyond the practitioners of the American metallic Renaissance.[16]... It is in every point of view fortunate that the modernization of the town was reserved for the better-trained designers of a younger generation.[17]

The first of these "better-trained designers" was William LeBaron Jenney, who launched into the current established by the Nixon Building with his Portland Block, built in 1872 at Dearborn and Washington Streets, where it survived until 1933.

Jenney was perhaps the most original structural talent of a group of the "younger generation" architects that later became known as the Chicago School. He belonged with "the type of American genius of which John A. Roebling and James B. Eads were leading representatives"[18] as Carl Condit puts it. Jenney's background was excellent. He had received the best technical training available at the time at the Ecole Centrale des Arts et Manufactures in Paris, from which he graduated in 1856. The son of a successful owner of a whaling fleet, Jenney was born at Fairhaven, Massachusetts in 1832. He studied at Lawrence Scientific School for about two years and in 1853 enrolled as an engineering student at the École Centrale des Arts et Manufactures. After his Paris graduation, he received his early practical experience as an engineer in Sherman's corps during the Civil War and was discharged in 1866 with the rank of major.

The Major came to Chicago in 1867 and established an architectural office in the following year. Except for a brief appointment as professor of architecture at the University of Michigan in Ann Arbor, Michigan, in 1876, he remained at his Chicago office which became the training ground for the future architects of Chicago. A few of them later became leading figures of the Chicago School. "William LeBaron Jenney," observes Giedion, "played much the same role in training the youger generation of Chicago architects that Peter Behrens did in Germany around 1910, or Auguste Perret in France. He gave young architects the preparation they needed to tackle the new problems for which the schools could offer no solutions."[19] Giedion goes on to say that in Jenney's studio French engineering combined with the methods of his German specialists in ornament to produce a curious mixture. Besides Louis Sullivan who worked in Jenney's studio in 1873, his staff at one time or another included Martin Roche, William Holabird and even Daniel Burnham.

The technique of combining cast-iron columns with wooden beams was standard during the 1870s and persisted until the 1880s in Chicago. The high point of this system of construction was attained in 1879 in Jenney's first Leiter Building (figure 2) which is still standing at Monroe and Wells Streets. The construction of the five-story Leiter included three of the basic techniques in common use at the time; cast-iron columns and girders, timber beams and joists, and brick piers. If Jenney had placed the wall columns in the piers, which function entirely as fireproof envelopes and as supports for windows and mullions, and had added three more columns to the party wall on the north, he would have built a work of true skeleton construction which Jenney was to achieve five years later in his famous Home Insurance Building erected between 1884 and demolished in 1931. It took Jenney four years to move from the tentative and awkward use of the framed construction in the first Leiter Building to relatively mature iron and steel framing on the grand scale in the Home Insurance Building (figure 1). No edifice in America has been investigated more thoroughly than it, for none has had a more decisive effect on the construction techniques of our time. This celebrated building marked the culmination of a century's progress in iron-framed construction. It was the first tall elevator building to be supported, both inside floor and outside walls, by a fireproofed metal frame. In a technological sense, the Home Insurance Building was generally acknowledged as the first skyscraper. In reality, the metal skeleton construction began only above the rough-hewn masonry base for the main floor and the lower part of the skeleton was of wrought iron while the upper part (above the sixth floor) contained Bessemer steel.[20] However, it was the first extensive application of the internal skeleton and the curtain wall to a high office building that had been designed to meet the most rigorous functional requirements. The criteria that established Jenney's program were chiefly these: maximum durability and fire-resistance, utmost economy of construction, maximum admission of natural light, and open interior space for maximum freedom in arrangement of internal elements. Skeleton construction alone provided the comprehensive answers to these demands, and by thoroughly exploiting its utilitarian possibilities in both the exterior form and the planning of the large commercial building, Jenney and his fellow architects in Chicago succeeded in creating a new architectural style, the first since the beginning of the eclectic revivalism at the end of the previous century. The style was categorized by the compilers of *Industrial Chicago* as "Commercial Architecture." In characterizing these utilitarian structures, they showed the awareness of the new "Style" that had appeared in the Chicago downtown. In the formation of Chicago commercial architecture, the Portland, the first Leiter Building and the Home Insurance were key buildings for future development, and Jenney seems to be the one who provided the impetus for the movement.

Between 1880 and 1890, while the new commercial style was being formed, Chicago also was undergoing tremendous changes. Its population doubled, from a half a million to more than a million but the center of the city remained only nine blocks square. Julian Ralph, the earlier-mentioned visiting journalist from New York, remarked in 1892 that the only leeway for expansion is upward. The increasing centralization of the business process, along with other social and economic determinants arising from urban growth, led to an ever-increasing intensity of land use. Carl Condit reports that by 1880 in Chicago the price of land in the Loop district was $130,000 per quarter-acre. By 1890 it had risen to $900,000 per quarter-acre. As long as the price of land kept going up, the center of the city would be subjected to an unceasing transformation. Most visitors at the time sensed this and some came to a conclusion that the huge commercial buildings had been calculated solely in terms of materialistic speculation. Paul Bourget said he could sense in the streets of Chicago a business fever rushing along like an uncontrollable element, and, behind the windows of the skyscrapers, the quivering hot breath of speculation. And, again on the subject, Julian Ralph remarks:

> The city has been thought intolerant of criticism. The amount of truth there is in this is found in its supervoluminous civicism. The bravado and the bunkum of the Chicago newspapers reflect this quality, but do it clumsily, because it proceeds from a sense of business policy with the editors, who laugh at it themselves. But underlying the behavior of the most able and enterprising men in the city is this motto, which they constantly quoted to me, all using the same words, "We are for Chicago first, last and all the time." To define that sentence is, in a great measure, to account for Chicago. It explains the possession of a million inhabitants by a city that practically dates its beginning after the war of rebellion. Its adoption by half a million men as their watchword means the forcing of trade and manufactures and wealth... In order to comprehend Chicago, it is best never to lose sight of the motto of its citizens... the whole business of life is carried on at high pressure, and the pithy part of Chicago is like three hundred acres of New York Stock Exchange when trading is active. European visitors have written that there are no such crowds anywhere as gather on Broadway, and this is true most of the time; but there is one hour on every week-day when certain streets in Chicago are so packed with people as to make Broadway look desolate and solitudinous by comparison. That is the hour between half-past five and half-past six o'clock, when the famous tall buildings of the city vomit their inhabitants upon the pavements.[21]

Those were the exact words of Julian Ralph, a journalist from New York who visited Chicago in 1891-92, that gave vivid description of the central business district of Chicago at the time. Long before Ralph saw Chicago, the city had already become the center of commerce in the Middle West of the United States. The prairie land had been opened to intensive agricultural exploitation. With agriculture came the institutions of finance and the facilities for the storage and milling of the grain. The meat packing industry soon followed the establishment of the grain exchange. The Union Stock Yards was founded in 1865 to centralize the process of slaughter. Along with the development of agriculture was the growth of the railway network. The Galena and Chicago Union were joined by the Union Pacific Railroad in 1869 and provided the first rail route to the Pacific Coast. Besides all the companies that provided links to the Middle West, the New York Central and the Hudson River Railroad offered connecting service to Albany and New York. By the 1880s, rail lines extended from Chicago in all directions to the Eastern seaboard, the midwestern waterways and the Pacific Coast. With respect to waterway transportation, Chicago was ideally located. In the 1880s traffic on the Great Lakes was busier than ever. A network of canals provided means of transportation of agricultural products from the farms to the slaughterhouses and grain elevators of the city. The constant extension and improvment of the canals of the Midwest ultimately made Chicago the focal point of the largest system of inland waterways in the world. With the railroads, the canals, and the Great Lake traffic came the steel, coal, and lumber industries. These economic demands clearly established the need for a highly developed building art. Condit states the case succinctly:

> Many changes in the size, design, and construction of large urban buildings would have occurred whether the architects were capable of directing them or not. As we have seen, enormous pressures lay behind the whole building process. The architects and engineers had first of all to develop a new type of structure, the big office block of the crowded commercial area. The growing complexity of modern industry demanded concentrated administrative centers where large numbers of people could work at detailed and correlated tasks.[22]

There had been unsympathetic remarks, particularly those of the Easterners, about Chicago's lack of cultural, intellectual, and artistic developments in those days. Condit vehemently disagrees. He says that the material achievements of Chicago reveal only part of the picture and that it is true much of the city's life reflected a brutal concentration of naked industrial power, attended by all the possibilities of corruption, indifference, and cruel exploitation. It is equally true, however, that the intellectual and artistic life of the city flourished with surprising vigor. By 1865 the Historical Society, the Academy of Science, an art museum and school, and a number of large private libraries had been established. The personal lives of the wealthier and better-educated citizens included extensive travel abroad, cultivated taste in their domestic life and a remarkable receptivity to new ideas. Says Condit:

> Before the end of the century, these qualities were to expand into a brilliant flowering of the civic spirit. Chicago became very much aware of itself, conscious of its differences from the East, determined to perpetuate and enhance them, dedicated to creating an original American culture free from stultifying traditions. For a generation or two around 1900 it was marvelously successful. It is only when we realize the intellectual vigor as well as the industrial power of the city that we can understand how the forms and techniques of contemporary urban building are in good part a Chicago achievement.[23]

It is not so difficult as Condit might have anticipated in his statement to understand that in many ways the forms and techniques of the present-day urban architecture derive from the achievements of Chicago architects and engineers of the late nineteenth century. Their most celebrated and important achievement in the technology of building construction lies in their invention and development of the skeleton construction.

> The skeleton of the steel or concrete frame is almost certainly the most recurrent motif in contemporary architecture,

writes Colin Rowe in his essay entitled "Chicago Frame, Chicago Place in Modern Movement" published in the November, 1956 issue of *The Architectural Review*,[24]

> and is among the most ubiquitous of what Dr. Giedion would describe as its "constituent elements." Perhaps the role of the frame is most aptly summarized in the drawing by which LeCorbusier illustrated the structural system of his experimental Domino houses, but while its primary function is evident, apart from this practical value, the frame has obviously acquired a significance which is universally recognized. Apparently the neutral grid of space which is enclosed by the skeleton structure supplies us with some particularly cogent and convincing symbol, and—for this reason—the frame has established relationships, defined a discipline, and generated form. The frame has been the catalyst of an architecture, but one might notice that it has also "become" architecture, that contemporary architecture is almost inconceivable in its absence. One recalls innumerable buildings where the frame puts in an appearance even when not structurally necessary; one has seen buildings where the frame appears to be present when it is not and, since the frame seems to have acquired a value quite beyond itself, one is often prepared to accept these aberrations. Without stretching analogy too far, it would be fair to say that the frame has come to possess a value equivalent to that of the column for classical antiquity and the Renaissance. Like the column, the frame establishes throughout the building a common ratio to which all the parts are related; and like the vaulting bay in the Gothic cathedral it prescribes a system to which all the parts are subordinate. It is the universality of the frame and the ease with which it has apparently directed our plastic judgment which has led to the focusing of so much interest upon the Chicago commercial architecture of the 'Eighties and early 'Nineties. In Chicago seemingly our own interests were so directly anticipated that if the frame structure is the essence of modern architecture then we can only assume a relationship between ourselves and Chicago

comparable to that of the High Renaissance architects to Florence, or of the High Gothic architects to the Ile-de-France, for although no doubt the steel frame did make occasional undisguised appearances elsewhere, it was in Chicago that its formal results were most rapidly elucidated.[25]

The skeleton construction was not the only technological triumph in building art of the Chicago architects and engineers in the 1880s and 1890s. With economic pressure bearing down upon them and the huge tall commercial buildings in great demand, architects and engineers were forced to invent and develop various new methods of building construction all of which worked together as a unit. William Fryer in his "Skeleton Construction" published in the November-December 1891 issue of *The Architectural Record*[26] summarizes:

> High buildings are demanded, and today there is simply no limit to the height that a building can be safely erected. This result has been reached mainly through three inventions, all of which are distinctively American: 1. The modern passenger elevator, 2. The flat-arch system for fireproof floors; and 3. The skeleton construction. The last enumerated one has only joined the combination in which the first two were so long inseparable, but it has come to stay, and the three work in unity for a common purpose.[27]

To be correct, the second one in the Fryer passage should be just simply "the fireproofing," for it covers more broadly and it was among the important factors in the development of Chicago commercial architecture that will be discussed in more detail later.

As Fryer said, the elevator had been in use for some time before the skeleton construction was introduced into tall buildings. Obviously, the high buildings now characteristic of American architecture could not have been developed without similar progress in elevator design. Before the elevator was put into use, there were a number of four or five-story buildings the upper floors of which provided warehouse space and housed their custodian underneath the cornices for the stores at the ground level. The lower the stories were, the more expensive they became. But eventually the elevator reversed this rental hierarchy. It first appeared around 1850 and received wide publicity with its demonstration at the 1853 New York World's Fair. By the middle fifties steam-powered grain elevators were in use, and in 1857 the first passenger elvator, operated by steam, was installed in New York City. Chicago had a steam elevator first in 1864 in the Charles B. Farwell Building on North Wabash Street. In 1870 C.W. Baldwin of Chicago invented and installed the first hydraulic elevator in a store building for Burley and Company on West Lake Street. This led to the designation of "elevator building" for the new multistory commercial structures. The Baldwin invention was the first practical elevator, and the passenger elevator of this type came into general use in 1877 both in Chicago and New York City as William Fryer recalls:

Chicago Commercial Architecture 73

> Up to the year 1870 the elevator was not used to any great extent for passenger service. Many persons will recollect the old elevator in the Fifth Avenue Hotel, with its vertical iron screw extending the whole height of the elevator well, and passing through a sleeve in the centre of the car; very slow in movement, but safe, although frequently getting out of order. This was one of the first passenger elevators in this city. Improvements rapidly followed, until now great speed with absolute safety has been attained. It was the elevator that taught men to build higher and higher, for without the elevator a high building is impractical.[28]

It was not only the elevator that marked the increasing number of stories in the 1870s, the demands of commerce made the increase a necessity as well. The hydraulic elevator was almost universally used until several years after the first successful electric elevator appeared in 1887.

In order to be able to thoroughly realize the essence of the Chicago commercial architecture and the achievement of its architects and engineers, it is obligatory that one acquire the knowledge of the structural techniques that were invented in Chicago in the 1880s and 1890s. Therefore, a discussion on major methods of construction is included here. We may start from the ground up.

Foundation

The foundation will, to a great extent, depend upon the soil upon which it is built—the most durable are those built directly upon rock; but engineering, even in the 1880s and 1890s, can adapt to the nature of the soil, though whether this be rock, clay, sand or gravel will largely determine what kind of foundation is to be used. The foundations of high building employed by the Chicago architects and engineers in the late nineteenth century may be divided broadly into two categories: continuous foundations and isolated foundations.

Continuous Foundations

As their name implies, continuous foundations are solid, uninterrupted walls, carried wholly or in part around the building. They may rest on earth or rock; on piles; or on beds of concrete. A continuous foundation on earth simply requires that the soil be of sufficient density to support the weight that will be applied to it through foundations. A continuous foundation on piles is a type not much used in the largest buildings and continuous foundation on a bed of concrete is not frequently built.

Isolated Foundations

Building practice in Chicago at the time was chiefly concerned with isolating foundations for high structures. Interesting and sound advice on the construction of isolated foundations was published in 1893 by Frederick

Bauman, an architect with twenty years of practice up to that date. As is often the case with improved techniques, Bauman's recommendations for locating and proportioning the size of footings were not followed by all builders. This isolated foundation system was devised to distribute the heavy loads of high buildings on earth foundations over a wide area, in order to effect a uniform distribution of the weight in an economic manner. They were formed of (a) piles, (b) brick or concrete or stone footings, (c) beams or rails, and (d) caissons.

Pile foundations for high buildings offered few features in construction that were not familiar to engineers at the time. Their long-continued use rendered them, in many respects, highly desirable foundations where the rock bed could not be reached, and where there was a hard stratum to which they could be driven. Piles had been almost universally employed prior to the introduction of the isolated pier system, but were somewhat neglected after steel rails began to be used. However, their employment was revived later in the Schiller Theater (1891) and the Stock Exchange Building (1893). Good practice required that the piles should be driven to rock or to hard pan and they should be cut off below water-level at a sufficient depth to permit any timber grillage erected on them to be permanently under water.

Brick or concrete or stone footings were seldom employed in the best construction, on account of their poor economy of space. The first isolated footings of dimension stone as recommended by Bauman were pyramidal in form and were employed in the Calumet Building (1884) and the Royal Insurance Building (1885) designed by Burnham and Root, and the Insuarnace Exchange Building (1885) by W.W. Boyington.

The raft or rail footings were devised to overcome the difficulty of supplying an adequate support to the great office buildings on the compressible soil, largely clay, of Chicago. At first, they consisted of old rails, then of I-beams for the upper course; later on I-beams especially manufactured for the purpose were used. This type of footing is relatively simple: a layer of concrete to protect the steel and supporting a casting to which is applied the base of the column of the frame. It has many advantages, particularly space saving. A steel foundation whose height between its concrete bed and the bottom of the column rests is one foot, eight inches, will be equivalent to a masonry foundation seven feet high, when the latter is stepped out to transmit the load over the same area. This space-saving amounts to the height of a basement. At the same time, the steel foundation is much lighter in weight and this permits the addition of an extra story to the building without adding to the load on the soil. However, steel foundations are more expensive than stone ones, but the great economy in space, in weight, and in the time necessary for the erection, more than compensates for their price. That is why they were employed in most of the tall office buildings in Chicago in the 1880s and 1890s, namely the Fair, the Manhattan, the Rookery, the Monadnock, the Woman's Temple, the Masonic Temple, the Marshall Field, and the Reliance.

While the raft system was found practically sufficient to carry the heaviest buildings of Chicago, it was thought desirable, by some architects and engineers, to carry the foundations down to the rock level. For the purpose, the caissons, sunk by pneumatic or hydraulic processes, came into use. Local circumstances would determine the process of sinking them. As foundations, they consisted of circular, rectangular, or various shaped cylinders or enclosures of sheet metal, filled with concrete and brick. These were covered with a proper cap, to which was applied the casting for the base of the columns. They were, in fact, simple columns or piers of masonry, which carried the weight of the building to the rock below. The first "Chicago" caissons were used under the west party wall of the Chicago Stock Exchange on North LaSalle Street, completed in 1894. The Herald Building adjoined the Stock Exchange on the west, and it was feared that the driving of piles would cause disturbance of the Herald presses. William S. Smith, who had designed the first pneumatic caisson sunk in this country, solved the party-wall problem by the use of open wells to hardpan, filled with concrete. The first use of caissons as the foundation of an entire building was in the construction of the eleven-story Methodist Book Concern (1899), on Washington Street. Thereafter the use of caissons became general, especially for the higher buildings.

As far as foundations for tall buildings are concerned, Barr Ferree, in his "The Modern Office Building" published in the March, 1896 issue of *The Inland Architect and News Record*, writes:

> The nature of the foundation of a high building depends on the weights of the structure, the nature of the soil, the nature of the adjoining edifices and their foundations, and economy or cost. Economy, which usually comes first in mechanical operations, is the least important of the conditions, since, as the object of the foundation is to carry its building, no economical arrangement can be employed that does not recognize this fact. The adaptability of the building to its foundation need not be considered, since any sort of a steel frame can, in practice, be applied to any sort of a foundation.[29]

Skeleton Construction

The "steel frame" or the skeleton construction is a term applying to all building in which all the load is transmitted to the foundation by a skeleton or framework of metal or reinforced concrete, either separately or in combination. Its birthplace is Chicago. In the 1880s and 1890s, as a common practice of Chicago architects, the skeleton construction consisted of iron or steel columns, with twin curtain walls between, in place of solid thick brick walls. The curtain walls themselves were carried on wrought iron or rolled steel girders spanning the distance between the columns, which was usually about fifteen feet. In addition, the weight of floors was also transmitted to the columns, so that the latter supported the entire building and contents. The columns were encased with brick-work and when the building was plastered and finished on the inside there was no visible evidence of the novel construction.

Chicago's claim to the origin of modern skeleton construction lies in the fact that plans prepared in 1883 by Jenney for the ten-story Home Insurance Building embodied the first clear conception of skeleton construction, although the party walls of this structure helped to support the floors. Jenney, who is regarded as the inventor of the skeleton construction, himself stated that this method was not a sudden invention, but that it evolved gradually from old forms of construction. A number of specific buildings, American and European, clearly constituted precedents for the structural system of the Home Insurance Building. William B. Mundie, who was Jenney's partner from 1891 to the latter's death, recorded that Jenney got his first ideas of the possibilities of framed construction when he spent three months as a youth in Manila, on a voyage of his father's whaling ships. The Filipinos used whole tree trunks as columns and lighter cuts of wood for lateral and diagonal braces, floor supports and partitions, binding them all together at intersections with thongs and pegs. These buildings survived typhoons and earthquakes with slight damage. What Mundie or even Jenney himself probably did not know is that the type of building construction as described above has for ages been employed not only in the Philippines but also in most other Southeast Asian countries, particularly in the lower countries where buildings have to be built on stilts in order to avoid floods. In some locales, better-developed and more sophisiticated methods, based on exactly the same principle of the metal frame Jenney designed for the Home Insurance, have been and indeed still are in active use; only the materials are different. Beside the Asian source, there are several European and American ones, such as Hippolyte Fontaine's warehouse of the St. Ouen docks in Paris built in 1864-65; Viollet-le-Duc's "Lecture on Architecture," translated and published in the United States in 1881, in which he proposed a skeleton construction for a vaulted enclosure with all structural members of iron; and James Bogardus' shot tower built in 1855 for the McCullough Shot and Lead Company of New York. The question of Jenney's sources and how directly or consciously he was influenced by them is only a matter for the historian's speculation. Whatever the source, the skeleton construction was developed and employed to its fullest capacity in the tall commercial buildings of Chicago, and it has come to stay.

The utilitarian advantages of iron and steel framing were enormous and immediately obvious to architects, builders, and owners. First of all, the advantage of using this composite construction was the room space gained by the difference between the thick wall and the thin wall. In the ordinary wall-bearing method of building, the higher a brick wall the thicker it must be in its lower parts. The lower stories of a building were the most valuable for rental. Every inch gained in the width or length of the inside measurement of a costly building increased the availability of the structure, and when this gain of space was feet instead of inches, the reasons became obvious why the new method of construction, which took up one-half or less of the area of the plain brick wall, should immediately become popular after a few demonstrations. Secondly, the shedding of the thick supporting walls, with the consequent reduction in weight led to an immense increase in height. The steel necessary to carry a tall building weighed only one-third as much as bearing masonry for an equal number of stories. Thirdly, the virtually unlimited increase in glass area, up to a hundred percent of coverage, allowed the maximum admission of natural light, besides the fact that the slender columns and wide bays offered greatly increased freedom in disposition of interior partition. In the Home Insurance Building, the deciding factor seems to have been the admission of the greatest amount of natural light available on a narrow, closely built street. In this respect, Burnham and Root's Reliance Building (1894-95) on North State Street presented the fullest development of what has become known as "the Chicago Window" which is composed of a single pane of glass that fills most of the bay and is flanked by a narrow sash at either end immediately adjacent to the columns. The sash windows were introduced for ventilation. The Chicago windows were usually raised about two feet from the floor. The final advantage of the skeleton construction was economy both in the cost of materials and in speed and efficiency of construction. Once the materials were delivered on the ground, the erection of the framework progressed very rapidly. Two stories could generally be erected in six ten-hour working days. In the Unity Building of seventeen stories designed by Clinton J. Warren and erected in 1891-92, the metal-work from the basement columns to the finished roof was accomplished in nine weeks, as Joseph K. Freitig reported in his *Architectural Engineering* (New York), published in 1895.

Among the Chicago buildings that exemplify the transition to skeleton construction was Jenney's first Leiter Building (figure 2) on West Monroe Street, built in 1879 and characterized by decided preference for skeleton rather than wall-bearing construction. The Home Insurance Building in addition to embodying the first true metal-frame construction known anywhere, was also noteworthy because in it the first substitution of Bessemer steel rolled beams for wrought iron was made. The Manhattan Building on South Dearborn Street also designed by Jenney in 1889 is of true skeleton construction, although still using cast and wrought iron. It was also the first sixteen-story building to be built in Chicago. The framing system of the Manhattan, designed by the engineer Louis E. Ritter, exhibits an unusual combination of advanced innovations and traditional materials. The continuing high cost of steel led to the adoption of cast iron for the columns and wrought iron for many of the secondary girders and beams. Steel was restricted to the main girders and joists and to the channels used for spandrel beams. The Manhattan frame was also the first for which an American designer recognized "windbracing" as a necessity. The engineers employed both diagonal and portal bracing for wind resistance. The columns at the basement floor level, where the shearing forces, bending moments and increased axial load induced by wind are at a maximum, are joined by double diagonals extending across the bays in the form of wrought-iron rods fitted with turnbuckles to maintain tension. This is generally known as "cross-bracing" or "portal-bracing." Above the first floor windbracing is secured through deep girders riveted throughout the depth of the web to the angle fixed to the columns.

On the subject of the skelton construction, William Fryer perhaps offers the best summary:

> The skeleton construction imposes no new conditions on the architect. It calls for no skillful treatment to make it appear what it is. The metal frame, like the bones in a human body, is concealed from sight. Indeed, the architect is relieved from many troublesome conditions. He may design his structure without regard to width of piers, so that a front of brick or stone may be made nearly as light and airy in appearance as one of cast iron, and with as large window openings as desired. The building is so tied together laterally and vertically as to resist wind pressure or any other strain with impunity... New opportunities are opening up for architects to display their skill in treating problems of height, such as their professional brethren of a few decades ago never dreamed. It remains to be seen whether the aesthetic spirit will keep pace with the mechanical progress of the art of building, and bring forth designs of grace and beauty for the tower-like structures, notwithstanding any pre-conceived notions of disproportion between height and width.[30]

This essay was written and published in 1891; what an enlightened mind its author had!

Fireproofing

The development of fireproofing parallels chronologically that of the elevator. Earlier, fireproofing depended upon the extensive use of stone, brick or cast or wrought iron. Heated stone usually cracks and scales, especially when cold water hits it; and heated metal turns ductile or melts. Only brick can offer most fireproofing possibilities. When a metal-frame structure is suitably encased in a fireproofing material, its vulnerability to fire damage diminishes markedly. The principal lesson of the great fire of 1871 was that brick or stone walls alone are not sufficient to prevent destruction by fire. The Nixon Building (1871) was so little damaged by the fire that it was finished only one week later because it was of "fire-resistive construction" as it was often said to be after the fire. However, its good fortune may not have been due entirely to its superior construction. Several historians have reported one incident of the great fire that left its mark on subsequent building construction. At the time, John Van Osdel was supervising the construction of the new Palmer House. As the fire approached, he gathered his plans and ledgers, hurried by the shortest route to the hotel basement while fire thundered from street to street closing in on the building. Van Osdel dug a hole and placed the documents in it. He covered the hole with two feet of sand and a thick layer of damp clay. The records survived the fire, and his method of preservation suggested a system of fireproofing with fired clay or terra-cotta. It was used for wrapping the metal frames of the buildings. This coating for the metal frame was especially effective against fire when a dead air space existed between the terra-cotta skin and the structural members. George H. Johnson had developed hollow tile for partition and subflooring based on this insulating property of a dead air space between skins of fired clay around 1870. But others also were working toward the same end, such as Peter B. Wight, who came to Chicago after the fire and later on devoted several years of his career entirely on the development of fireproofing materials and methods. Johnson also came to Chicago after the fire in 1871 to promote his new invention. He won the contract for fireproofing the Kendall Building. Coincidentally, the building was designed by John Van Osdel and was erected on North Dearborn Street during 1872 and 1873. It was originally six stories in height but later increased to eight. The floors rested on hollow terra-cotta arches spanning between the wrought-iron joists, and the fixed partitions were built of hollow terra-cotta blocks. The Kendall was considered the first fireproof structure in Chicago. It was demolished in 1940. The first flat-tile arches were used in Chicago in the Montauk Building designed by Burnham and Root and erected in 1882, although they had been invented and used in New York several years earlier as William Fryer proudly reports:

> It was in the Post Office Building in this city that for the first time in this or any other country was introduced hollow-tile flat arches between iron floor beams. This was the invention of Mr. Kreischer, a well-known manufacturer of fire-brick. His was not the invention of a flat arch in itself, but of a flat arch, whose end sections abut against rolled iron floor beams, and recess around the bottom flanges of the beams, having on top wooden sleepers and wooden flooring, thus forming a level ceiling underneath and a walking surface above. Previous to Mr. Kreischer's invention the method of filling in between iron beams was by means of common brick arches, leveled up on top with concrete, and floored over. On the underside the bottom surfaces of the beams were left exposed and painted. A ceiling of a room then consisted of a series of curved arches between iron beams, which were very unpleasant in their appearance and effect on the eye. If a level ceiling was determined upon, it had to be obtained by wooden or iron furrings and lathing, fastened up to the underside of the beams and then plastered. The flat-arch system provided a level ceiling at once, at a less cost and with much less weight of material than before. The iron beams were covered in and protected from fire, and the side walls had a lighter load to carry. A new impulse was given to fireproofing construction, and following the great fires in Chicago and Boston the Kreischer system came into general use all over the country.[31]

With the rapid progress in the technology of building construction, particularly of the various methods of erecting foundations and the advanced techniques of skeleton construction, came many possibilities of even more radical changes in the design of the large, tall commercial building. The elevator made such a building practical from the standpoint of fast and easy movement to upper floors. Fireproof construction made it safe. Within a few years the exploitation of these technical factors brought about the revolution in form and construction of the Chicago commercial architecture that became the basis of a fully modern building art liberated from the last trace of dependence on the past.

The decade of 1872 to 1882 was not only the time for the technology and aesthetics of the commercial architecture in Chicago, but also the time of the gathering of the men responsible for the group development. The city had attracted a large number of architects and engineers ever since the ashes of the great fire of 1871 cooled down. Their talents and skills were unrivaled anywhere in the country and for the most part they were young men who came to Chicago primarily from the Eastern states as a visitor once remarked that the State of New York and the state of New England had sent the very best of their youth to the task of rebuilding Chicago. Hardly anyone was a native of Chicago, not even John M. Van Osdel who arrived from New York in 1837 before anyone else. S.S. Beman, another native of New York came to stay after designing a whole town for George Pullman. Otis Wheelock and Francis Whitehouse were also from New York and Asher Carter was from New Jersey. William Le Baron Jenney, it will be remembered, was a native of Massachusetts. Of the younger men who were members of Jenney's staff at one time or another, Sullivan was born in Boston and Burnham in upstate New York. However, both came to Chicago at an early age after their families had moved to the city. Martin Roche came from Cleveland, Ohio while William Holabird was born and grew up in American Union, New York. Erving K. Pond originally was from Ann Arbor, Michigan and William B. Mundie, a Canadian, joined Jenney in 1884 and later became his partner in 1891 until Jenney's death. Henry Ives Cobb and Charles S. Frost had emigrated from Boston and, of course, Peter B. Wight and Root had forsaken New York simply because of the great opportunity the burning of Chicago had presented. These were the men who built and rebuilt Chicago and who brought the Chicago commercial style into being. They were all energetic, substantially self-educated, direct in action and bold in vision, and most importantly they all were highly conscious of Chicago as a uniquely "American" city. With these qualities and this conviction was endowed the human component responsible for the growth of the commercial architecture in Chicago from the time of its conception to the time of its fullest maturity.

Of the early group of architects who both "built" and "rebuilt" Chicago, Root in 1891 fondly recalled:

> Among these men, to whose integrity and ability so much is due, several are with us—some in active practice. Mr. Van Osdel does not now undertake much work; Mr. (Asher) Carter, whom everybody loved, is gone where the materials used in architecture are more splendid than here; but Mr. Boyington and Mr. Wheelock, Colonel (Stephen V.) Shipman and Mr. (S.M.) Randolph, Mr. (L.D.) Cleveland, Majors (James R.) Willet and (William) Le Baron

Jenney, Mr. (William H.) Drake, Mr. (Edward) Burlington and others take their share of work in these new and less pressing days, and by their ability keep their younger confreres from too great vanity. Mr. Boyington's career has been in every way remarkable. During all the years of his practice, young men have gone from his office all over the continent remembering him as friend and preceptor.[32]

Of other architects, Root continues:

> S.S. Beman began his career under most favoring auspices. Endowed with fine talents and well equipped in his profession, he was entrusted with the erection of the town of (George M.) Pullman... Mr. (Joseph L.) Silsbee has also built many dwellings, especially of the suburban type, which are in the main thoroughly architectural and interesting. Mr. (Henry I.) Cobb came here from the East to erect the Union Club, which remains one of the most attractive ornaments of the North Side. In his hands also has been the Newberry Library, from which we anticipate so much. His influence for good has been very marked, especially in the great number of dwellings designed by him, whose great charm is their honesty, simplicity and refinement.... The gentlemen mentioned above upon the whole confer honor upon the profession; alas, that there should be others of whom this may not be said! "Unconscious assimilators" of the designs of others which reappear in distorted and mutilated form; worshipers of all the cheap tin goods of architectural art; coarse and self-assertive in every line and mass of their work; constantly destroying by their monstrosities the beauty of whole streets, and making the ends of vistas hideous nightmares, it is a comment upon the large charity of Chicago that they are suffered to exist. Men like these, however, disgrace all professions, but despite them, the architectural profession in Chicago stands in ability and integrity well abreast of that in any other city, and of any other profession.[33]

By the 1880s, with the leadership of William LeBaron Jenney and six younger men—Daniel Burnham, John Wellborn Root, Dankmar Adler, Louis Sullivan, William Holabird, and Martin Roche—the architectural profession in Chicago not only stood abreast of but even well ahead of that of any other city. All were to make decisive contributions to commercial architecture in Chicago. However, it is very important to note here also that the credit to such achievement should be shared with a group of influential men who played an important role, though usually in the background, in the evolution of commercial architecture in Chicago. They were those wealthy and powerful businessmen who happened to be the architects' clients and whose decisions on important matters in planning and erecting those famous buildings were—to put it mildly—taken very seriously by the architects. In an essay entitled "A Critique of the Works of Adler and Sullivan," published in the December 1895 issue of *The Architectural Record*, Montgomery Schuyler writes:

> Now that the Chicago construction has come to prevail, they are still noteworthy in comparison with the sky-scraper of other towns for these same qualities. And this brings me to remark upon the very great share which the Chicago "businessmen" has had in the evolution of commercial architecture in Chicago, a share not less important than that of the architects, and not less important for being in the main negative.[34]

82   Chicago Commercial Architecture

Schuyler went on to quote Paul Bourget's comment on the commercial architecture of Chicago in his *Outre Mer*. The Schuyler version of the translation is slightly different in the employment of some English terms from the one I have quoted earlier but the essence of the passage is the same. In part, it reads:

> The sketch appears here of a new kind of art, an art of democracy, made by the crowd and for the crowd, an art of science in which the certainties of natural laws gives to audacities in appearance the most unbridled the tranquility of geometrical figures.[35]

With the above remark of Bourget in mind, Schuyler made his analysis in the respect of the relationship of the Chicago architects and their clients as follows:

> It is noteworthy that the observer had seen and described New York before he saw Chicago. The circumstance makes more striking his recognition that it is in Chicago that the type of office building has been most clearly detached and elucidated. One is arrested by the assertion that this art, so evidently made "for the crowd," is also made "by the crowd," since a crowd cannot be an artist, one is inclined to say. But there is not only the general consideration that in architecture an artist cannot even produce without the cooperation of his public, and cannot go on producing without being popular. There is the particular consideration that in this strictly utilitarian building the requirements are imposed with a stringency elsewhere unknown in the same degree, and vary greatly to the advantage of the architecture. Elsewhere the designer of a business building commonly attempts to persuade or to hoodwink his client into sacrificing something of utility to "art," and when he succeeds, it is commonly perceptible that the sacrifice has been in vain, and that the building would have been better for its artistic purpose if it had been better for its practical purpose... I asked one of the successful architects of Chicago what would happen if the designer of a commercial building sacrificed the practical availableness of one or more of its stories to the assumed exigencies of architecture, as has often been done in New York, and as has been done in several aggravated and conspicuous instances that will readily occur to the reader familiar with recent building here. His answer was suggestive: "Why, the word would be passed and he would never get another to do. No, we never try those tricks on our businessmen. They are too wide-awake."... The architects of Chicago are not so radically different as all this from architects elsewhere. They are different on compulsion. They have "frankly accepted the conditions imposed by the speculator" [the word I translate "frankly" is brutalement, and I wish that M. Bourget had chosen to say "loyally" instead], because they are really imposed, and there is no getting away from them, if one would win and keep the reputation of a "practical" architect. And mark that the businessmen who impose these conditions are not the most private-spirited; they are the most public-spirited body of businessmen of any commercial city in the world. They are willing to make the most generous sacrifices for their city to provide it with ornaments and trophies which shall make it something more than a centre of pig-sticking and grain-handling. They are willing to lay the part of Maecenas to the fine arts, only they insist that they will not play it "during business hours." They are too clear-headed to allow themselves or their architects to confuse their several and distinct capacities of money-makers and Maecenases. If they allow themselves to be confused upon this point, in the first place they would not have so much money to do their public benefactions withal, and in the second place their commercial architecture would not have the character that in fact it has, and that comes from their insistence upon a rigid

adherence to the real requirements of their commercial undertaking. Into that architecture, then, their influence enters as a very potent factor, and whatever the architect beginning his practice in Chicago with head full of "classical embellishments" may have thought or said, it enters, as every discerning beholder must now perceive, as a very beneficient factor.[36]

If one wants to illustrate the fact that, indeed, the clients of the Chicago architects at the time exerted a great deal of influence upon the planning, the designing and even the erecting of a commercial building as Schuyler explains above, the experience of John Root with his Eastern clients would be a classic case to be picked as an example. The Brooks shipping family of Boston with Peter and Shepard Brooks as the principal intermediaries, wanted to make some money through ownership of a building in Chicago. The Brooks brothers in 1881 engaged Owen F. Aldis of the Aldis Company which was a real estate firm as their agent and financial adviser to direct their investment for the largest possible return. Aldis commissioned Burnham and Root to design the building that had become known as the Montauk Building since its completion in 1882. It stood at the corner of Dearborn and West Monroe Streets until it was demolished in 1902. Aldis worked very closely with the architects in planning and designing the building. He had told them that the steeply rising prices of land in the Loop area meant that any commercial structure to be built must rise high; to ensure future profits, the Montauk had to have at least ten stories. The building's tremendous dead load forced Burnham and Root to employ what the latter called "the floating raft system" for the foundations instead of the usual isolated piers. The Brookses were so satisfied with their investment, after the Montauk's opening in 1882, that they came back three years later and started negotiations to put up another large building under the same auspices, with Owen Aldis controlling the investment, and the firm of Burnham and Root in charge of design and construction. The Brooks brothers evidently did not believe in meddling with success. And they had their reward. The new Monadnock (1884-85) Block turned out to be a hit, both as a commercial project and an example of commercial art. At first, many Chicagoans doubted that the Brookses had another winner in their hands, and thought the promoters and builders had invited bankruptcy by locating on Jackson Street, which at the time did not deserve the title of boulevard. In fact, the south side of Jackson from State Street to the river presented nothing but an array of sheds and shanties. Harriet Monroe, Root's biographer, recorded that Owen Aldis kept urging and pressing the architects to come up with "extreme simplicity" in the design, rejecting one or two of Root's sketches as "too ornate." Before long, John Root was saying he thought he would "throw the thing up without a single ornament," and the result was the building we have today. What is now called the Monadnock was originally conceived as four separate buildings united within a single block, each with its own street entrances, elevators, heating plant, and utilities. This arrangement was felt desirable because four branches of the New England family were included in the Boston trust that financed the enterprise. The units of the quadripartite whole were separated from one another by bearing fire walls, thus permitting any one of the four branches of the family to sell its portion of the building and seal it off from the rest. The four units were whimsically named for as many New England mountain peaks, to symbolize the rise of the composite building from what were then the low structures in its immediate vicinity: from north to south, the Monadnock, Kearsarge, Katahdin, and Wachusett. Since Burnham and Root were responsible for the first half of the two-stage building program (the second half was designed by Holabird and Roche in 1889-91), their segment actually included the Monadnock and the Kearsarge. This plethora of topographical allusion became confusing to both management and tenants, however, and by the late nineties the four buildings became collectively known as "The Monadnock." Besides the Montauk and the Monadnock, the Brooks family also financed a few other commercial buildings in Chicago among which are the Rookery and the Marquette.

In the 1880s, there was a general belief among the people of Chicago, which was shared by a large body of Americans, that the rapidly growing city was destined to become ultimately the largest and most important in the United States. Its unrivalled advantages and unexampled expansion would seem to foreshadow this, for it was pushing ahead with boundless energy, and was enjoying an amazing accumulation of wealth and an astonishing development in all directions. The amount of business transacted in Chicago at the time was second only to that of New York and it steadily attracted the shrewdest from all over to take part in its vast and profitable enterprises. Almost all of these men came to Chicago after attaining adulthood, being attracted by its business advantages. They were young and full of energy; and they were destined to become the chief builders and developers of Chicago, and by the 1890s they all were the city's most prominent men in public spirit, in trade, and in wealth, as Julian Ralph writes:

> It seems to have ever been, as it is now, a city of young men, one Chicagoan accounts for its low death rate on the ground that not even its leading men are yet old enough to die. The young men drifted there from the Eastern states after the close of the war all agree that the thing which most astonished them was the youthfulness of the most active business men. Marshall Field, Potter Palmer, and the rest heading very large mercantile establishments, were young fellows.[37]

One of the most prominent among these powerful and wealthy businessmen of Chicago was Potter Palmer, a New York State man, who came to the city in 1852. A visitor to Chicago is always impressed with the great State Street, lined with splendid buildings and crowded with busy people. This famous street owes much of its development to Potter Palmer who in a single night during the fire of 1871 had lost his magnificent new hotel—the first

Palmer House. Borrowing nearly two million dollars from an insurance company—the largest loan ever made to an individual at the time—Palmer scoured the country buying materials to rebuild his beloved State Street, the centerpiece of which was, of course, his new hotel. Using Van Osdel's plans for the lost building, Palmer had them greatly expanded to create one of the most sumptuous edifices in the United States. His new Palmer House was also the most profitable hotel property in the country. From the time of the Civil War until the end of the century, the dry-goods and department store business of Chicago was dominated by the partnership of Levi Z. Leiter and Marshall Field. The latter, having come to Chicago in 1856, began work as a clerk for Cooley, Wadsworth and Company. In 1861 he was made general manager, and in 1862 he was admitted to partnership. The firm was now named Cooley, Farwell, Field and Company. In 1865, when Potter Palmer offered his department store business for sale to concentrate his time on his hotel enterprise and others, Field and Leiter who had joined him in the business a year earlier withdrew from the firm to take over the new store. In time Field developed it into the largest department store in the world and he himself became the wealthiest citizen of Chicago. The first Field and Leiter Store was built in 1868 at the northeast corner of State and Washington Street, only to fall before the fire three years later. The second store, on the same site, was opened in 1873, to be followed by a larger building in 1878. Up to the turn of the century, this building continued to be known as the Field and Leiter Store, although the partnership was dissolved before that time. Leiter had moved his business to a newer building designed by Jenney which was then known as the second Leiter Building. It still retains the name of Levi Z. Leiter on the State Street face of the parapet, although it is now a store of Sears, Roebuck and Company, founded in 1886 by Alvah Roebuck and Richard Sears. The building stands on the southeast corner of State and Van Buren Streets, where it was erected between 1889 and 1891. There are scores of other great Chicago merchants whose "stores are architecturally imposing piles that cover acres, and whose wealth and trade have also made them multi-millionaires,"[38] as one visitor remarked in 1887. Prominent among them were the Farwell brothers. They were also in the front rank of the builders and developers of the city. John V. Farwell arrived in Chicago in 1845. Five years later he was admitted into partnership in Cooley, Wadsworth and Company. In 1862, when Marshall Field became a partner, the name was changed to Cooley, Farwell and Company, and in 1864 to Farwell, Field and Company. After the withdrawal of Field and Leiter, the firm's name became John V. Farwell and Company. His brother, Charles B. Farwell, in 1864 purchased an interest in his brother's store and became general manager. He went to Congress in 1870 and in 1887 became a United States senator from Illinois.

In still other types of business, Chicago claimed men of wealth, power and influence equal to those mentioned above. Philip D. Armour was among them.

A native of New York, Armour in 1863 went to Milwaukee and joined the firm Plankington, Armour and Company, meat packers and grain dealers. In 1875 he came to Chicago to head the Armour and Company, a firm dealing in meats and grain, established by his brother H.O. Armour some years before. Philip Armour was the first packer in the modern sense of the word, and his products were known all over the world. He was known to be a bluff, hearty, vigorous, and hard-headed businessman, whether it be in meats or in wheat or in railways, or in anything else with the expansive and versatile spirit of Chicago that made the city great. At the time probably the Chicago name best known throughout America and the world was that of George M. Pullman, a name which had become a word synonymous with all the phrases that described the complete comfort in railway travel. Pullman, a New York cabinet maker, migrated to Chicago in 1856. His first services to Chicago were in devising ingenious methods for raising its buildings, among them the famous Tremont House, to the new grade level. In 1859, using his experience as a cabinet-maker, he remodelled two sleeping cars; and, although they did not compare with his later palace cars, they were a big improvement over the old sleeper. In 1864-65, he built the first palace car. In 1867, the Pullman Palace Car Company was incorporated, and in the 1880s he commissioned S.S. Beman to design and erect the Pullman City whither he promptly moved all his shops. He enlarged his business so as to include freight cars, street cars, and other types. His was soon the largest car-building company in the country.

All businessmen mentioned above were important and wealthy figures who wielded considerable power. As clients of the Chicago architects, they played pre-eminent roles in the development of commercial architecture in the city and thus cannot be ignored. Thanks to the East where most of these architects and businessmen originated, their firmly-joined skillful hands and Yankee ingenuity helped to make Chicago as great as it is today.

6

Adler and Sullivan

A very important building by an Eastern architect—Henry Hobson Richardson—that exerted great influence on all Chicago architects in the 1880s and 1890s as far as commercial architecture was concerned was the Marshall Field Wholesale Store (figure 3). In 1885, while Jenney was busy at work on his Home Insurance Building, Richardson was commissioned by Marshall Field to design a wholesale store and warehouse to be erected in the block bounded by Adams, Wells, Quincy, and Franklin Streets. Completed in 1887 the building stood until it was demolished in 1930. Unfortunately, Richardson[1] at the early age of forty-seven and at the height of his power died before the Marshall Field Store was finished. The building—its size and its site, its austerity of conception and the force of its presence, impressed the local architects tremendously. Louis Sullivan proclaimed the building "an oasis."[2] Sigfried Giedion, in his *Space, Time and Architecture,* thinks that Richardson's massive stone walls belonged to another period, and that it showed Chicago architects how unobtrusively a great volume could be integrated. He also says that Richardson injected into this building something of the vitality of the rising city, in a treatment redolent of dignity.[3]

Montgomery Schuyler, who knew Richardson personally, saw the Marshall Field Store during his visit to Chicago in 1891 and appreciate the "thing itself." He correctly observed the significance of it as the inspiration for much that was severely relevant to the stripped style of Chicago commercial buildings of the eighties and early nineties. In that same essay, "Glimpses: Chicago" (1891), Schuyler describes the building as follows:

> One of the earliest of the more modern and characteristic of commercial structures of Chicago, the Field Building is by Mr. Richardson also, a huge warehouse covering a whole square, and seven stories high. With such an opportunity, Mr. Richardson could be trusted implicitly at least to make the most of his dimensions, and large as the building is in fact, it looks interminably big. Its bigness is made apparent by the simplicity of its treatment and the absence of any lateral division whatever. Simplicity, indeed, could scarcely go further. The vast expanses of the fronts are unrelieved by any ornament except a leaf in the cornice, and a rudimentary capital in the piers and mullions of the colonnaded attic. The effect of the mass is due wholly to its magnitude, to the disposition of its openings and to the emphatic

exhibition of the masonic structure. The openings, except in the attic, and except for an ample pier reserved at each corner, are equally spaced throughout. The vertical division is limited to a sharp separation from the intermediate wall veil of the basement on one hand, and of the attic on the other. It must be owned that there is even a distinct infelicity in the arrangement of the five stories of this intermediate wall, the two superposed arcades, the upper of which, by reason of its multiplied supports, is the more solid of aspect, and between which there is no harmonious relation, but contrariwise a competition. Nevertheless, the main division is so clear, and the handling throughout so vigorous, as to carry off even the more serious defect. Nothing of its kind could be more impressive than the rugged expanse of masonry, of which the bonding is expressed throughout, and which in the granite basement becomes Cyclopean in scale, and in the doorway Cyclopean in rude strength.[4]

Schuyler elaborated this interpretation more completely in an essay, "American Cathedral," which was published with his Chicago essay in his *American Architecture*. In it, he presented Richardson as a modern prophet, who in the Marshall Field Store had very nearly freed architecture of its eclectic borrowings. All his life Richardson wanted to design a great commercial structure that would reflect the power, organization, and boldness of modern commerce. The store was his chance and in its daring simplicity, directness and severe economy of details, he came very close to his ideal. The Marshall Field Store was a forerunner of the new architecture of industry and commerce where volume, surface texture and the free expression of structure were to determine aesthetic effect. Louis Henry Sullivan was overwhelmed by the building. So were other Chicago architects at the time. The Marshall Field Store immediately inspired three most impressive commercial buildings in Chicago to rise in the Loop during the late 1880s. All still stand today: the second Leiter Building of Jenney; the Monadnock Building of Burnham and Root; and most importantly and most apparently, the famous Auditorium designed by the firm of Adler and Sullivan.

Seven years before the completion of Richardson's Marshall Field Store, the firm of Adler and Sullivan was formed and during their fifteen years of partnership the firm became one of the nation's most famous and most productive architectural offices. Says Condit:

Adler by himself or in association with men of only ordinary competence produced little to command the attention of historians. It was the partnership with the imaginative Sullivan that gave him exactly the opportunity he needed to exploit his amazing technical virtuosity. While Sullivan concerned himself with the problems of planning and architectonic design, Adler handled the matters of business and engineering. It was a perfect symbiosis.[5]

In his article entitled "Louis Sullivan—Return to Principle" published in the February, 1948 issues of The Liturgical Arts,[6] Joseph Salerno writes:

One cannot speak of Louis Sullivan apart from his gifted engineer-partner, Dankmar Adler. Sullivan was 24 when the partnership was formed in 1880; Adler 36. It was an association in direct contrast to the usual "business" partnership so characteristic of professional practice to-day. To Adler must be given great credit for the influence he undoubtedly exerted on his young partner, both professionally and intellectually.[7]

Actually, Adler's "young partner" entered his office in 1879 as head draftsman. In that year, Adler was working on his first independent commission and his most important until 1881—the Central Music Hall—after the partnership of Burling and Adler was dissolved in 1878 and succeeded by Adler and Company. The completion of the Central Music Hall found Adler's office deluged with building commissions which had to be conscientiously executed. Adler obviously would be yearning for help. Sullivan had been drafting for various Chicago firms since 1876 when he returned from Ecole des Beaux Arts. John Edelman, an old friend and fellow draftsman when both were in Jenney's office during the winter of 1873-74, knew of Adler's seeking for a good designer and suggested to Sullivan that Adler was the man to be associated with. So Sullivan called on Adler as described in his *The Autobiography of an Idea* and arrangements were made. Sullivan, up to then, had had no opportunities to show his genius in buildings completely designed himself, though he was known locally as a good draftsman and designer. Adler, progressive, open-minded, and farsighted, took Sullivan in and gave him scope that permitted the development of his genius. In May of 1879, Sullivan accepted an offer of a one-third share in the business and a year later the firm adopted the name of Adler and Sullivan, with partnership on an even basis. Sullivan's personality was not such as to attract clients, and all the clients were Adler's and remained Adler's. Confidence of clients in Adler was unbounded and well deserved, since no effort was too great or time devoted to a problem too much to tire Adler in his efforts to achieve the best results. It must be further admitted that Adler defended Sullivan against the attack of clients for what appeared often to them to be unreasonable desires on the designer's part. Together striving more than any others of their time to advance the cause of architecture as a science and an art in America, Adler and Sullivan created buildings that were truly distinctive and revolutionary. Adler always had his hand on the lever. He was entirely familiar with every intricacy of plan and he gave approval before the work was executed. Frank Lloyd Wright, in his "Louis Sullivan—His Work," published in the July 1924 issue of the *Architectural Record,* said of Sullivan:

> His genius burst into full bloom with the impetus of the success and fame that great enterprise brought to him and Adler. Dankmar Adler, his partner, was a fine critic, a master of the plan and of men. His influence over Louis Sullivan at the time was great and good.[8]

The work of the firm during the seven years before the Auditorium can be divided roughly into three classes: (1) several medium-sized commercial buildings, average six stories in height, the best of which were the Borden Block, Rothschild Store, Revell Building, Ryerson Building, and Troescher Building; (2) about thirty residences, more or less Queen Anne in style; (3) a number of theater interiors, for which Adler had a special talent. The firm did not enjoy the prestige of Burnham and Root, which had been established in 1873 and under the suave salesmanship of Daniel Burnham had won commissions for the ten story Montauk Building (1881), first tall building in Chicago, the equally tall Counselman Building (1883), and the Rookery (1885). Nor did the firm's early commercial work match the scale of S.S. Beman's Pullman Building (1883). However, Adler and Sullivan gained rapidly in prestige and were the envy of the profession when they captured the Auditorium commission in the summer of 1881. After that, all was well for the firm. Great commissions, some of which will be discussed later in this study, poured in to the office.

A serious financial panic in 1893, resulting in a depression of several years, put an end to most construction and thus hit the architects hard. Adler, at the solicitation of Richard T. Crane, severed his connection with Sullivan, dropped the practice of architecture, and decided to accept the high paying position of consulting architect and general sales manager of the Crane Elevator Company. Crane and Adler, both strong, aggressive types, could not for long work together. After only six months, the ten-year contract was terminated by mutual agreement. At that time, Adler was 51; Sullivan 38. Adler wanted to re-establish the partnership, but Sullivan felt that Adler had deserted the firm in a trying period and refused to rejoin his former partner. This was a critical business error on his part, for Adler was far more able in obtaining commissions. On this matter, Carl Condit says:

> The refusal to reform the partnership may have been Sullivan's greatest mistake. Adler, the steady and practical man, was the necessary balance to Sullivan's reckless pride. The number of his commissions declined rapidly. He received only two more in Chicago before the dismal period from 1900 to his death in 1924, during which his business as an architect virtually disappeared. One was for the Gage Building, which involved only a facade; the other was for the Carson Pirie Scott Store. The latter was the pinnacle of Sullivan's achievement and the climax to the heroic age of the Chicago School.[9]

Betty Chamberlain, in her "Louis Sullivan"[10] wrote that for thirty years Sullivan carried on a dwindling practice, despite his ever-present creativity and imagination, and grew in cynicism and bitterness. Chamberlain went on to quote the noted Swedish artist, Anders Zorn, on a visit to the United States as saying:

> What is the matter with you Chicago people? There in the Auditorium Tower sits your country's greatest living architect, one of the world's leaders in his profession, doing nothing. This could not happen in Europe.[11]

But alas, such a thing did happen in America. In an article entitled "Frank Lloyd Wright on Louis Sullivan" published in the August, 1949 issue of *The Architectural Forum*,[12] an anonymous writer comments:

> But the mob takes an "unconfessed revenge" for the kind of independence shown by those it calls "genius." The firm of Adler and Sullivan did not survive the depression which followed the great success of the Columbian Fair, while the classic revival generated by the fair architecture eclipsed for many decades Sullivan's contribution to American building. Sullivan died broke; even the commissions for small town banks had long since dwindled away and the great architect had been thrown out of his offices in the Auditorium Tower. A few terra cotta manufacturers and a few architectural cronies stuck with him to the end, visiting him in his disreputable room in a South Side hotel. Wright saw him weekly. A few days before he died, Sullivan gave Wright a bundle of drawings, the ornaments he had designed in the years of his great building. "Frank, you will be writing about these, someday?" he asked. Sullivan left over one hundred buildings, most of them done in partnership with the "big chief" Dankmar Adler, whose brilliant grasp of structure matched Sullivan's gift of design. It will surprise many students of Sullivan, who believe that when Sullivan turned his back on Richardson's Romanesque the whole course of contemporary architecture turned with him.[13]

The very last article John Root wrote for publication entitled "Architects of Chicago" had been printed earlier in *America* anonymously. It was reprinted as a tribute to Root in the January 1891 issue of the *Inland Architect* after his death. In it, Root says of Sullivan:

> One of the most individual personalities and the author of some of the most characteristic works, is Mr. Sullivan. Cultivated in many directions, with a bold, alert, vigorous and imaginative mind bending its energies into many channels, self-confident and enthusiastic, ideally supplementing Adler his partner, Sullivan has accomplished much admirable work, and will achieve much more. The Ryerson Building on Randolph Street, and [the Revell Building] on Adams Street and Wabash Avenue, are his; his are the designs for the Auditorium with its decorations, as well as many other buildings, all of which attest the boldness, freshness and ingenuity of his mind. So exuberant is he that he sometimes seems to neglect the larger questions of mass, of light and shade, of sky-blotch in his care for delicacy, beauty and significance of detail, and even in this respect at times forgets that this detail should assume different expressions when executed in different materials.[14]

Meanwhile, Adler founded his own architectural practice with increasing dependency on his sons Abraham and Sidney. Together, they built warehouses for the Meyer Estate, work for the Chicago Dock Company, for Wright and Hill Linseed Oil Company and two dormitories for Morgan Military Academy in 1897 and 1898 along with some other works of insignificance. Only five years after his separation from Sullivan, Adler died on April 16, 1900, following an apoplectic stroke. Writes Root of Adler in his aforementioned last essay:

> Among the highest in all the profession stands Mr. Adler. For some time after the fire a partner of Mr. Burlington, and the "designing" member of the firm. Of late Mr. Adler has

passed the artistic crayon to Mr. Sullivan, but work designed by him in the earlier days—such as The [Dickey] building opposite the Tremont House, on Dearborn Street, that at No. 97 Dearborn Street, and Central Music Hall—shows a strength, simplicity and straightforwardness, together with a certain refinement, which reveal the true architect. No professional man has pursued a more consistent and dignified course than he, and no man is more respected by his confreres. The Auditorium, a really wonderful building, stands as a monument to his and Sullivan's talent.[15]

Adler's Central Music Hall mentioned above by Root was completed by 1879. It came as a surprise after eighteen rather undistinguished years of engineering and architectural experience. Adler had come to Chicago in 1861, at the age of seventeen and had begun his career in the office of Augustus Bauer. He was born in Lengsfeld, Germany where his father was a public school teacher. In 1854, the elder Adler migrated with his family to America, settling in Detroit where he became the rabbi of Congregation Beth-el. In that city, Dankmar Adler attended the public schools but he cut his education short to become an apprentice draftsman in the office of the Detroit architect, E. Willard Smith, where he learned architectural history and the philosophy of architectural design, besides gaining first-hand experience in drafting. Later at Bauer's office in Chicago he acquired knowledge of designing and building construction. In 1866 after serving four years in the Union Army during the Civil War, he returned to Chicago and re-entered Bauer's office for a short time and then joined the office of O.S. Kinney, an architect whose practice included churches, schools and courthouses. Adler rose rapidly in Kinney's office, and at Kinney's death in 1869, Adler and O.S. Kinney, Jr. formed the partnership of Kinney and Adler. Shortly after the fire following the establishment of the firm Burlington and Adler in 1871, commissions for office buildings came to him. Among the prominent buildings turned out by this office were the old Tribune Building at Dearborn and Madison Streets and the First National Bank at State and Washington. Adler was kept more than busy and felt that the senior partner, Edward Burlington, was perhaps unduly loading his shoulders with responsibilities. In 1879 the Burlington association was severed and Adler operated alone under the name of D. Adler and Company for two years. During these two years, Adler devoted himself to the design and erection of the Central Music Hall whose chief importance is historical and possibly technical. "In it," observes Condit, "lay the genesis of the great Auditorium Building which was to follow it by a decade."[16] It stood on the southeast corner of Randolph and State Streets and was demolished in 1901 to make way for the first block of the present Marshall Field Store by Burnham. The Central Music Hall was thus Adler's most important work until 1880 when he was joined by Louis Sullivan.

The younger of the partners—Louis Sullivan—had been born in Boston of Irish and German-French parentage in 1856. Although his parents moved to Chicago in 1869, Louis remained in Boston, where he entered the English High

School in 1870 and then in 1872 the school of architecture of the Massachusetts Institute of Technology. At M.I.T., he found the architectural courses offered "architectural theology" which was made up of "boring, empty, and repetitious" classical styles, orders and details. Sullivan was at M.I.T. not over a year. Either he could not endure M.I.T. or M.I.T. could not endure him. Sullivan then went to work for the firm of Furness and Hewitt in Philadelphia as an apprentice draftsman with the intention of going to study at the Ecole des Beaux Arts. He did not make it to Paris yet though. Fate and destiny brought him into the office of William LeBaron Jenney in Chicago in 1873 at which he shortly found himself in the company of William Holabird, Martin Roche, and Daniel Burnham. Who would realize at the time that within a few years these extraordinary men with progressive minds together could change the course of commercial architecture of Chicago, perhaps of the world! Sullivan went to the Ecole des Beaux Arts in 1874 where he studied under an obscure instructor of descriptive geometry—M. Clopet. In his *Autobiography of an Idea,* discussing the advanced technology of building construction in Chicago in the 1880s and the problems of designing tall buildings at the time, Sullivan writes:

> The problem of the tall office building had not been solved, because the solution had not been sought within the problem itself—within its inherent nature. And it may be here remarked after years of observation, that the truth most difficult to grasp, especially by the intellectuals, is this truth: That every problem of whatsoever name or nature contains and suggests its own solution; and the solution reached is invariably found to be simple in nature, basic and clearly allied to common sense. This is what Monsieur Clopet really meant when he said to Louis in his Paris student days: "Our demonstrations will be such as to admit of NO EXCEPTION." Monsieur Clopet carried the principle no further than his mathematics, but Louis saw in a flash the immensity and minuteness of its application, and what a world of research lay before him; for with the passing of the flash he saw dimly as through a veil and it needed long years for the vision to reclarify and find its formula.[17]

As an architect, throughout his life, Sullivan devoted himself to a search for that rule that "shall admit of no exceptions."

The same as any place else, the young and restless Sullivan could not stand academic venture. He stayed at the Ecole des Beaux Arts no more than a year. He felt that what was taught there he had already acquired at M.I.T. Therefore, Sullivan in 1875 decided that he had to return to Chicago to refresh himself once more through direct contact with the constituent facts in the structural art of his time. Through his friendship with John Edelman, whom he met while working at Jenney's office, Sullivan was offered the job of draftsman in the office of Johnston and Edelman. As already mentioned, it was the latter who introduced him to Dankmar Adler.

To appreciate Sullivan's architecture, it is important that one must understand his concept and philosophy of architecture which he expressed in his numerous writings. Like Le Corbusier and Frank Lloyd Wright, Sullivan enlarged his position in the history of modern architecture by creating through extensive writing his own legend. Only Wright and Le Corbusier wrote more. His writings have brought him fame as a hero in modern culture; in his case as the neglected genius and "prophet" of modern architecture in the United States. Sullivan has become a martyr. By the last decade of the century, Sullivan had developed in preliminary terms his organic theory of building art, a system which was later to be presented at length in his major writings, *The Kindergarten Chats* (a series of essays published in 1901-02) and *The Autobriography of an Idea* (1924). The philosophy of architecture offered in these works contains extensive ethical and social, as well as formal and aesthetic elements. Of *The Chats*, Sullivan once confided to a friend:

> The Kindergarten Chats will strike deeper than you are inclined to imagine. As a psychological study they will be far and away beyond anything I have hitherto attempted. The key to them, you will find, is the development proceeds, slowly but elaborately,—in the development of the character and artistic nature of the young man, FROM WITHIN. It will be the first serious attempt ever made to test architecture by human nature and democracy. Don't let a certain flippancy of treatment mislead you. Try to spread them as far as you can among the laity, for they will be free from technicalities. I am writing for the people, not for architects.[18]

In his *The Autobiography of an Idea*, besides his attack on the Columbian Exposition of 1893, Sullivan encapsulated his ideas of "form follows function." The slogan, together with LeCorbusier's "A house is a machine for living in," has become canonical in modern architecture. Both slogans have been misinterpreted, especially by conservative architects who condemned them as reducing the roles of architects to the role of a skilled automaton or human computer for design; fed by the client's program, an architect regurgitates the inevitable arrangement to meet practical needs. But the conservative did not mention that even the most austerely practical problem in engineering, not to mention a problem in architecture, involves choices of conceptions, materials, structure, dimensions, and so on. The quality of these choices determines whether or not works of engineering are also works of art.

Of Sullivan's writings, Joseph Salerno writes:

> Sullivan's achievement was two-fold: it lay in what he said as well as in what he did. His doctrine was as important in its influence as the structure he built, if not more so. It is significant that the two provinces do not contradict, but complement and reinforce each other. With his words, as well as with his work, Sullivan waged a war against four hundred years of encrusted imitation. It seems great men are bound to suffer the abuses of misunderstanding and misinterpretation. There are those who see no further than Sullivan's ornament. Extraordinary as it was, it cannot be considered as the same significance as the buildings themselves. There are others who dispose of Sullivan with the facile reiteration: "Form follows function," as though it were a political slogan. But the implications of function and form, poetic as well as practical were infinite. Nowhere in Sullivan's writings is this more eloquently expressed than in *The Kindergarten Chats*, a series of essays in dialogue, remarkable for the excellence of its prose as well as the clarity of its exposition:

"The interrelation of function and form. It has no beginning and no ending. It is immeasurably small, it is immeasurably vast: inscrutably mobile, infinitely serene; intricately complex, yet simple...a universe wherein all is function, all is form: a frightful phantasm, driving the mind to despair, or, as we will, a glorious revelation of that power which holds us in an invisible, a benign, a relentless—a wondrous hand." For his contemporaries Sullivan had nothing but justifiable contempt. The legacy of the fifteenth century, which inevitably degenerated into ill-concealed sham, has played itself out in a welter of indiscriminate and promiscuous revivals.[19]

It is always interesting to hear from other writers who hold an opposing view on the same matter. In his unsympathetic article entitled "Is Sullivan the Father of Functionalism"—a highly critical essay on Sullivan that was published in the December, 1956 issue of *Art News,* Philip Johnson comments:

After the Wainwright and Guaranty Buildings in the mid 90's, nothing Sullivan did ever could be called anything but second rate. The ornament, which was always Sullivan's first love rather than structure or massing, became painfully ugly and the fenestration more and more arbitrary and ill-proportioned. He seemed not to have become aware of Wright's great revolution of 1900 in architectural form. Wright's "breaking of the box", which became the basis of all thinking in modern architecture, Sullivan never noticed. He remained a man of the "pencil" in his designs and a Richardson in his building. History has been kind to Louis Sullivan. The alcoholism, the sex troubles, his rejection by the public before he was fifty, the lonely death are all grist to the romantics' mill. In addition, being exiled in a sense from architecture by 1904, he had twenty years of life in which to write his apologia. Like Napoleon at St. Helena, he created his own myth while he was alive, but luckier than Napoleon, he was survived by a much greater pupil, his mythographer, Frank Lloyd Wright, who still calls him Leiber Meister (a phrase he can easily afford without loss of ego or arrogance). Artists who write (was this always so?) have a great advantage, especially if they have a broad theoretical bent. Le Corbusier, Wright, Neutra and Mendelsohn are good architects, but their reputations are surely enhanced by their voluminous publication. An example of the power of the pen has been the invective Sullivan poured on the 1893 Fair. Not many of us now living ever saw that famous exposition, but if one can judge from pictures, the White City was a far more unified and splendid sight than New York 1939 or Paris 1925. In fact, Sullivan's little revolt in one wing of the Fair, the Transportation Building with its forty-seven kinds of ornament, "colored in gold, brown, green and crimson" (what a combination!) was not even a unified piece of design. Richardson would have integrated the great Saracenic portal into the total composition. Sullivan's furious antagonism to the Classic Revival, which swept into Chicago from the East, has been taken much too literally in the history books. Wright himself did distinguished Classical work in the 90's. It was in the air. Perhaps Sullivan's feeling was that everybody was out of step but himself.[20]

The early application of Sullivan's complex philosophy of architecture to a specific building problem appeared in a document which has become a classic of modern theory, "The Tall Office Building Artistically Considered" first published in *Lippincott's Magazine* for March, 1896 and later reappeared in the January, 1922 issue of *The Western Architect*[21] and the January, 1957 issue of *Progressive Architecture.* In this particular essay lies Sullivan's solution to the problem of the tall commercial building. Richardson died before the problem really existed, Root soon after, and Sullivan rose to the challenge. He was, as every critic agrees, even Philip Johnson, the first to give architectural expression to the tall building of steel. And it seems that any architect facing the design of such a building truly cannot but be influenced by Sullivan's two great examples—first the Wainwright Building in St. Louis (1890-91) which is the perfect embodiment and the realization of Sullivan's theory in an actual commission and then the Guaranty, later Prudential, Building in Buffalo (1894-95) in which the same system is developed and perfected. Both buildings represent Sullivan's greatest achievement. In the late 1880s and early 1890s, the problem that Sullivan and other architects of the Chicago School were facing was the problem of the steel-frame office building. Sullivan himself grasped at once that the new form of engineering was revolutionary demanding an equally revolutionary architectural mode; to Sullivan, masonry construction, insofar as tall buildings were concerned, had become a thing of the past, to be forgotten so that the architect's mind might be free to face and solve new problems in new functional forms. The old idea of superimposition had to give way to the imperatives of vertical continuity of a tall office building. "Thus has come about that form of lofty construction called the 'modern office building.' It has come in answer to a call, for in it a new group of social conditions has found a habitation and a name," writes Sullivan in his "The Tall Office Building Artistically Considered." He continues:

> Up to this point all in evidence is materialistic, an exhibition of force, of resolution, of brains in the keen sense of the word. It is the joint product of the speculator, the engineer, the builder. Problem: How shall we impart to the sterile pile, this crude, harsh, brutal agglomeration, this stark, staring exclamation of eternal strife, the graciousness of those higher forms of sensibility and culture that rest on the lower and fiercer passions? How shall we proclaim from the dizzy height of this strange, weird, modern housetop the peaceful evangel of sentiment, of beauty, the cult of a higher life. This is the problem; and we must seek the solution of it in a process analogous to its own evolution,—indeed, a continuation of it,—namely by proceeding step by step from general to special aspects, from coarser to finer considerations. It is my belief that it is of the very essence of every problem that it contains and suggests its own solution. This I believe to be natural law. Let us examine, then, carefully the elements, let us search out this contained suggestion, this essence of the problem.[22]

There was an interesting editorial note that accompanied the article when it was published in the *Western Architect* in 1922 in which the editor remarked:

> The decade will witness the construction of many large structures in all the great cities of the country. On the eve of this new are it is regarded as extremely desirable that tenets of this article be given hearing. In fact, another hearing, for it first appeared in 1895, in Lippincott's Magazine, and is given here just as it was published at the time. After nearly thirty years of high building construction, much of which, unfortunately, cannot be considered as artistic, Mr. Sullivan's clear reasoning, based upon his logical solution of the high building problem, is as fresh and worthy of study as in 1895. Mr. Sullivan, himself, states that he has nothing to add nor to subtract from his early statement.[23]

After Sullivan's death in 1924, *The Architectural Record* in its April, 1925 issue published a very long essay entitled "Louis Sullivan—An Old Master" written by Fiske Kimball as a tribute to the architect. It included excerpts of Sullivan's "The Tall Building Artistically Considered" and Kimball's comments on Sullivan's article and his successful application of the theory to actual buildings—the Wainwright and the Guaranty. Kimball writes:

> The achievement was widely recognized and acclaimed. Almost without exception, tall buildings from 1897 to 1912 showed its influence by accented vertical lines. This was scarcely more true in the work of consistent "modernists" like Sullivan, who sought to abandon all historical forms, than of their antagonists, the eclectics. They gave at least lip-service to "structural expression," and turned often to Gothic with its soaring lines. Even the most consistent devotees of abstract form did not remain untouched. In their New York Municipal Building, designed in 1908, McKim, Mead and White marked the lines of steel columns by shallow vertical strips. Thus in the treatment of the skyscraper Sullivan's creative work attained a historical influence corresponding to its artistic significance.[24]

Finally, on May 9, 1946—twenty-two years after the architect's death, the American Institute of Architects belatedly recognized Louis Henry Sullivan's stature as "architect" by awarding him posthumously the Institute's highest gift, its Gold Medal. The citation was read by the A.I.A. president as follows:

> His profession of architecture was a lifetime dedication of all his energies of mind and spirit. By esteeming practical requirements as esthetic responsibilities he unfolded a new discipline of design. He believed that the dimensions of American architecture are the dimensions of American life, and thus directed us to an art of, by, and for our own people. He approached each task afresh, believing that each problem contains and suggests its own solution. He demanded of himself an emotional and spiritual expenditure to endow each building with its own identity of beauty. He attacked entrenched beliefs. He repudiated false standards. He scorned the stylistic gods of the market-place. He fought almost alone in his generation, lived unhappily, and died in poverty. But because he fought, we today have a more valiant conception of our art. He helped to renew for all architects the freedom to originate and the responsibility to create. The standards he set have contributed much to the achievement of today and will augment the promise of tomorrow.[25]

In the 1880s and 1890s, after the partnership of Adler and Sullivan was formed and during their fifteen years of working together until the establishment was dissolved, the technical means of a new building art in Chicago were available to Sullivan. It remained to him to transmute the structural solutions to these unprecedented fuctional requirements into a symbolic art. His organic philosophy had already come to exist at least in an incoherent form, but so broad an approach to architectural design could not lead directly to a specific kind of formal expression. The key to the process of transmutation of the advanced building technology and the architectural concept of Sullivan may be found in those passages of his writings in which he expresses his feelings about particular architectural and structural achievements of the time. He writes in his *Autobiography of an Idea:*

98   Adler and Sullivan

> Thus the year 1880 may be set as the zero hour of an amazing expansion, for by that time the city had recovered from the shock of the panic of 1873. Manufacturing expanded with incredible rapidity, and building industry took on an organizing definition. With the advance in land values, and a growing sense of financial stability, investors awakened to opportunity, and speculators and promoters were at high feast. The tendency in commercial buildings was toward increasing stability, durability, and height, with ever bettering equipment. The telephone appeared, and electric lighting systems. Iron columns and girders were now encased in fireproofing materials, hydraulic elevators came into established use, superseding those operated by steam or gas. Sanitary appliances kept pace with the rest... The Bessemer process of making "mild" steel had for some time been in operation in the Pennsylvania mills, but the output had been limited to steel rails; structural shapes were still rolled out of iron... Meanwhile the use of concrete in heavy construction was spreading, and the application of railroad iron to distribute concentrated loads on the foundations, the character of which became thereby radically changed from pyramids to flat affairs, thus liberating basement space; but this added basement space was of comparatively little value owing to deficiency in headroom due to the shallowness of the street sewers. Then joined in the flow an invention of English origin, an automatic pneumatic ejector, which rendered basement depths independent of sewer levels.... so in this instance, the Chicago activity in erecting high buildings finally attracted the attention of the local sale managers of Eastern rolling mills; and their engineers were set at work... Thus the idea of a steel frame which should carry all the load was tentatively presented to Chicago architects. The passion to sell is the impelling power in American life. Manufacturing is subsidiary and adventitious. But selling must be based on a semblance of service—the satisfaction of a need. The need was there, the capacity to satisfy was there, but the contact was not there. Then came the flash of imagination which saw the single thing. The trick was turned; and there swiftly came into being something new under the sun. For the true steel-frame structure stands unique in the flowing of a man and his works; a brilliant material example of man's capacity to satisfy his needs through the exercise of his natural powers... The architects of Chicago welcomed the steel frame and did something with it. The architects of the east were appalled by it and could make no contribution to it... The social significance of the tall building is in finality its most important phase. In and by itself, considered SOLUS so to speak, the lofty steel frame makes a powerful appeal to architectural imagination where there is any. Where imagination is absent and its place usurped by timid pedantry the case is hopeless. The appeal and the inspiration lie, of course, in the element of loftiness, in the suggestion of slenderness and aspiration, the soaring quality as of a thing rising from earth as a unitary utterance, Dionysian in beauty. The failure to perceive this simple truth has resulted in a throng of monstrosities, snobbish and maudlin or brashly insolent or thick-lipped in speech; in either case a defamation and denial of man's finest powers.[26]

The building construction situation and the architectural problems facing Chicago architects at the time as Sullivan vividly described above prevailed in every architectural office, whether it be Adler and Sullivan, or Burnham and Root, or any others, and the solutions to the problems were being searched for. In the midst of all these came a great influence from the East—the erection and completion of Richardson's Marshall Field Store (1886-87) as mentioned at the beginning of this chapter—that deeply ingrained itself in the creative mind of every architect in Chicago, particularly Louis Sullivan and John Root in their early goings. On the matter of Richardson's influence on Chicago architects, Montgomery Schuyler, while analyzing the work of Burnham and Root in his

"Great American Architects Series" published in the February, 1896 issue of *The Architectural Record*, writes:

> The commercial buildings of Burnham and Root were in the main, though very loosely and generally Romanesque in origin and suggestion. The designer was inspired by the success of Richardson, which, indeed, from 1876 onward affected almost every architect in the United States who was not too old to learn. But generally the effect of Richardson's "impetuous and overbearing" talent had been to induce the admirers of it to become its indiscriminating imitators, and to reproduce especially the excesses and the errors in it which were most easily reproducible. A very few designers subjected the effectiveness of it to intelligent analysis and maintained their own individuality in works which nevertheless would clearly not have existed in their present form but for this admiring study of Richardson's work on the part of their designers. One of these, as I have already had occasion to say, is Mr. Sullivan. Another was John Root. A very typical and a very brilliant example of his essays in an enriched romanesque is the entrance of the Phoenix Building, of which it is equally plain that it could not have been designed except for Richardson, and that it could not have been designed by Richardson. It is Richardson chastened and restrained. Whatever else it is, it remains after a decade, one of the most noteworthy examples in this country of the art of architecture, admirable alike in composition and in detail. Alas, it remains also, like so many other things, as monument to our inconstancy, and another proof that no sooner do we approach a common way of working and begin to attain some skill in it than the promise of a style is broken by the capricious introduction of a new fashion.[27]

Richardson's Marshall Field Store and other buildings he designed in Chicago, namely the MacVeagh House and the Glessner House, all of which were planned and completed at about the same period of time (1885-87), were brilliant examples of his final phase—a phase characterized by unparalleled penetration and freedom in the handling of American nineteenth-century requirements. Their superficial quality, their "Romanesque Style," was to go exfoliating in the work of Chicago architects for two decades. Sullivan distilled from these now-famous buildings their true meaning and permitted it to crystallize that drive toward the commercial architecture in which he was to be engaged, and with which he, in turn, inspired Frank Lloyd Wright who reported for duty at the Adler and Sullivan office while Sullivan was working on the Auditorium designs. It is easy to imagine how the sight of these plans exhilarated Wright and made him feel that he was at last in the main currents of contemporary architecture. But, as a matter of fact, Sullivan himself was a newcomer to these currents, having just passed through a period of awkward dependence upon such cumbersome styles as the Egyptian and others; and having just become aware of Richardson's work. In his "Louis Sullivan—His Work" published in the July, 1924 issue of the *Architectural Record*, Wright writes of Sullivan on this matter as follows:

> H.H. Richardson, great emotionalist in architecture that he was, elected to work in the "style" Romanesque. The Master dug deeper and made style for himself out of the same stuff the Romanesque was made from and the Gothic too. With all these examples before us of

"styles," surely man may penetrate to the heart of style and unveiling its secret be master of his own. And as a master of this type was Louis Sullivan—estoeric though synthetic style may be.[28]

And in his *An Autobiography*, Wright describes the influence of Richardson on Sullivan in wry terms:

> Richardson at this time had a decided effect on Sullivan's work, as may be seen in the outside of the Auditorium building itself, the Walker Warehouse, and other buildings. The effect is unmistakable, although he seemed to hold Richardson in no very high esteem.[29]

Wright was wrong. There was one essay in *The Kindergarten Chats* series—Number VI, "The Oasis"—in which Sullivan clearly acknowledged his debt to Richardson. He described, in ironic and impressionistic metaphors, the deep emotional impact of Richardson's Marshall Field Store:

> Let us pause, my son, at this oasis in our desert. Let us rest awhile beneath its cool and satisfying calm, and drink a little at this wayside spring...
>
> You mean, I suppose, that here is a good piece of architecture for me to look at—and I quite agree with you.
>
> No; I mean here is a MAN for you to look at. A man that walks on two legs instead of four, has active muscles, heart, lungs, and other viscera; a man that lives and breathes, that has red blood; a real man, a manly man; a verile force—broad, vigorous and with a whelm of energy—an entire male.
>
> I mean that stone and mortar, here, spring into life, and are not more material and sordid things, but, as it were, become the very diapason of a mind rich-stored with harmony...
>
> Four square and brown, it stands, in physical fact, a mounument to trade, to the organized commercial spirit, to the power and progress of the age, to the strength and resource of individuality and force of character; spiritually it stands as the index of a mind, large enough, courageous enough to cope with these things, master them, absorb them and give them forth again, impressed with the stamp of large and forceful personality; artistically, it stands as the creation of one who knows well how to choose his words, who has somewhat to say and says it—and says it as the outpouring of a copious, direct, large and simple mind.[30]

It is clear that Sullivan was profoundly moved by Richardson's building. James Marston Fitch explains:

> The design had an electrifying effect on the 30-year-old Sullivan, an effect he was always to acknowledge with winning candor. For the Field building taught him a lesson he never forgot—that of modeling a building plastically so that it could be immediately perceived as a whole, as a total sculptural entity, irrespective of the detailed treatment of its component parts. With this in mind, he quickly recast the entire exterior of the Auditorium in a frankly Richardsonian mold, thereby converting a mediocrity into a work of distinction.[31]

The lesson for Sullivan in Richardson's Marshall Field Store was exactly what he needed to free himself from his preoccupation with irrelevant details and give direction to his inchoate powers. Burchard and Bush-Brown further describe what the Field Store could teach Sullivan:

> We know that Sullivan learned from it how to express what was really central in architectural composition, and that this pulled him out of the morass of minor themes and decorative touches in which he was floundering. Here in the sight of this building, Sullivan found what others would find later, a way of form so that the technical need not be ugly and the aesthetic would be neither borrowed nor flimsy. Richarson, gave to many architects a goal of quality, and index of scale, a sense of stateliness possible in architecture for industrial civilization.[32]

Richardson's Marshall Field Store was a special and inspiring gift from an eastern architect to the commercial architecture of Chicago.

The influence of Richardson's Marshall Field Store began to manifest itself in the Standard Club (1887-88), at the southwest corner of Michigan Avenue and Twenty-Fourth Street. It was demolished in 1910. The Romanesque details, the rusticated limestone facing, the simplicity of the wall treatment, the horizontal division of the elevations, the sense of mass together with a rich plastic quality—all reveal Sullivan's debt to the Eastern architect. A much more important work of the Adler and Sullivan firm in the Richardsonian manner was the Walker Warehouse (1888-89), on Market Street. Demolished in 1957, it was perhaps architecturally more significant than the celebrated Auditorium Building. The influence of Richardson was obvious, but the influence was assimilated and developed into a form which pointed more clearly in the new direction. It was a solid mass of masonry, and no rustication interrupted the smooth rectangular profile. Hugh Morrison characterizes the Walker Warehouse as a pure revelation of the fundamental architectural forms of the pier, the lintel, and the full-centered arch. For all its intrinsic excellence, however, the Walker Warehouse, like the Marshall Field Store, stood at a great distance from Sullivan's later work which shows a superb mastery of the new structural techniques.

Adler and Sullivan's Auditorium Building (figure 4) is the triumph of the firm in the traditional materials of masonry and iron and the structural forms appropriate to them. Indeed, the reputation of the firm, and for that matter, of Chicago itself, was made and secured by the Auditorium Building. One of the largest and most complex buildings in the country at the time of its construction, matched only by the great railroad terminals, it embodied civic and aesthetic more than commercial motives. The Auditorium, which extends the full block from Michigan to Wabash Avenue and embraces a ground area of 63,350 square feet, stood for forty years after its completion in 1889 at Congress Parkway and Michigan Avenue, and its complex facilities—the Auditorium Theater, the hotel and the office block—continued in full and profitable use until 1929 when the Civic Opera Building was completed. It was then that the life of the magnificent theater was mortally threatened. Bankruptcy came in 1940. Parts of the building were used as the Chicago Center of the United Service Organization during the war years of 1942 to 1945. In the following year the entire property was purchased by Roosevelt University and the hotel space was transformed into the classrooms and other facilities of an educational institution.

By then, fifty-seven years had passed since the time the Auditorium was completed and first opened to the public in 1889. The dedication that year was a glamorous occasion: President Harrison was ensconsed in a special box at the side of the stage; Madame Adelina Patti sang; and publicity was sensational. The Auditorium Building illustrated to the world:

> How the versatile Western American combines sentiment with thrift, and demonstrates how he can endeavor to cultivate the service of Mammon simultaneously with an effort to attain his higher artistic ideals... Whether or not the enterprise is an unqualified financial success can hardly be definitely stated. So much, however, is certain: Chicago has an Auditorium far better as an opera house or a concert hall or a ballroom than the Metropolican Opera House or the Music Hall of—New York, and the certainty that its owners will not be assessed to secure its maintenance is already established beyond the possibility of doubt.[33]

These were the words of the architect Adler himself in his "The Chicago Auditorium" published in the very first issue of *The Architectural Record* (Volume 1, October-December 1891). The earliest published comments and criticism on the Auditorium are probably those which appeared in an article entitled "The Auditorium Building" and written anonymously right after its opening ceremony in the December 1889 issue of *The American Architect and Building News*. The author writes:

> At length the great Auditorium Building has been officially opened, with all the accompaniment of pomp and ceremony consistent with democratic institutions. Not only the various State and municipal officers were out in full force, but both the President and Vice-President of the United States were here and dedicated the building within whose half-finished walls they had been nominated eighteen months ago. The opening ceremony was certainly the most gorgeous spectacle of its kind ever beheld in the West. The audience-room, in itself an impressive sight, was made still more magnificent by 4,000 people arrayed in all their very best "purple and fine linen," not to mention gold and precious stones. In the eyes of all of the architects and many of the public there was, however, one thing lacking in all the ceremony and that was that Messrs. Adler and Sullivan, the architects to whose thought, study, and conscientious work the whole magnificent pile was due, were not even mentioned by name in the exercises and received no public recognition whatsoever. Now that the building is at length opened to the public, one may at least be able to judge of the general result even if some of the very minor details do still require a little going over and polishing and general finishing up.[34]

The Auditorium Building embraces much more than a theater. The auditorium proper, with a seating capacity of 4,237, occupies the center position of the enclosure; the west, or Wabash Avenue, end is a typical commercial office block; the east, or Michigan Avenue, end is a hotel; at the center of the south elevation is a tower that provides additional high rent office space. Condit comments:

> The problem of integrating this complex of separate and diversified elements within uniform elevations taxed the ingenuity of Adler and Sullivan to the utmost. That they succeed is attested not only by the appearance of the building but by the fact that except for the theater it is in good condition and in active use today.[35]

Of this complexity of building and the problems facing the architects, Adler explains:

> The wish of Chicago to possess an opera house larger and finer than the Metropolitan, a hall for great choral and orchestral concerts, a mammoth ball-room, a convention hall, an auditorium for mass meetings, etc., etc., all under the same roof and within the same walls, gave birth to the Auditorium proper. The desire that the Auditorium be made self-sustaining, and not like the Metropolitan Opera House, a perpetual financial burden to its owners, rendered necessary the external subordination of the Auditorium itself to the business building and hotel, which, together with it, form the Auditorium Building.[36]

An article anonymously published in *The American Architect and Building News* for its December 1889 issue gives a more vivid description of the complex interior facilities of the Auditorium in connection with its vast external appearance as follows:

> "The Auditorium" as it is usually called, is a building occupying nearly one entire half a block. It has a frontage of somewhat less than two hundred feet on the great throughfares—Michigan and Wabash Avenues, and some three hundred and sixty upon a smaller cross street. This latter and longest side is considered the front proper of the building and here is the large tower, with the main entrance to the great audience-hall. The great building really includes three separate structures, viz., an opera house, an office-building and a hotel. With such variations and irregularities as the requirements of the different buildings demand, the hotel may practically be said to occupy the entire Michigan Avenue front and a portion of Congress Street: The office-building, the Wabash Avenue, and also a part of the Congress Street side. While the great inner portion of the edifice is mainly occupied by the opera house, which in itself is really the "Auditorium". It goes without saying that the whole construction is supposed to be absolutely fireproof. The office-building and the Auditorium proper are now opened but the hotel is still in the hands of the workmen and will not be finished for several weeks yet, although it is even now a most interesting portion of the building to visit. Externally the building is effective more by its size than by any architectural composition, and its dignity is due to its vastness. At the south but not at the center of the facade rises the large rectangular tower (41 by 70 feet in size) to a height of about 240 feet, while on top of this

for another 30 feet higher is a so-called lantern for the convenience of sight-seers and also for the protection of the various instruments in use by the U.S. Signal-Service station, which is in the seventeenth story of the tower. This tower is, of course, the great exterior feature of the building and both from the lake and from the south is an important object in the landscape. Probably for constructional reasons, a rather unusual form was adopted, the width of the face being nearly twice the depth. From many points of view this shape is certainly not as satisfactory as a square one would have been, and consequently the first sight is to strangers often rather disappointing, although it certainly does grow upon one since it has already become an object that every true Chicagoan has an affection for. The material of the building is gray granite and Indiana buff (Bedford) limestone: the lower three stories rock-faced and the upper seven dressed. The general form and outlines of the openings, together with the main features of the building, mark the style as the modern Romanesque, although not extremely pronounced. The principal entrance to the Auditorium proper is through three massive arches in the tower which lead into the main vestibule and lobby.[37]

The three massive arched entrances of the Auditorium not only lead us into the main vestibule and lobby, they also lead us into a special world of Adler's ingenious technical and engineering skills and Sullivan's brilliantly creative and artistic power in architectural design. Frank Lloyd Wright, who was put to work mainly on the interior details of the Auditorium project when he first reported to work at the Adler and Sullivan office, wrote an essay entitled "Louis Sullivan—His Work," published in the July 1924 issue of the *Architectural Record*. In it, Wright has none but good words of praise for the Auditorium as follows:

Work must be studied in relation to the time in which it presented its contrasts, insisted upon its virtues and got itself into human view. Remember if you can the contemporaries of Louis Sullivan's first great work, the Chicago Auditorium. Those contemporaries were a lot of unregenerate sinners in the grammar of the insensate period of General Grant Gothic. Imagine this noble calm of the Auditorium exterior, the beautiful free room within, so beautifully conceived as a unit, with its PLASTIC ornamentation, its deep cream and soft gold scheme of color, the imaginative PLASTIC richness of this interior, and compare both with the cut, butt and slash of that period—the meaningless stiffness that sterilized the Chicago buildings for all their ambitious attitudes and grand gestures. They belong to a world to which the sense of the word "PLASTIC" had not been born. That the word itself could get itself understood in relation to architecture is doubtful—and then see what Louis Sullivan's creative activity from that time on meant to architecture as an art. Back of that first great performance of his was a deepening knowledge, a tightening grasp on essentials. Much in the great effort got away from him; it wore him out; it was all at tremendous pressure, against fearful odds—but the Chicago Auditorium is good enough yet to be the most successful room for opera in the world. I think I have seen them all.[38]

I have mentioned earlier the powerful influence of the clients upon the designs of Chicago commercial buildings such as in the case of Burnham and Root's Monadnock Block. Adler and Sullivan's Auditorium is another such instance. Interestingly, in both cases, the influence of clients proved singularly beneficial to good design. The Auditorium Building was planned as a huge opera house set into the heart of a masonry shell with a hotel on the lake side and offices on the city side in order to make the large investment financially solvent. The chief promoter of this scheme was Ferdinand W. Peck who had staged the successful Opera Festival in the spring of 1885. Adler, who had an uncanny gift of building theaters with almost perfect acoustical results, successfully put up a temporary opera hall for the Festival in the Old Exposition Building on the site of the present Art Institute. That achievement probably secured the firm the commission for the Auditorium. To execute this ambitious program the Chicago Opera Association was formed in 1886. The commission for the design of its building went to Adler and Sullivan as expected in the same year. The preliminary design was a huge Romanesque building with angle towers, pavilions, dormers, projecting oriels and pitched-roof tower not unlike that on Van Brunt's Memorial Hall at Harvard. The most immediate inspiration seems to have been Root's design for the Rookery just then finished. Almost as close at hand was S.S. Beman's Pullman Building (1883). The final design of the Auditorium is much simpler. The pyramidal roof and the many oriels have been eliminated so as to stress the overall cubic mass. This, the lower story rustications and the rhythms of window spacing make no disguise of the influence of Richardson's Marshall Field Store which was being completed during the year 1887. There is a tradition, vouched for by Paul Mueller, Adler and Sullivan's chief engineer, that Root, seeing the preliminary design, remarked that Sullivan was about to smear another building with ornament. Whereupon, Sullivan called in the plans and redesigned the building. Ferdinand Peck, the Auditorium's chief promoter, and Sullivan both admired the Field Store; and the board of the Opera Association saw many possible economies in the adoption of its exemplary simplicity. The preliminary designs were constantly modified at conferences with Peck and the director of the Opera Association. Writes Condit:

> Fortunately for architecture everywhere, Sullivan abandoned his propensity for elaborate exterior ornament and concentrated on the architectonic effect of the mass, texture, and the proportioning and scaling of large and simple elements.[39]

Adler himself attested the influence of clients upon the design of the Auditorium in an article of 1891 published in *The Architectural Record:*

> When the design of the Auditorium Building was first entrusted to its architects only two-thirds of the ground and less than half the money finally absorbed by the work were placed at their disposal. But, little by little, the enthusiasm of Mr. Fred W. Peck, the chief promoter of the enterprise met with such response from businessmen of Chicago as to warrant the acquisition of greater area for the building site and expansion of the scope and scale far beyond the limits contemplated in the conception and development of original design. The form in which we find this bulding is, therefore, the resultant of many conflicting causes and influences ... It is to be regretted that the severe simplicity of treatment rendered necessary

by the financial policy of the earlier days of the enterprise, the deep impression made by Richardson's "Marshall Field Building" upon the Directory of the Auditorium Association and a reaction from a course of indulgence in the creation of highly decorative effects on the part of its architects should have happened to thereby deprived the exterior of the building of those graces of plastic surface decoration which are so characteristic of its interior treatment.[40]

The final outcome of the external appearances of the Auditorium was impressive enough to attract attention of a young visitor with a critical mind from the East—Montgomery Schuyler—who came to take his first glimpse of the city in 1891 and recorded his visit in his "Glimpses of Western Architecture: Chicago." Fittingly enough, Schuyler's own active roles as both architectural critic and chronicler of the American skyscraper began with his articles on the Chicago School. These articles, mostly published in the various issues of *The Architectural Record* have become classics in this standard interpretation of the school—most especially in the perception of the significance of Richardson's Marshall Field Store to the city's architects, and the intensely rationalistic bias of the architects abetted by the no-nonsense attitude of Chicago clients, the block-like quality of the buildings on generous sites as compared to the tower development in New York, and the important role of the firm of Burnham and Root in the creation of the Chicago type. Therefore, Schuyler, through his numerous essays laced with his sharply defined personal views, helped to make the ideas and creations of the Chicago School common knowledge both to the professional and to the public.

In his "Glimpses of Western Architecture: Chicago," following his discussion of the original modest home of the Chicago Art Institute earlier erected by Burnham and Root (1886-87), Schuyler begins his remarks on the Auditorium as follows:

In part, as we have just intimated, this modesty may be ascribed to the modest dimensions of the [Art Institute] building. At any rate, it was not out of the question, in another important quasi-public building, which is the latest, and, at this writing, the loudest of the lions of Chicago—The Auditorium. Whatever else a ten-story building, nearly 300 feet by more than 350 in area and 140 in height, with a tower rising 80 feet farther, may happen to be, it must be conspicuous, and it is no wise possible that its designer should make it appear bashful or unobtrusive. Of however retiring a disposition he may be, in such a situation he must brazen it out. It is in his power to adopt a very simple or a very elaborate treatment, and to imperil the success of his work by making it dull on the one hand or unquiet on the other. Messrs. Adler and Sullivan, the architects of the Auditorium, have chosen the better part in tracing their huge fronts with great severity, insomuch that the building can scarcely be said to exhibit any "features," except the triple entrance on the lake front, with its overhanging balcony, and the square tower[41] that rises over the southern front to a height of 225 feet. While they did wisely in showing that monotony had fewer terrors for them than restlessness, the monotony that undoubtedly amounts to a defect in the aspect of a completed work is by no means wholly or mainly attributed to them. A place of popular entertainment, constructed upon a scale and with a massiveness to which we can scarcely find a parallel since

Roman days, would present one of the worthiest and most interesting problems a modern architect could have if he were left to solve it unhampered. It is quite difficult enough to tax the power of any designer without any complications. The problem of design in the Chicago Auditorium is much complicated with requirements entirely irrelevant to its main purpose. The lobbies, the auditorium, and the stage of a great theatre, which are its essential parts, are all susceptible of an exterior expression more truthful and more striking than has yet been attained, in spite of many earnest and interesting essays.[42]

In this 1891 article, Schuyler entirely left the magnificent interiors of the Auditorium undiscussed simply because "we are not dealing with interiors, however, and they were required to envelop the outside of their theatre in a shell of many-storied commercial architecture which forbade them even to try for a monumental expression of their great hall."[43] Of the exterior of the building, Schuyler continues:

In the main, their exterior appears and must be judged only as a "business block." They have their exits and their entrances, and it is really only in these features that the exterior betrays the primary purpose of the building. The tower, even, is evidently not so much monumental as utilitarian. It is prepared for in the substructure only by a slight and inadequate projection of the piers, while it is itself obviously destined for profitable occupancy, being a small three-story business block, superimposed upon a huge ten-story business block. Such a structure cannot be converted into a monumental feature by making it more massive at the top than it is at the bottom, even though the massiveness be as artistically accentuated as it is in the tower of the Auditorium by the powerful open colonnade and the strong machicolated cornice in which it culminates. Waiving, as the designers have been compelled to do, the main purpose of the structure, and considering it as a commercial building, the Auditorium does not leave very much to be desired. The basement, especially, which consists of three stories of granite darker than the limestone of the super-structure, and appropriately rough-faced, is a vigorous and dignified performance, in which the expression of rugged strength is enhanced by the small and deep openings, and in which the necessarily large openings of the ground-floor are prevented from enfeebling the design by the massiveness of the lintels and flat arches that enclose them, and of the piers and pillars by which these are supported. The super-structure is scarcely worthy of this basement. The triple vertical division of the wall is effectively proportioned, but a much stronger demarcation is needed between the second and third members than is furnished by the discontinuous sill-course of the eighth story, while a greater projection, a greater depth, and a more vigorous remodelling of the main cornice, and an enrichment of the attic beneath, would go far to relieve the baldness and monotony that are the defects of the design, and that are scarcely to be condoned because there are architectural faults much worse and much more frequent, which the designers have avoided. It is only, as has been said, in the entrances that they have been permitted to exhibit the object of the building. Really, it is in the entrance on the lake front, for the triplet of stilted arches at the base of the tower is not a very felicitous or a very congruous feature. The three low arches of the Lake front are of a Roman largeness—true vomitoria—and their effectiveness is increased by the simplicity of their treatment, by the ample lateral abutment provided for them, and by the long and shallow balcony that overhangs them. With the arches themselves this makes a very impressive feature, albeit the balcony is a very questionable feature. Even to the layman there must be a latent contradiction in the intercalation of the pillar to relieve the bearing of a lintel, when the pillar is referred to an unsupported shelf, obviously lighter and weaker than the lintel itself. This contradiction is not explained away by the vigor and massiveness of the shallow corbels that really account for the alternate columns, and it suggests that the construction so exhibited is not the true construction at all, and leaves this latter to be inferred without any help from the architecture. Even if one waives his objection to architectural forms that do not agree with the structural facts, it is surely pedantic to require that the construction asserted by the forms shall be plausible to the extent of agreeing with itself. It is a pity that there should be such a drawback from a feature so effective; but the drawback does not prevent the feature from being effective, nor do the shortcomings we have been considering in the design of the Auditorium, nor even the much more serious obstacle that was inherent in the problem and imposed upon the architects, prevent it from being a very impressive structure, and justifying the pride with which it is regarded by all patriotic Chicagoans.[44]

All patriotic Chicagoans were also very proud of the famous interiors of the Auditorium Building with which Sullivan allowed a free hand. He especially used ornament on a lavish scale in the hotel lobby, the main dining room and the striking great hall or theater. In the last, its greatness is not due so much to the beauty of decoration, for that is comparatively simple, but it is almost due entirely to the result of the splendid architectural lines. With the exception of a very limited number of boxes, all parts are open, free and light. They conceive as integral parts of the scheme of construction. Over the stage springs the splendid perfect ellipse of proscenium-arch, while parallel to it over the auditorium at intervals spring ever larger identical ellipses, reiterating the same line of beauty. It is astonishing, given these strikingly impressive features of the Great Theater and its ornaments; that the interiors of the Auditorium went unnoticed in Schuyler's 1891 discussion. Only in 1895 would Schuyler turn to the interior:

But of course the exterior is a compromise, the environment and concealment of a monumental theatre by a commercial building, and it is the interior that alone affords a gauge of the capacity of the architect for monumental design. The success of this interior is striking and unchallenged. The type of an opera-house, which the auditorium essentially is, is so well settled and so universally accepted that the variations ordinarily attempted upon it, even by architects of original force, are comparatively slight. While the component parts of the accepted type are retained in this interior, they are transmuted into an entirely new result. The general forms are determined, as Mr. Adler has explained, entirely by acoustical considerations, and it is pleasant to know that in this instance the science of acoustics, which so many architects deny to be for their purpose a science at all has been vindicated, and that the auditorium is in fact an excellent place in which to hear. But the devices adopted for this purpose have been treated as to produce a most impressive and quite unique interior. The succession of the concentric elliptical arches which frame for the spectators the spectacle of the stage has the result of bringing all parts of the audience, huge as in fact it is, into much closer relation with the performers than is attained in theatres more conventionally treated, even much less dimensions, and it attains a very noble largeness and simplicity, which the designer has been careful not to impair by his detail, rich and intricate as this often is, or by his color-decoration. It is not fanciful to say that this great and simple interior, with its expanding arches above, and its expanding terraces below, extending and proclaiming a hospitality as nearly as may be equal and undistinguishing, illustrates, as plainly as the exterior of the many-storied office building, and in contrast with the "royal" and "imperial" opera houses, M. Bourget's conception of "a new kind of art, an art of democracy." It was in this building that was announced URBI ET ORBI, first beyond Chicago if not first in Chicago, Mr. Sullivan's singular endowment as a decorator. This is so eminent and remarkable, indeed, that it has induced some of his professional brethren to regard him and describe him as a decorator only. The Auditorium alone would suffice to refute that unjust limitation, for the largeness and simplicity and liberality of the general scheme are eminently "architectonic" qualities, and these qualities are equally exhibited in the treatment of the features, of the exterior features, the balcony on the lake front and the crowning tower, and of the interior features, the auditorium proper, the public banquet room and dining room of the hotel, in which a perfectly straightforward following out of the indications of the plan has issued in a highly artistic and a very original apartment. Any one of these features in its general composition, without a single ornament, would suffice to vindicate its author as an architect in contradistinction to a decorator. Nay, the adjustment of ornament, in place and in scale, so that it heightens and carries further the inherent expressions of the disposition and the structure is the work of the architect and not the decorator. It remains true that the ornament of the Auditorium and of Mr. Sullivan's work in general is extremely well worth looking at on its own accounts.[45]

No less astonishing that in his essay of 1891, Schuyler not only failed to take note of the interior of the Auditorium, but also to discuss the great Chicago invention of skeleton construction. If he did not notice Jenney's Home Insurance Building (1883-85), at least Holabird and Roche's Tacoma Building which was erected in 1888-89 should have caught his eye. The probable explanation is that, to Schuyler in 1891, the contribution of the Chicago School was not a new kind of structure but the beginning of a new aesthetic and a new form of commercial architecture with its frank austere "shell" appropriate to the no-nonsense spirit of commerce. However, by 1895 the importance of skeleton framing was too obvious to be ignored. His 1895 discussion on the works of the architects of the Chicago School reveals the most enlightened account of the great impact of the skeleton construction on Chicago and vice versa. In his discussion on Adler and Sullivan's Auditorium, for instance, Schuyler continues:

Still, it seems to me fortunate that the Auditorium, young as it is, antedates the Chicago construction. Its admirable basement would have lost either its impressiveness or its pertinency if it had not been an actual wall, and had not had an actual wall to carry. Indeed, we must own that the Chicago construction in its latest development, has not yet found its artistic expression, that no designer has yet learned to deal successfully with a structural change so radical that it has abolished the wall, which is the chief datum of every one of the historical styles of architecture, excepting only the developed Gothic. Looking at the steel cage that forms the skeleton of the sky-scraper, and that is run up so many stories in advance of the architectural envelope, which is also a structural necessity! There is the problem crudely stated, and it does not seem to suggest its own solution. It contradicts almost every assumption of the schools. It contradicts especially the fundamental assumption of a building that it is composed of walls, and that is that it must be more solid at the bottom than at the top. In the steel cage which here is the structure there is no sensible diminution of massiveness as it rises. The diminution which does or may take place as the load is lightened is slight enough to be negligible, is too slight to have been thus far found expressible. In the project we have been considering [The Auditorium Building], the aesthetic necessity of a more massive base to the structure has been recognized, and the base has been provided, but by ignoring the structure of a cage and by making it an actual wall, apparently adequate to its own support and that of the superstructure, which reveals or rather betrays itself as a cage in uprights evidently too slender to do their work if they were built of the material with which they are faced. To give a cage a solid base and an enriched top, and to leave the interval as a cage is the method adopted by our best designers to meet the new requirements, and it would be difficult to suggest a better. But it is always to be borne in mind that this is provisional and tentative, rather an evasion than a solution, and that it is the work of more than a decade, of more than a generation, to carry so far the analysis of the new mode of building as to produce the artistic expression of it which it is yet an article of artistic faith that it supplies in itself the means for attaining. Meanwhile, the architects who undertake to reconcile so far as may be the old artistic requirements with the new structural requirements, to observe the Aristotelian precept of a beginning, a middle and an end, with a cosntruction that is uniform and virtually equivalent from the ground to the sky line are entitled to be judged by their success in their own aim and some of the successes have been very brilliant.[46]

This was exactly the kind of constructive architectural criticism that was badly needed at the time and the one that has helped to make American architecture great. On the same matter, presented ten years later was another excellent criticism by another critic with sharp eyes and an enlightened mind. In his article entitled "The Riddle of the Tall Building: Has the Skyscraper a Place in American Architecture?" published in the April 1905 issue of *The Craftsman*,[47] H.A. Caparn writes:

Not one of the architects who most deplore and despair of its [a skyscraper's] artistic problems but would jump at the opportunity of building the highest that could be made to stand and frown insolently down on the roofs below. Not one but would, for the sake of the fat commission and the glory, do his best to get out the complete working drawings as soon as he possibly could, to satisfy his client's haste and save him from the loss of rent not received and taxes paid out that would accrue with every day's delay. No one would insist upon months or years to think over and digest the problem that such an outlay as goes into one of these steel structures calls for in these days not only of great buildings but great building. Partly for reasons like these, not wholly because of the inherent difficulties of the problem, most of the skyscrapers hitherto put up are crude and ugly, and none of them is entirely satisfactory. Most are hasty, potboiling copies of the previous ones, a few are what they all ought to be—honest experiments, attempts to find a solution for an architectural problem. The skyscraper has not yet developed a type of recognized excellence, or even lines along which evolution may advance, and so until it does, each new one should be an attempt to find a solution, cautious or bold, according to the powers or temperament of the designer. The trend of contemporary architectural thought is along logical or classical lines, the outward expression of and obedience to structural conditions. So it seems quite natural that long and assiduous search should have been made for some outward and visible sign of the inward and structural steel, for some way of making the necessary masonry sheathing tell the story of the metal uprights it conceals and protects.

This appears to naturally result in vertical ribs or piers encasing the columns with panels between to make the walls. This, in one form or another, is the idea of the average tall building. Starting in a similar way to reason from first principles, builders of skyscrapers have reasoned that because the walls are high and obviously ponderous, they must have a base that looks massive enough to support such weight. Thus many-storied buildings are apt to have a base of huge stones with exaggerated rustication, intended not merely to be, but to appear an adequate support of the vertical mass above them; the structure must not only BE, but it must LOOK secure. In other words, the base tries to appear able to support the superincumbent wall as if all were of masonry, a set of conditions contradictory and impossible: for if the walls were thick enough to support themselves, there would be little or no room left for floor space, so that the primary object of the skyscraper, the multiplication of floors without loss of floor space, would be defeated. Thus this apparent truthfulness entails a denial of the very essentials of the fabric... This would be a bold departure from the convention, a resolute way of expressing real structural essentials, not by searcing for, but by building them. It might lead wholly away from the traditions of string courses, piers, cornices, and the other conventionalities into a new set of forms and a new kind of decoration, and develop a new style, a new principle of construction... Many architects have sought light and air (and, perhaps unintentionally lightness and airiness) in other ways. They have made the central stories a mere frame work of iron and glass with solid looking side piers, cornice and upper story... More notable instances of this kind of design are Mr. Louis Sullivan's Garrick Theatre, in which the strong and resolute piers seem to run up to the top of the structure with power to support their own weight and the iron frame between them without need of it for lateral bracing.[48]

The Garrick Building (figure 5), mentioned by Caparn as a good example of honesty of construction, exemplified the unparalleled flexibility that the steel frame could offer in dealing with the structural problems. These were problems that always attended buildings designed to house a diversity of functions and the wide range of techniques that were called upon for a single structure such as the Garrick. Originally known as the Schiller Theater, the Garrick Theater Building was constructed between 1891 and 1892 on West Randolph Street and demolished in 1961 in "a tragic act of architectural vandalism" as Condit sharply remarks, after a lengthy legal battle to save the building which Condit reports in detail in his *Chicago School of Architecture* (1964). The building was designed to include a theater with its associated stage and mechanical equipment, a seventeen-story office tower that extended back over the theater in a thirteen-story wing, and club and banquet rooms in the two top stories. The result was a work that presented a great many difficulties of design and construction. Its foundations and framing constituted an intricate system of construction embracing a great diversity of materials and techniques, but the whole work was the outcome of a careful investigation illustrative of the new scientific spirit. It represented the most complex, the most thoroughly studied, and the most advanced structural system available to the builders at the turn of the century. The Garrick Theater Building was certainly among "some of the successes" that "have been very brilliant" in which the architects undertook "to reconcile the old artistic requirements with the new structural requirements" as Schuyler observed. He writes:

> In the Schiller Theater, Mr. Sullivan was able to carry out imperfectly and on a smaller scale the scheme of "progressive recessions from base to pinnacle," which he projected in so

complete and so grandiose a fashion for the Fraternity Temple. Here the problem was to design on an inside lot an office building containing a theatre. The stopping of the wings at the ninth story evidently secures permanently by the reservation of the space on each side the effective lighting of the offices above that point, while the architectural advantage of the central tower, flanked by the lower wings and rearing its detached and unbroken shaft through fifteen stories is equally manifest. The bowed balcony was very bold, but also a very successful expedient of designating and emphasizing the base, and the summit with its spreading cornice and its belvedere-finial is a picturesque object from any point of view. In the interior, the theatre suffers, of course, in comparison with a theatre so monumentally conceived as the Auditorium, by the cramped dimensions from the sense of which it is difficult to escape but it shows the same felicity of detail.[49]

Another "monumentally conceived" building of the skeleton steel frame that came out of the Adler and Sullivan office and caught Schuyler's sharp, critical eyes was the original Stock Exchange Building (figure 6) on North LaSalle Street. It was designed in 1893, and erected in 1894. It was the largest commission of the firm after the Auditorium and the one that entered most fully into the mainstream of the Chicago School. The building, demolished in 1972, had become one of the most popular office-buildings in the Loop after the Exchange moved into the present Board of Trade Building in 1930. Even during the Depression of that decade, it was 95 percent occupied. Comments Condit:

The exterior form of the Stock Exchange is an organic outgrowth of steel framing without being a direct expression of it. Sullivan abandoned the plastic surface texture of the Wainwright and the Garrick Theater and treated the wall as a repetitive series of largely transparent plans. The general impression made by the street elevations is that of a great box composed largely of glass and poised lightly on the arcade of the third story... Throughout its major area the wall becomes a thin curtain drawn in neutral tension over the projecting bow windows and the flat areas between them. The quality of a skin-like envelope is heightened by the shallow reveals and by the absence of continuous courses of bands, the narrow moldings around the windows forming closed rectangles. But there is an ambiguity in the treatment of the Stock Exchange Building, that seems more pronounced than in other commercial designs of Adler and Sullivan. It rises from the tension between the personal expression of the artist's individualistic temperament and the more impersonal statement of the structure and function of the building. The conflict appears primarily in the fenestration of the Stock Exchange. The narrow windows of the projecting bays standing independent of the large Chicago windows with their horizontal orientation. The two separate window sizes break up the elevations into numerous facets of glass that form a vivid play of light but are not unified into a coherent pattern.[50]

This is probably the "strongest" unfavorable criticism that has come out of Carl Condit on a work of the Chicago School of architects. To Condit whatever the architects of the School did seems great and often becomes the object of unreserved praise. In so doing, he has knowingly taken the role of the School's apologist and its architects' hagiographer. However, his mild comment quoted above on Adler and Sullivan's Stock Exchange is indeed justified. Schuyler has similar objections. In his 1895 discussion of the two architects' work, Schuyler observed:

> In the Chicago Stock Exchange the main motive of the composition is supplied by the necessity for the unusually spacious and lofty apartment required by the institution from which the building takes its name. Though it is but an incident of such a pile, it seems that a still more specialized treatment of it might have been adopted, with great advantage to the expressiveness of the building, and without too much sacrifice of uniformity. As it is, the Exchange is not distinguishable from the offices of the same level, of which its height includes two ranges. Neither is the relation between the basement and the superstructure fortunate, nor the demarcation sufficiently signalized. the decorative detail of the basement is rich and refined, it is true, when one comes to look at it, but it is scarcely emphatic enough to take its proper place. What impresses one in looking at the building and what one carries away from it is the effective treatment of the cornice, including the plain colonnade beneath, that gives value to the enrichment of the cornice itself, in which the ornament is as well adjusted in scale as it is effective in design; this cornice and the principal entrance, which is excellently composed and excellently detailed, and which has in Chicago no rival in its own kind, excepting always the entrance to the Phoenix Building, in which carving in stone takes the place of modelling in terra cotta.[51]

In order adequately to understand Sullivan's range and validity in the architectural design for tall commercial buildings, it is necessary here to introduce two structures erected outside Chicago which represent Sullivan's deliberate and most thorough attempt to create a special form appropriate to the multistory office block as "programmed" in his famous document entitled "The Tall Office Building Artistically Considered" first published in *Lippincott's Magazine* in 1895 and considered earlier in this chapter. Sullivan's theory was first applied to the Wainright Building in St. Louis, constructed in 1890-91 (figure 7) and was perfected in the Guaranty (now Prudential) Building in Buffalo, New York, which was completed four years later in 1895 (figure 8). The Wainwright was, as Hugh Morrison, Sullivan's biographer, writes:

> ...the first true skyscraper built by Adler and Sullivan, and the surety, the justness, the completeness of this first attempt at solving a new architectural problem are astounding evidences of Sullivan's creative imagination and power of design. In the architectural world, it was like an Athena sprung full-fledged from the brow of Zeus; the problem had been solved, a new need had called forth a new form.[52]

Actually, the problem had not been completely solved as testified in the two essays discussed earlier by two critics who were Sullivan's contemporaries—Schuyler and Caparn—but the Wainwright was the first truly radical turn made toward that goal. It was Adler and Sullivan's first commission involving the use of complete iron and steel framing, and all the new technical features that had become standard desiderata of the Chicago office building are present in the ten-story Wainwright—the raft footings of reinforced concrete, the braced and riveted steel frame, the wall bays carried on

114   Adler and Sullivan

spandrel shelf angles, the fireproof-tile covering of all structural members, and the movable interior partitions. The formal and functional program derived from the structural basis and utilitarian demands had clearly been grasped by Sullivan in all its essentials. On the Wainwright, in his 1891 essay Schuyler comments:

> The Wainwright Building in St. Louis is of a simpler composition and of a plainer treatment, and it is distinctly more successful, partly by reason of its greater simplicity and plainness, mainly by reason of its superior coherency and unity, to which the greater emphasis of its distribution conduces. The basement, in brownstone, is absolutely bare of ornament, excepting the enrichment of the doorway, and this is confined to the reveals. The emphatic string-course that divides this from the superstructure of red brick and red terra-cotta is not even molded and it is judiciously stopped at the angles so as not to interrupt the vertical mass of the pier; but the baldness does not here give the sense of crudity or want of faith. In the superstructure, the skeleton, the cage, is confessed, and although the envelope is of brickwork it rather dissembles than accentuates the stark continous posts of which the lines are nowhere interrupted between base and cornice. Only at the angles is a mass permitted of such magnitude as to deserve to be called a pier. At the top alone is there any contradiction of the actual structure. To crown a vertical post of coated steel with a pilaster capital, is, however, plainly by weight, and expands in order to receive a load of greater area than that of the shaft. The arrangement is irrelevant and unmeaning when applied to a frame of uprights and cross beams that are riveted together, and produces confusion in the minds even of those spectators who do not analyze the cause of the confusion. The solids of the building, apart from the beams, are only the panels filling the spaces between sills and floor-lines, and these are treated as the mere screens that they are, being withdrawn from the plane of the piers, or rather of the posts, and being very properly decorated, for the decoration not only promotes the understanding that they are insertions extraneous to the stark structure, but also defers to the material. To leave plain a material so plastic is almost, if not quite, to deny its character. That the decoration is effective by design and by scale need scarcely be said. The real enrichment of the structure, however, is in the cornice-story, where it forms an appropriate crown and here the richness, intricacy and refinement of the ornament amount to a signature.[53]

The Guaranty Building in Buffalo is similar to the Wainwright in St. Louis in its functional characteristics and its formal quality, the "main difference being the substitution of terra cotta both for the masonry of the basement and for the brickwork of the superstructure" in Schuyler's words of 1895. It is the last commission of the firm of Adler and Sullivan as the partnership was dissolved in the year the Guaranty was completed. After 1895, Adler and Sullivan went their separate ways for the rest of their lives. Philip Johnson, again, in his critical essay on Sullivan's functionalism discussed earlier, appreciatingly analyzed the building:

> Sullivan saw that the problem of such tall facade is somehow to unify it, make it a comprehensible whole, not a disjointed collection of floors and columns. The Reliance Building, for example, as skeleton-like as it looks, had no over-all design discipline. Sullivan, following as usual the basic elements of Richardson's Marshall Field Warehouse of 1885, which we know he admired, with great originality has stretched out the main arcade to

include ten floors instead of the Marshall Field Building's three, or the Auditorium Building's four, and then confined the upper stories to an attic floor of OEIL-DE-BOEUF windows that merge into the magnificent flaring cornice. He has extended the base story of the Marshall Field Building to two, making a more proportionate relation to the ten above. The corners of the building are thickened for visual stability as in the Marshall Field and Auditorium Buildings. The piers project in front of the spandrels, thus creating a vertical accent similar to but much simpler and grander than, the Auditorium Building. It is a fine design and suited to a tall building. Some critics see as a functionalism here which I fail to find. Sullivan said "form follows function," but he went on to define it very differently from today's architects who mean either "suited to purpose" or "expressive of structure." Sullivan had a third meaning. An oak should look like an oak, a rose like a rose. Then Sullivan goes on to say what function means in a tall building. He felt it had a basic organic shape: at the bottom there are shop windows. (Naturally, but then why two stories? The second story of the base is useless.) Then it has a middle section of repeated office units. Right. Then it has a top. Why? It seemed inevitable, "functional," to Sullivan; but hardly to us. We cannot escape the conclusion that Sullivan found a cornice inevitable simply because he was used to it and liked it. That is a good reason, but let us not call him a functionalist or a proto-modern for clinging to cornices. And most especially, let us not, as some critics do, call him a functionalist in a structural sense. The Guaranty is a steel cage building but its exterior is expressive only of masonry. A layman could never guess that only every other pier concealed a steel column, or that the thicker corner pier concealed a column no larger than the rest. No; Sullivan's interest was not in structure, but design; and indeed more and more, in the ornament which covers his later buildings. At the time of the Guaranty Building, he had not yet reached the extremes he was later to achieve, but he had passed beyond the truly architectural phase of his ornamentation which had been so effective in the Wainwright Building of 1890. In that earlier building, only the spandrels and the cornice were ornamented; the piers and base stories remained magnificently plain. But by now everything is covered.[54]

Of the same building, Schuyler, in his 1895 essay, says:

The Guaranty Building at Buffalo is in its scheme a variant upon that of the Wainwright. The main difference being the substitution of terra cotta both for the masonry of the basement and for the brickwork of the superstructure. The more facile material is recognized throughout in the treatment of reticulations of surface ornament differing in density and character of design, according to the function of the surface treated and to the function of what is behind it. I know of no steel-framed building in which the metallic construction is more palpably felt through the envelope of baked clay. The designer has in this respect fully availed himself of the plasticity of his enclosing material. Here again it is the capital which forms the questionable feature, for this is formed by arches turned from post to post, a cornice-story of bulls' eyes aligned above the voids and an unbrageous cornice, the only continous horizontal line above the strong molded and enriched string-course that divides the basement from the superstructure. Effective as the cornice is in itself, with its bold projection and the emphatic arcade forming the lunettes of the round openings, the failure to bound the attic underneath entail an incertitude and confusion that render the broad and definite belt at the summit of the Wainwright a more eligible termination. In this respect, however, of an appropriate and effective finial for the very lofty building, the treatment of a projected work on the site of the old Burnet House, in Cincinnati,[55] is more successful than any of the executed works we have been considering. This mode of crowning such an edifice will be recognized as that of the "roof garden," whether or not the terminal story is devoted to that purpose. Such as an expansion is as evidently logical in a structure of metal as in one of timber, whether in either case it is managed by the projection of brackets, or by the mere prolongation of the floor beams, and it gives to the building to which it is applied a capital that may be made a suitable counterpart to the richest base. The treatment of it here is very admirable, both in the design of the crowning feature itself and in its adjustment to what is beneath it. The terminal arches of the Buffalo building are here reproduced, but on a larger and more effective scale, being turned not between every pair, but between alternate pairs of piers, the intermediate piers being subordinated to mere mullions so slight that they may be stopped above the base without incongruity. The system gives scope for a larger treatment, insomuch that the unit of the design may properly be called a bay, and it gives scope also for the introduction in the window heads of a rudimentary but very effective tracery. The shaft is also noteworthy for the modelling of the piers. While the angle piers are left plain and get the benefit of their dimensions, the intermediate piers that are connected above by arches are contrasted by modelling, and the piers between these which perform the office only of mullions are reduced each to a single moulding. This treatment promises to be very effective, and equally expressive, since the form assumed by the brickwork wrapping very strikingly suggests a flanged column of metal. The basement is masonry, again of a ground floor and an entresol, is signalized by the modelling of the angle pier into a group of columns, forming a feature of which it does not yet support what it shall be, and of which the effect will be apprehensible only in execution, and of a portal of which the actual entrance is a Romanesque archway, while above it is a canopied archway of a form derived from the Italian Renaissance. This latter is also employed at the entrance of the Buffalo building. It is of a rather disagreeable recent association, as having been so frequently employed perched upon two columns and standing free. Mr. Sullivan's sense of construction is altogether too keen to admit of his building an arch without any visible abutment, and in the entrance at Buffalo there is no difficulty with the feature on this score, nor indeed on any other. But in the Cincinnati building the superposition of it upon an arch of so different dimensions, proportions and treatment threatens a troublesome complication of forms. But even if this be not averted, it is that does not compromise the architectural success of the building as a whole, as one of the most interesting and perhaps the most organically complete and most satisfactory of its author's contributions to the most urgent of the architectural problems of the present in this country.[56]

At the time Schuyler wrote this 1895 essay, one of Sullivan's commercial buildings that later has become "the most interesting and perhaps the most organically complete and most satisfactory of its author's contributions to the most urgent of the architectural problems of the present in this country" had not been planned and erected yet. It was not until 1899 when Sullivan began the design of his most important commission after the dissolution of the partnership of the Adler and Sullivan firm in 1895—the Schlesinger and Mayer Store (figure 9) at State and Madison Streets on what Chicagoans termed the world's busiest corner. Lyndon P. Smith describes in his "The Schlesinger and Mayer Building," published in the July 1904 issue of *The Architectural Record:*

The tide of commerce ebbs and flows along State Street, in Chicago, and as the observer moves with the passing throng, his attention will be drawn toward the corner of Madison Street, and retained there by a building recently completed. It is one of many devoted to the retailing of goods, but on an extensive scale and including a large percentage of women among its patrons. This function is unmistakably expressed in the design. The city in which the building is located has the peculiarity of concentrating its commercial district in a comparatively limited area, within which there has been erected a large number of buildings of like purpose and character. The one in question is not of colossal type. Its facade is not based on "features", but its individuality is distinct. Its exterior frankly betokens its structural basis and rises in no uncertain fashion from sidewalk to cornice. It is a logical solution of the commercial building, such as a department store, the latest and best achievement produced in this country.[57]

Smith was an architect whose chief claim to fame seems to have been his continuing friendship with Sullivan. In his 1904 article on the Schlesinger and Mayer Building, Smith continues,

> This result has taken some time to accomplish and is the culmination of a long series of previous efforts, all working toward the better expression of what is regarded as our most unsatisfactory architectural problem. It is the outcome of careful preparation, skillful study and its application, maturity of mind and full sympathy between the maker of ideas and the makers of materials. The design is thoroughly modern. It shows fully the structural function of the steel frame with the enclosing protection of terra cotta, treated with full knowledge of its plasticity in its natural state and hardness and durability after treatment in the kiln. The lower portion on the street is equally straightforward in its qualities of "plate glass" architecture. Here are the largest openings possible for display windows and their attractions to feminine eyes are framed by a surrounding of elaborate decoration in cast metal. These forms immediately attract attention. They are full of vitality, of movement, grace and line. They twine and intertwine, divide and subdivide in marvelous fashion, yet they are ever traceable to their parent source and strongly organic. In the Prudential (Guaranty) Building, in Buffalo, which emanated from the same head, the essential element is masculinity. It is an American office building dominated by men and devoted to the transaction of their business in all its multitudinous forms—the elements of activity, ambition and directness of purpose, are all shown thereby in the architectural forms. The Schlesinger and Mayer Building is a differentiation of the commercial problem and has been treated entirely on its own merits, both in the general design and in the detail. This is frankly a department store—an establishment where goods of many kinds may be retailed to many people and so displayed over large floor areas that ease of examination and accessibility to products may be specially achieved. Hence, throughout its typical floors, the window openings are of maximun size and form a distinct basis of the exterior design. The detail of the decorative treatment around these openings enhances the outlook, and gives additional values to the exterior effect. The building terminates in a cornice based on the projecting roof beams and rationally functional.[58]

The work on the Schlesinger and Mayer Store was planned to be executed in three sections, in 1899, 1903-04, and 1906. The first unit was nine stories high and three bays on some 60 feet in width; the second was twelve stories high and 150 feet wide, but otherwise identical in design with the first. In 1904, the establishment was taken over by the Carson, Pirie and Scott firm and the store has been called after its name ever since. The third unit was designed for it by Burnham and Company, but Sullivan's scheme for the first two sections was retained, with only a few unimportant changes. Two years after Sullivan's second unit was completed, H.A. Caparn wrote an article in the April 1906 issue of *The Craftsman* concerning the problems of the steel-frame skyscrapers that were facing American architects at the time. In this same article, Caparn analyzes Sullivan's Carson, Pirie and Scott Store as follows:

> Chicago possesses one of Mr. Louis Sullivan's latest, most original and successful experiments in the Schlesinger and Mayer Building, and New York has the new Singer Building on Broadway and Prince Street, a skeleton of steel with its rib spaces filled with crude terra-cotta, a thing economical and unashamed, displaying its inmost secrets for all the street to see. Hasty people—even, and perhaps especially, architects—describe it as hideous and with other glib epithets of disapproval, but it is a work to make the judicious stop and think, and perhaps pronounce it the best, because the truest and most courageous thing yet done in tall buildings. Such a structure may look gawky and ephemeral to one who has passed his life in learning to judge architectural proportions on traditional standards. But we have learned to judge proportions on the basis of brick or stone being clearly able to do the work required in them, and have come to think that such and such relations of height and thickness of support to the thing supported are the only corrections, and that anything else is not "architectural". But how if we use steel, a material capable of doing the work with a small fraction of the mass of brick or stone? Is it not reasonable to suppose that there may be another system of proportions discoverable adapted to steel and yet in its way "architectural"? The fault may be in us, not in the steel; we can feel only one kind of design. Even if the architectural expression of steel framing in its own sizes and shapes has not yet been found it may be possible for someone to find it and for us to learn to appreciate it, to get an impression of strength and durability from a new set of dimensions... The true expression of the skyscraper, then, is not weight, but lightness; the appearance of doing the most work with the least effort, of supporting the greatest number of stories with the least quantity of steel. The building should rest on its uprights, not its walls, and be braced by girders, and should appear to do so. Its walls should not only BE, but should seem to be, panels. It is of no use to say that a seemly and dignified exterior treatment of a really candid edifice cannot be discovered, for the experiment has hardly been tried on a daring and untrammeled scale until the building of the Schlesinger and Mayer and the Singer Buildings. The designers of these buildings have not feared to discard conventional models and to make modern structures in a modern way with modern means and materials, even as the ancient Greeks and Mediaeval masons did, and, like them, to even found a new style in architecture, expressing the needs and taste of a nation.[59]

This is a great example of the far-cry for a new form and new expression in architectural design from a handful of critics at the turn of the century. It certainly was heard soundly and clearly by architects and those powerful clients at the time, but whether they chose to listen to it or not was another matter. Whatever critics like Caparn saw in Sullivan's Carson, Pirie and Scott, amazingly enough, is exactly the same thing that the present day critics and historians see in it a half-century later. In an article published in the Winter 1959 issue of the *Technology and Culture,* Carl Condit writes:

> In the Carson, Pirie and Scott Store Sullivan turned to an entirely different kind of expression, one derived from the dominant mode of the work of the Chicago School. Where he used the close vertical pattern in the older buildings, in the department store he opened the main elevations into great cellular screens which exactly express the neutral steel cage behind them... In the Carson Store it is a weightless screen, glass and opaque covering (cast iron)

forming one unbroken plane, making the cellular wall above literally seem to float free of the earth below it.[60]

and James Marston Fitch, in his *Architecture and the Esthetics of Plenty* (1961), quickly adds:

> The Schlesinger store presents us with Sullivan's brilliant resolution of these contradictions. Structurally the steel cage of the skyscraper is static, inert: horizontal and vertical members have identical importance. And functionally the walls are certainly no more important than the floors. The esthetic expression of these facts would be a nondirectional design. Moreover, since the wall of the skyscraper is a mere membrane stretched around the skeleton like a skin, it would be expressed most clearly as one taut, unbroken vertical plane. And this property would be further emphasized if the windows are mere perforations in the wall. All these subtleties are subsumed in the Schlesinger. Now the volumetric fact of the interior is made explicit—a honeycomb of identical bays slipped like shoe boxes into a cellular skeleton. Thus the whole story is told with diamond-sharp clarity, without the least deviation from either structural or functional fact.[61]

In 1956, the same year the noted modern architect Philip Johnson wrote his critical essay on Sullivan, Professor Hugh Morrison, who wrote *Louis Sullivan: Prophet of Modern Architecture* in 1935, sent a reply to the editor of the *A.I.A. Journal*[62] at the latter's request to commemorate Sullivan on the 100th anniversary of his birth. Concerning the Wainwright Building and the Carson, Pirie and Scott we have just discussed, Morrison replies:

> I am not really interested in writing any more about Sullivan. Such an occasion as this might properly demand a reassessment of what I had to say about him a generation ago, but I have very little reassessment to do. Either my interpretation of him at that time was extraordinarily durable—which would be for others to say—or I am extremely inflexible and stubborn in my viewpoint! Actually the only change in my viewpoint has been a reinterpretation of the Wainwright Building. I then took it as a good illustration of Sullivan's thinking anent the skyscraper, as revealed in his 1896 article on "The Tall Office Building Artistically Considered", and differing only in detail from later skyscrapers because of differences in the program. I now consider it essentially a classical work: modern classicism, to be sure, but a work whose composition was essentially governed by traditional principles of classical composition. A profound change had occurred by the time the Carson, Pirie Scott Store: That was the big leap forward; dynamic rather than static, esthetically articulated according to the new structure rather than "composed" in accordance with a traditional esthetic. The Wainwright was a great masterpiece of traditionalism; the Carson-Pirie jumped forward into the mid-twentieth century in one bold stroke.[63]

If Montgomery Schuyler had read Professor Morrison's remarks on Sullivan in 1956, he would have completely agreed. It was almost like a commemorative tribute to Sullivan in the way Schuyler ended his 1895 discussion on the work of the Adler and Sullivan firm. In its very last paragraph, he writes:

We must not, however, take leave of Mr. Sullivan's work with a negation. The work is too positive and too vital for that. It would be unthoughtful to seem to ignore how much he has done in laying excessive stress upon what he might have done,—upon what, indeed, he may yet do. For I think nobody who really pays attention to his work, even as it is herewith shown, can imagine that he has said his last word, or has had tasks to draw out his utmost powers. It is not difficult to imagine problems more interesting than an unvaried series of those pronounced in the ordinary course of architectural practice in Chicago. But in the solution of these problems he has shown a power of design that makes his one of the most striking and interesting individualities among living architects.[64]

In analyzing Schuyler's architectural criticism on the work of the architects of the Chicago School, it is interesting to note that his first essay written in 1891 after his earliest visit to Chicago represents a more impressionistic treatment of the School than his later essay of 1895. The rightful high point in his first essay is his discussion of Richardson's Marshall Field Store. He gave much attention to, but was also quite critical of, Adler and Sullivan's Auditorium as the outstanding structure derivative from Richardson's example. Although his criticism was generally justified, there is so much of it to suggest that he thought less of the Auditorium than of some of the comtemporary buildings by Burnham and Root. This may, however, have been simply because he believed that the Burnham and Root designs represented the more relevant contribution to the continuation of Richardsonian Romanesque or he might have thought of the firm of Burnham and Root as the leader of the Chicago School at the time as well as his specific wish to memorialize Root in particular.

7

Burnham and Root

John Wellborn Root's premature death from pneumonia, which he contracted while preliminary design meetings were underway for the Columbian Exposition, occurred on January 15, 1891. A month later, on February 12, 1891, Montgomery Schuyler delivered a speech on architecture at a final banquet meeting of the week-long convention of the Fifth Annual Meeting of the National Association of Builders held in the Lenox Lyceum in New York. Schuyler began his address by quoting Leopold Eidlitz's famous remark already familiar to the reader:

> It has also been said by an honored friend of mine, himself an architect, whom I hoped to see here to-night, that American architecture was the art of covering one thing with another thing to imitate the third thing, which, if genuine, would not be desirable.[1]

Schuyler's address was published under the title of "Architecture" in the February 1891 issue of *The Inland Architect and Building News,* and later appeared as the first essay in his *American Architecture* (1892) under the title, "The Point of View." In his address Schuyler proceeded to explain Eidlitz's criticism:

> That is the origin of the exclusive practice of working in architectural styles, as it is called. Why, before the fifteenth century, I don't suppose any man who began to build a building ever thought in what style he should compose it any more than I thought before I got up here in what language I should address you; he simply built in the language to which he was accustomed and which he knew. You will find this perfect truth is the great charm of Grecian architecture, and ten or fifteen centuries later it was the great charm of Gothic architecture, that is to say, that it was founded upon fact, that it was the truth, that it was the thing the man was doing that he was concerned about, even in those pieces of architecture which seem to us the most exuberant, the most fantastic, like the front of Rouen, or like the cathedral of which Longfellow speaks, as you all remember:
>
> How strange the sculptures that adorn these towers!
>   This crowd of statues, in whose folded sleeves
>   Birds build their nests; while, canopied with leaves,
> Parvis and portal bloom like trellised bowers,
> And the vast minster seems a cross of flowers.[2]

> Even in those things there was that logical, law-abiding, sensible, practical adherence to the facts of construction, to the art of building, which we have so long lost, and which I hope we are getting back again. There are examples, in the work of our modern architecture, of architects who design with this same truth, with this same reality, with this same sincerity that animated the old builders before the coming-in of this artificial and irrelevant system of design... There is one example that I would like to mention here, because many of you know his work; I mean the late John Wellborn Root, of Chicago. I shouldn't mention him either if he hadn't, unfortunately, gone from us. Root's buildings exhibit the same true sincerity—the knowledge of the materials with which he had to do, the fulfillment of the purpose which he had to perform. I don't know any greater loss that could have happened to architecture of this country and to the architecture of the future than the man dying before his prime.[3] These are stimulating and fruitful examples to architects of the present time to bring their art more into alliance, more into union, more into identity, with the art of building; and it is by these means, gentlemen, and by these means only, that we can ever gain a living, a progressive, a real architecture—the architecture of the future.[4]

In that same year, only seven months after Root's death, Schuyler wrote his first essay on the architecture of Chicago entitled "Glimpses of Western Architecture: Chicago" which was published in the August 1891 issue of *Harper's Magazine* and was later included in his *American Architecture* (1892). In this 1891 discussion Schuyler writes:

> We have been speaking, of course, of the better commercial edifices, and it is by no means to be inferred that Chicago does not contain "elevator buildings" as disunited and absurd and restless as those of any other American town. About these select few, also, there is nothing especially characteristic. They might be in New York, or Boston, or Philadelphia, for any local color that they exhibit. It is otherwise with the commerical buildings designed by Messrs. Burnham and Root. With the striking exception of Mr. Richardson's Field Building, the names of these designers connote what there is of characteristically Chicagoan in the architecture of the business streets, so that, after all, the individuality is not local, but personal. The untimely and deplorable death of John Wellborn Root makes it proper to say that the individuality was mainly his. It consists largely in a clearer perception than one finds elsewhere of the limitations and conditions of commercial architecture, or in a more austere and self-denying acting upon that perception. This is the quality that such towering structures as the Insurance Exchange, the Phoenix Building, and the "Rookery" have in common, and that clearly distinguishes them from the mass commercial palaces in Chicago or elsewhere.[5]

A few generations later, Carl Condit, chief chronicler and spokesman for the Chicago School of Architecture, would wholeheartedly have agreed with Schuyler's statement above. States Condit:

> Richardson, Sullivan, and Wright are always regarded as the great triumvirate of American architecture. If a fourth were to be added, the choice would be difficult, but it would certainly have to give serious consideration to John Wellborn Root. His death at the age of forty-one was a calamity. In addition to his talent as a designer, he knew where the structural art ought to be going, and he had the courage, idealism, and conviction to keep it to its path. As a philosopher of the new movement in architecture, he was second only to Sullivan, but he often spoke with greater force and clarity than his more widely read colleague.[6]

Root was a native of the South. His father came from England and later became a wealthy dry-goods merchant in Georgia before the Civil War. John, the eldest son, was born January 10, 1850, in Lumpkin (Georgia). But while the child was yet an infant, his parents moved to Atlanta where he spent his boyhood. When the South was being ravaged in the Civil War, in 1864, the boy was sent to England with a business associate of his father for safekeeping. At the age of fourteen he began to attend a school at Claremont, near Liverpool, where he took special courses in architecture and music. At sixteen, he passed the preliminary examination for entrance to Oxford University. Instead of entering Oxford, he returned to his family, by then living in New York, where he was enrolled as a sophomore at New York University in 1867, and in 1869, graduated with a Bachelor of Science degree in civil engineering—an education for his chosen profession perhaps equal to any available in America at the time. After his graduation, Root became an unsalaried apprentice at the office of James Renwick, the architect of St. Patrick's Cathedral, for a year. Then he went on to work for John B. Snook, a fashionable New York architect, patronized by the Vanderbilts, who was busy with the old Grand Central Station at Park Avenue and Forty-Second Street. Root, at twenty-one was made superintendent of construction. After the Great Fire of 1871, Root went to Chicago at the persuasion of Peter B. Wight. He was made foreman and chief draftsman for the firm of Carter, Drake and Wight in early 1872. A little later, destiny led in another young man—Daniel H. Burnham—to the office. In 1873 Root and Burnham were to form a partnership that was to make history in American architecture.

Wight, in his article, "John W. Root as a Draftsman," written on January 21, 1891, only a week after Root's death and published in *The Inland Architect and News Record* number for that month, recalls:

> I came to Chicago and sent for him in January, 1872. When he came he was made foreman of the office, in which place he remained until the formation of the firm of Burnham and Root about a year later. Mr. Burnham was employed by us during that time, and there they made their acquaintance... Mr. Root was essentially a self-taught man, possessed in his youth of the greatest acquisitiveness I have ever witnessed. His experience in offices of New York architects cannot be considered in the light of his education, for his early designs showed no evidences of the influence of those he had been with....[7] I consider that the great excellence in Mr. Root's designs was due to the fact that he was quick in seizing on the capacity of all building materials for architectural expression; that he designed for the materials, and did not have to find materials for carrying out his designs. He was in this a thorough exponent of the principles of Viollet-le-Duc. It was the keynote of his great versatility in design. He sought to make everything he touched beautiful rather than architectural. His works have done more than those of any other man to free us from the architecture of the schools and give us an architecture of perfect freedom. But his freedom never led to license, as has been the case with others who did not possess the self-discipline which he practiced, which was all the more necessary in one possessed of such an active imagination. His works have demonstrated, not that we can develop an American style of architecture, but that the best architecture of the nineteenth century is not trammeled by precedents; that the best works of

past ages are models for study only and not for repetition; and that if we only grasp the knowledge of the best architecture of other days, seize upon the capacities of the materials of today and mold them into things of beauty, we will develop architecture worthy to be associated with the other arts of the nineteenth century.[8]

Wight was right in stating that Root was "essentially a self-taught man, possessed in his youth of the greatest acquisitiveness." Root was certainly familiar with the writings of the great architectural thinkers and philosophers of his nineteenth century. With his friend Fritz Wagner, he translated parts of Gottfried Semper; and clearly he knew and was deeply influenced by the rational and organic principles in *The Discourses* of Viollet-le-Duc. The basic principle was that of organic metaphor. Architecture was to parallel the process of nature: analogies to a creation of nature, a work of architecture was to possess unity, consonance of parts, an integral relationship of parts to the whole, and a compelling and individual reality. The organic notion, a vital theoretical force of modern architecture today, had been developing through the early years of the nineteenth century and even before, and had been expressed in varying degree by many writers, many of them not architects. Among others were Carlo Lodoli, in Italy; numerous German Romantic philosohers and the architect Semper; Coleridge, Pugin, Ruskin, and Edward Lacy Garbett, in England; Viollet-le-Duc, in France; and Greenough, Emerson, Thoreau, Whitman, and the often-forgotten great architect and thinker, Leopold Eidlitz, in America.

Root's architectural philosophy is almost as important as the buildings he designed. Along with Sullivan, he was one of the few architects in the late nineteenth century who clearly and fully understood the necessary character, importance, and purpose of the structural art in an age of mechanized industry. For some years, with the encouragement of Robert Craik McLean, the then-editor of *The Inland Architect and News Record,* Root had written about architecture reflecting many aspects of what today is regarded as organic-functional theory. Noteworthy is the fact that his words were heard and read before any of those of Sullivan and Wright. Most of Root's numerous speeches, essays, and comments were published in *The Inland Architect and News Record.* This was the official organ of the Western Association of Architects and was one of the progressive journals of the day. Root's concern with the theory of architecture and of art in general led to an interest in some of the metaphysical aspects of the subject. In an unpublished paper entitled "A Utilitarian Theory of Beauty," he tried to relate art and science in a logical unity by turning to the biological basis of color and form as the basis for the "utility" of the art to mankind. The idea was certainly organic in a narrow Darwinian sense. In this paper Root writes:

Art and science are of a co-related whole, complements of each other, standing to each other as the intellect to the affections, as the thought to the act. Utility is the idea of use, of fitness—

in a sense, of goodness itself; beauty, all those pleasure-giving qualities we define by words from "exquisite" to "majestic." Beauty is utility, but not always an obvious utility... Let him, so-deceived, pass but one hour considering, from an art standpoint, such magnificent scientific theories as Laplace's "Nebular Hypothesis" or Darwin's "Development of Species," and then ask if this poetic imagination need look further. When artists thus faithfully study nature by the light of science, we shall no longer be in doubt as to the value of the arts. Portraying in forms of idealized beauty the natural principle of eternal fitness, each work of art becomes a lesson for better living. Based upon uses, art becomes useful. Artists will be then, as now, priests of the temple of natural beauty. But from that temple will then be lifted the veil of mystery, and men will see their goddess face to face—a deity surpassingly fair, because divinely good.[9]

As early as 1883, Root wrote a brief and generalized discussion of natural principles as a basis for art in which he revealed, at an early date, the organicism of his approach. This essay was published that year in the November issue of *The Inland Architect and Builder* under the title of "The Value of Type in Art." In part, it reads:

Let us look at these natural principles in a few of their manifestations, bearing in mind that Nature has within a few years received new revelation through modern science, and that the general attitude of art to science is one of at least covert hostility. The principles thus obtained from Nature we will find to underlie all good art of every sort—painting, sculpture, music, architecture or any other.[10]

And finally, in his first serious and forceful essay on architecture and its organic aspects, Root pleads for rationalism for the use of ornament as accent which looks to the organic creation of nature as a source of models in his "Architectural Ornamentation" published in the April 1885 issue of *The Inland Architect and Builder*. In it he says:

Unity of design we must have. But the unity must spring from within the structure, not without it. The great styles of architecture are of infinite value but they are to be vitally imitated, not servilely copied. Continually return to nature and nature's methods. From nature we may also draw suggestive lessons in the decorative use of color. In this direction we have a number of suggestions which as yet it does not seem possible to follow, but many are so full of meaning that they touch all we have to do. Among these none is more pertinent than this: that all things in nature tend as they become greater toward monochrome. It is the small things which are polychromatic. So obvious a law is certainly a thing that we should follow in our building... No general principle can be laid down in this respect, however, and it can only be said that the greatest works of great architects must be studied with nature for a hand book; and the greatest works of nature must be analyzed by us with great architects for guides.[11]

In his essays Root revealed much concern with architectural and art criticism of the time. Typical, for instance, is his "The Value of Type in Art." The very first paragraph declares:

> Nothing is more perplexing to both the artist and the layman than the status of art criticism. At present it is, for the most part, purely empirical, depending, in each instance, upon the personal whim of the critic. Many evils flow from this. Artists are not only discouraged, but also befogged, and hence do not attain good results; but laymen, having no just basis of criticism, extend their patronage at random. Of course, there are admirable critiques on each branch of art, and by careful reading and observation any man may become a competent critic in any department. But in order to accomplish this result he will be compelled to reject much that he reads, because the critic has his own opinion about each work of art, and these opinions are often contradictory. There are but few general principles confessed by every art critic, and one of these is that all art work should have in its method special reference to natural principles... The fact is that it is public criticism which make good art. And we have it in our own power to determine what the art of our time shall be. Criticism, once it is based on sound principles, cannot be too scrupulously excercised. It should be as swift to praise the good as to unsparingly condemn the bad. And there is no reason why the public should ever allow its judgment to be warped, and its criticism be clouded, by any of the technical jargon which is so often used to bolster up bad art. A design for a house is not good because it is Queen Anne, but Queen Anne is good or bad for certain inherent reasons. Nor does the signature of a great "impressionist" or of a great "Pre-Raphaelite" make a great picture, unless the picture be great when judged from its creator's point of view. And in all cases one of the best talismans of criticisms will be found to be the jewel CONSISTENCY.[12]

In another essay, "Architectural Ornamentation," he begins with sharp comments on architectural critics:

> So much has been written and said about architecture and architectural decoration that it seems hopeless to expect anything new, and yet it is true that very few critiques upon these subjects are satisfactory. They are often too technical in vocabulary for laymen, and not sufficiently technical in substance for architects. Or, if this be not true of them, they are deficient in interest by the general absence of critical qualification in the writers. Architectural critics are of two large classes. First are those who, being conscious of certain natural taste, assume this to be sufficient for all the uses of a prophet and apostle, as was a divine inspiration. Of this class are the vast numbers... Then there is a class of really educated critics..., whose whole canon of criticism is to be found in an architectural history. With these men, a good or bad building is known by its conformity to certain conditions, or certain rules, laid down by acknowledged theory-builders of remote ages. Both taste and learning are, of course, necessary to a good critic in architectural as well as other matter, but often all possible has been said and written by the best equipped of lay critics, something new can be added by the active practitioner, because of the difference in his point of view. The habit of analysis necessary for him to do this is one most desirable for him to cultivate, for it may be assumed, without fear of contradiction, that the commonest cause of that mental ossification among architects, that hopeless crystallization of style, is their failure to constantly refer all they do to the inherent reason of things. Ideally, the creator of any design ought to be able to assign a valid reason for every feature in it, and if the reason is not better than a matter of feeling or sentiment, he may well doubt the merit of the feature.[13]

Most importantly, throughout his writings, Root maintained his confidence that America someday would create her own architecture—her own American architectural style—free of any historical features. He said:

> The national mind is peculiarly open; it is freer from prepossessions than any other; it is fair and level, not set in certain grooves and fixed with unchangeable tendencies. To this are added quickness of receptivity almost unparalleled; readiness to receive impressions and acute sensitiveness to environment; humor broad and fanciful, veiling at times beneath its play the depth and seriousness of mind which is also typically American.[14]

This sentiment was expressed by Root before an audience at the Chicago Architectural Sketch Club on January 16, 1888, and was promptly revised by him for publication in the February 1888 issue of *The Inland Architect and News Record* under the title of "Broad Art Criticism." As far as architecture was concerned, Root had a clear sense of his message and his method. His great, creative architectural works during those productive years of his partnership with Daniel H. Burnham testify to this. The two men complemented each other professionally while their partnership was based on a strong mutual respect and affection. One can readily imagine the blow to Burnham of Root's tragically premature death. Yet, for Burnham, the life and building had to go on. Of Burnham, Carl Condit writes:

> If Daniel Hudson Burnham had lived anywhere except in the city of Chicago, he would not have had the architectural reputation that he now enjoys. He was an organizer and a merchant of work often designed by others. The great designs that came from the office of Burnham and Root were either the work of the latter or of men trained by him and designing under his direction. After Root's death in 1891, as long as original architecture flourished in Chicago, the work of Burnham's office continued in the commercial style. As soon as the powerful effect of the classical taste touched him, however, he willingly embraced the new fashion. He enjoyed the greatest success of the Chicago architects, but he did so by increasingly turning against what they stood for. Yet his appearance was necessary, and his contribution during the Chicago renaissance was valuable.[15]

Daniel Burnham was born in Henderson, Jefferson County, New York, September 4, 1946. His father was a country merchant in that upstate town and later in 1855 moved to Chicago where Burnham was to grow up. Daniel studied at Central High School in Chicago and graduated in 1865. After his graduation, he entered the office of William Le Baron Jenney to study architecture but soon gave up and joined a party that had been organized to carry out a colonization scheme in Nevada. In this party also was Gustave Laureau, a Frenchman whom Burnham met in Jenney's office. The scheme proved to be a failure, and he and Laureau returned to Chicago. He tried architecture again, establishing a partnership with Laureau in 1871 but the fire destroyed their business, and Laureau left town. Finally, Burnham's father, who had withdrawn completely from the drug trade at the time of the fire, wanted to set up the young and directionless Daniel and placed him as a draftsman in the firm of Carter, Drake and Wight—widely known and successful Chicago architects. In a paper originally delivered at a meeting held at the Chicago Art Institute on June 11, 1912 and later published in the August 1912 issue of *The Architectural Record,* Wight himself describes this episode:

> I first saw Daniel Burnham in my own office in Chicago in the winter of 1872-73. He was then 25 years of age. He was introduced to our firm by his father, the late Edward Burnham, the firm then consisting of Asher Carter, William H. Drake and myself... He was then put under my personal direction as a student. I introduced him to John W. Root, who had followed me from New York to Chicago in the winter of 1871-72, and was then the head draftsman in our office. We were very busy trying to do our share in rebuilding the burned city, and had just moved into our new offices in the corner suite on the second floor of the Morrison Block, now the Morrison Hotel, which we had rebuilt from the old plans which had fortunately been saved, for the first building was quite new at the time of the fire. A very close friendship was cultivated between Burnham and Root from the time that they first met. This resutled in the partnership which they formed in 1873, which deprived me of my head draftsman, who I had expected to become my partner after the death of Mr. Carter. They opened an office in the building which I had designed at 88 and 90 Washington Street. From that time Burnham furnished the clients and Root did the work.[16]

Similar to the case of Adler and Sullivan only in a different respect, the partnership of Burnham and Root proved to be another model of architectural symbiosis. Root possessed creative technical and artistic talent of a very high order. Burnham, an affable and friendly man, proved an excellent salesman and organizer. When the new office opened for business, it had one drafsman. The second one the partners hired was William Holabird. It is worthy to note that while working and studying under the personal guidance of Wight, Burnham had come to admire him greatly. Wight, a prominent architectural writer and critic as well as an eminent Gothic Revival architect, taught Burnham the practical part of building design and aroused in him an appreciation for scholarship. Suggests Condit:

> There is every possibility that Wight may have had a strong and lasting influence on him, which later appeared in the insistence on his designers' meticulous fidelity to the origins of ornamental detail.[17]

In his *Skyscrapers and the Men Who Built Them* (1928), W. A. Starrett vividly describes the Daniel Burnham known to him in his boyhood:

> I was a boy in Chicago when the first skyscrapers rose. I knew most of the architects and engineers who devised and erected them, and served as a cub under some of them... — "Uncle Dan," as he was affectionately called—one of the fathers of the skyscraper and master builders of America.... He had a forceful, if austere, personality, and his vision was practical as it was far-reaching. "Make no little plans," he counselled in 1907. "They have no magic to stir men's blood and probably themselves will not be realized. Make big plans; aim high in hope and work, remembering that a noble, logical diagram once recorded will never die, but long after we are gone will be a living thing, asserting itself with ever-growing insistency. Remember that our sons and grandsons are going to do things that would stagger us. Let your watchword be order and your beacon beauty." The big and noble plans he made for

Chicago, Washington, San Francisco, and Cleveland in particular and these United States in general, true to his prophecy, are living things today, sixteen years after his death, asserting themselves with ever-growing insistency.[18]

The organizing and business ability that Burnham demonstrated in the amazing rise of his firm and, of course, his concept of "make no little plans" as Starrett tells us above, brought about his election as chief of construction and after Root's death, chief consulting architect for the Columbian Exposition of 1893. Cass Gilbert, another important figure of the Fair, praised Burnham as follows:

His enthusiasm was unbounded; he measured the future by the past. He said to me once, "I think what this country was a hundred years ago, realize what it is today, and think what it will be a hundred years hence; you cannot plan for the future on too large a scale."... It was through his ability as a man of affairs that the Columbian Exposition became a triumph.[19]

It is necessary to introduce here an analysis offered by Montgomery Schuyler of the significance of Burnham's administrative ability to the works that came out of the firm and an important comment made by A.N. Robori in regard to Burnham's remarkable personality and his role in the evolution of commercial tall buildings in this country.

In his "D.H. Burnham and Company," published in the February 1896 issue of *The Architectural Record,* Schuyler writes:

In the correspondence concerning the Government architecture which, as president of the American Institute, Mr. Burnham conducted with the Treasury Department, he took occasion to say that the duties of the Supervising Architect were not so mysterious and difficult as that official tried to make out and that they could be efficiently discharged by "any good business man with a knowledge of building."[20] That may be taken as an expression, reduced to its lowest terms, of Mr. Burnham's own faculty. In the remarks introductory to this consideration of the work of the leading architects of Chicago, I have preferred to call it the faculty of administration in pointing out that it was the one faculty that was absolutely indispensable to the success of a practitioner of architecture in Chicago. It is the faculty which there must be in "the office," whether or not it be possessed, as it is not apt to be in a very high degree, by the actual designer. And certainly nobody will dispute that Mr. Burnham has shown himself a great administrator. The business of the World's Fair, in construction at least, was precisely the business to which the chief of construction had served a long apprenticeship as head of the firm of Burnham and Root. Although he did not appear in the architectural display of the Columbian Exposition as a designer at all, it did not need more than a brief inquiry into the manner in which that display came about to satisfy the inquirers that the one indispensable factor in the artistic success of the display was the architect who did not appear as a designer. He had exercised in preparing it the same powers of selection and coordination and supervision which had been required in his private business and which were now called into requisition on an ampler field and a larger scale. It is not at all wonderful that they should have been found equally efficacious in the services of administration which have nothing to do with architecture, but in which the same method is available that is necessary to administer a large architectural business. Such an administrator need not, it is evident, design at all nor employ any other than the critical faculty in the work of design. In the partnership of Burnham and Root, the junior partner was commonly esteemed to be the designer of the firm, and the estimate was in a general way correct, the services in this regard of the senior being for the most part consultative and critical rather than creative, but nonetheless valuable and indispensible. And indeed in the buildings of Burnham and Root the administrative faculty is not less conspicuous than the power of design.[21]

A.N. Rebori in his essay entitled "The Work of Burnham and Root" published in the July 1915 issue of *The Architectural Record* expresses similar sentiment:

Essentially a man of affairs, Mr. Burnham would have been successful in any calling of life, for the qualities which make for success were his to an unusual degree. A commanding figure in any group, his was the power to stimulate and bring forth the best efforts of those with whom he came in personal contact. By his convincing manner he compelled men to carry out his big ideals. He inspired confidence and left the impression of a great personality upon all who came within range of his powerful and positive nature, and upon thousands of those who only knew his name and works. It can be said with truth that Mr. Burnham lived during a period of opportunities in the making; a period during which the skyscraper was not only conceived, but in which it was carried to its ultimate structural development. That he played a tremendous part in the growth of this truly American problem is at once apparent. The majority of the commercial buildings designed and planned under his direct control will readily prove that he possessed a marvelous administrative faculty. He was the dictator who organized the work of the various mechanical and technical experts who contributed to the making of tall buildings. He considered it his first duty to permit the structure to serve in the most economical manner possible the combination of functions for which it was intended.[22]

Daniel Hudson Burnham lived in his busy world some twenty years longer than his friend and partner, John Wellborn Root. His enormous vitality in the last decade of his life was devoted to city planning and civic art, culminating in the celebrated Burnham Plan for the City of Chicago in 1909. Burnham died in Heidelberg, Germany while touring Europe with his family in June, 1912. It was just a little over a month after his sixty-fifth birthday. It is sad to mention here that of the approximately twenty-seven commercial structures that Burnham, together with Root, had sweated over in the Loop[23] area of Chicago, only three—the Commerce Building (1885-86), The Rookery (1885-88) and the Monadnock (1889-92)—are still in existence. All the rest have followed their architects to their untimely graves.

After the partnership of Burnham and Root was formed in 1873 and after their first building was completed, the office fared badly for a while. The financial panic of 1873 effectually stopped the building boom which followed the Great Fire and until 1876 Chicago's architects had to struggle to survive. With 1876 the building business in Chicago again came to life. It did not take very long for Burnham's tremendous energy to lift the firm up to the top of the profession in the city, not only in the quantity of the work done, but also in its architectural quality. By 1880 Chicago was in the type of unprecedented building boom which would last until the financial panic of 1893, the year that the Columbian Exposition was opened. Up to 1881, the work of the Burnham and Root firm included all types of buildings. The firm now began to attract attention of clients from various parts of the Middle West. This gave the opportunity to Root to display his great versatility and restrained originality. Burnham never let an occasion pass without proclaiming the great talents of his partner. In effect he relieved Root of any necessity of convincing their clients of his ability. This was one of the secrets of their success. Burnham attracted confidence from all those who came within range of his positive and powerful personality. Root had the ability to carry out successfully anything Burnham offered to do. Therefore, it was this special kind of a combination that gained for the firm its preeminence. Root, in his very last article written anonymously for publication, analyzed himself and his partner with fine acumen:

> Burnham and Root, occupying a high position, have been very uneven in their work. Mr. Root, upon whom has largely devolved their designing, seems to have been too facile always to carefully reconsider his designs, and to have been to a large extent the victim of his own moods. Much work by Burnham and Root—the Phoenix, the Insurance Exchange, the Rookery, Rand-McNally's and the Art Institute—is suggestive, and has borne its part in the architectural movement of the day, while much of it reveals crudities begotten of the haste or indifference of the hour. The position occupied by these gentlemen in connection with the Columbian Exposition gives them an opportunity of the welfare of the profession in America, the gravity of which it is hoped they will realize. It may be mentioned in passing, that the partnership between these two gentlemen seems to be admirably adjusted, Mr. Burnham adding to keen artistic perception remarkable executive ability.[24]

The first important commercial structure designed by the two partners was the Montauk Block (figure 10) on West Monroe Street in 1882. It was demolished in 1902. Condit writes:

> The Montauk was an epoch-making building, not only because of its intrinsic characteristics but equally because of its genesis and its architects' method of dealing with the problems it presented. It was the first large commercial project that came into being as the result of the painstaking investigation in the new scientific spirit of all the factors involved: the economic need, the costs, the financial possibilities, and the utilitarian requirements associated with the urban office building, and the technical means by which such requirements could be met and the possibilities realized.[25]

I have discussed earlier the influence of and the roles played by the wealthy clients and their agents, whom the Chicago architects of the time had to cope with, in the conception and development of the commercial architecture in the city. The Montauk project may serve a particularly apt example. It was commissioned by the two wealthy brothers of the shipping business—Peter and Shepard Brooks of Boston and their agent in Chicago was Owen T. Aldis. Carl Condit comments on the three as follows:

> The unprecedented and prophetic qualities of the Montauk were the consequence of Root's translation of Brooks's and Aldis' shrewd, daring, and original ideas into the design and construction of the skyscraper office building. It was an extraordinary union of talents, in which Peter Brooks issued the commands with the expectation of immediate and exact obedience.[26]

Condit states the case succinctly. The many letters that Peter Brooks wrote to his agent in connection with the planning and erecting of The Montauk survive as testimony. In them, one can discern not only the shrewd and no-nonsense attitude of those powerful clients, but also their immense influence upon the Chicago architects of the late nineteenth century. In one of the very earliest of these letters a prophetic sentence stands out: "Tall buildings will pay well in Chicago hereafter, and sooner or later a way will be found to erect them." These words were written by Peter Brooks to his agent—Owen Aldis—on March 25, 1881. In this same letter, he prescribed the functional purpose and the necessary utilitarian features of the new multistory commercial structures. In part, it reads:

> Enclosed are rough plans but sufficient to express my idea of the ground floor of a building for the lot on Monroe Street. The architect can improve on them or submit better, giving also an idea of cost. Let his preliminary plans be on a small scale and not expensive.[27]

Brooks knew precisely what he wanted and the letter clearly indicates his primary motive for commissioning the building. In the same letter, he continues:

> I prefer to have a plain structure of face brick, eight stories and also a basement, with flat roof to be as massive as the architect chooses and well braced with iron rods if needed. The building throughout is to be for use and not for ornament. ITS BEAUTY WILL BE IN ITS ALL-ADAPTATION TO ITS USE.[28]

The emphasis of the last sentence is my own, for in it lies a message that was to become a very important concept of the Chicago commercial architecture of the time. Burnham and Root completed the plans of the Montauk in July 1881. In the course of design they increased the number of full floors from eight to ten. When the building was under construction in the early part of 1882, Brooks expressed his satisfaction in a letter dated February 5, 1882. In it he says:

> I am well pleased with the construction of the Montauk Block in comparison with the New York Buildings—from your (Aldis') description; for its situation could not be better... For the future I should never build but of brick and terra cotta with iron and wood covered with fireproof tile—but I think hereafter I should, like the New York people, build ten stories high—the Chicago foundations with care will stand it, if broad enough—but there must be a limit to the cost of foundations beyond which it will not pay to go.[29]

The Montauk Block in its finished form was a completely fireproof structure of stone and brick, each story above the first identical with every other. Fireproofing was effected through hollow-tile subflooring and tile envelopes around the cast-iron columns and wrought-iron floor beams. Peter B. Wight, an expert on fireproofing at the time, was involved in the Montauk project as consulting architect on the fireproofing and foundation planning about which Peter Brooks expressed so much concern. In his 1912 essay on Burnham, Wight recalls:

> Before then there had been many office buildings, so-called, but the improvement in elevator construction and equipment made possible the erection of higher buildings as revenue producers, provided they could be safely erected. They must therefore be fireproof and we knew then how to make them so nearly as well as we now do, but the old methods were heavy and the substrata of Chicago soil was of doubtful consistency to carry heavy loads. High walls and heavy floors called for foundations of such great spread and size as to destroy the usefulness and revenue producing efficiency of basements. At that time Peter C. Brooks, of Boston, and his son,[30] who had done more than any other men... to improve Chicago with new and high class buildings, engaged Burnham and Root to design the Montauk block for offices and wanted to build it ten stories high. It seems strange now to call it a skyscraper, but that is what it was called at that time. At the same time, through their agent, Mr. Aldis, I was engaged as consulting architect with the duty mainly to plan the foundation, in association with Burnham and Root, and that was the first time that I had any business relations with them after they had been with me. What we did is now a matter of history and is not pertinent to this occasion, except to say that the building was successfully erected, and was the starting point in the career of Burnham and Root in the designing and erection of high office and mercantile buildings. We not only put in a foundation of concrete and old iron rails, to save room in the basement, but the weight of I-beam and hollow-tile floors was reduced to thirty-five pounds per superficial foot. The building went to the scrap heap many years ago, but it was the first successfully erected ten story building in Chicago.[31]

The Montauk Block actually "went to the scrap heap" ten years before Wight wrote the above essay after having been a great "revenue producer," as Wight puts it, for some twenty years for the Brooks family. Peter Brooks closed his investment in the building with a handsome profit: he sold the land and the building to the First National Bank of Chicago for $500,000 against a total expenditure on his part of $325,000. The bank demolished the structure in 1902 to make room for its office building.

In the matter of its external appearance, Brooks' prescription was well filled. The building was a perfectly functional structure, well proportioned, simple and dignified, with an almost "monastic austerity" as Condit suggests. It evolved in part from the vernacular propensity for flat, unadorned wall surfaces, which its owner must have known well in the warehouses and markets of Boston. As a client, Peter Brooks certainly made his idea and influence known and felt through the buildings he commissioned his chosen architects to design. The Montauk was not the only one in which Burnham and Root had to cope with Brooks and Aldis. Two more were on their way to the firm—The Rookery (figure 11) and the Monadnock (figure 12).

The technical excellence of the Montauk Block was not improved upon until the construction of the Rookery three years later. Like the Montauk, the building was commissioned by Peter and Shepard Brooks of Boston, who again employed Owen Aldis as their agent. Due to the fact that the location of the Rookery is bounded by three streets—La Salle, Adams and Quincy and an alley, and also due to the fact that in plan it is a hollow square surrounding an interior court, the structure possesses an unusual feature of being naturally lighted on four sides as well as the interior. Structurally speaking, the building embraces both traditional masonry elements and advanced techniques of iron framing. The exterior walls up to the top, or eleventh, story are composed of a series of stout, widely spaced granite columns surmounted by brick piers. On the periphery of the court, however, the wall and floor loads are carried on a rigidly bolted system of cast iron columns and wrought iron spandrel beams in true skeleton construction. The most important structural feature is the glass and iron vault covering the inner court, the interior ornament of which was designed by Frank Lloyd Wright in 1905. This kind of construction had become common in the nineteenth century after Paxton's Crystal Palace.

In Montgomery Schuyler's 1891 essay after his first visit to Chicago, the critic praised several buildings designed by Burnham and Root. To him they connoted "what there is of characteristically Chicagoan in the architecture of the business streets." They embodied larger and clearer conception than one found elsewhere of the limitations and conditions of commercial architecture. The three favorite buildings during his initial visit included neither the Monadnock, nor strangely enough anything in Adler and Sullivan. They were The Rookery, the Insurance Exchange,[32] and the Phoenix[33] Buildings all the early products of the Burnham and Root firm. Schuyler observed of them:

> There is no sacrifice to picturesqueness of the utilitarian purpose in their general form,... and no denial of it in detail,... Their first roofs are not tormented into protuberances in order to animate their sky-lines, and those of them that are built around an interior court are frankly hypaethral. Nor is there in any of them any incongruous preciousness of material. They are of brick, brown or red, upon stone basements, and the ornament is such, and only such, as is needed to express and to emphasize the structural divisions and dispositions. These are negative merits, it is true, but as our commercial architecture goes, they are not less meritorius on that account, and one is inclined to wish that the architects of all the commercial palaces might attend to the preachments upon the fitness of things that those edifices deliver, for they have very positive merits also. They are all architectural compositions, and not mere walls promiscuously pierced with openings, or, what is much commoner, mere ranges of openings scantily framed in strips of wall. They are sharply and unmistakably divided into the parts that every building needs to be a work architecture, the members that mark the division are carefully and successfully adjusted with reference to their place and their scale, and the treatment of the different part is so varied as to avoid both monotony and miscellany. Their angle piers, upon the visible sufficiency of which the effectiveness, especially of a lofty building, so largely depends, never fail in this

sufficiency, and the superior solidarity that the basement of any building needs as a building, when it cannot be attained in fact by reason of commercial exigencies, is suggested in a more rugged and more massive treatment no less than in the employment of a lavish stronger material. These dispositions are aided by the devices at the command of the architect. The angle piers are weighted to the eye by the solid corbelled pinnacles at the top, as in the Insurance Exchange and the Rookery, or stiffened by a slight withdrawal that gives an additional vertical line on either side of the arris, as in the Phoenix, while the same purpose is partly subserved in the Rookery by the projection from the angle of the tall metallic lantern standards that repeat and enforce this line. The lateral division of the principal fronts is similar in all three structures. A narrow central compartment is distinguished in treatment, by an actual projection or by the thickening of the pier, from the longer wings, while the coincidence of this central division with the main entrance relieves the arrangement from the unpleasant look of an arrangement obviously forced or arbitrary.[34]

In the same year in which Schuyler spoke these words of Burnham and Root, Henry Van Brunt also wrote an article in the January 1891 special issue of *The Inland Architect and News Record* commemorating Root's death. Surprisingly, Van Brunt, who was a noted architect and an architectural writer, and "one of the leaders of eastern architectural taste, who was seldom disposed to find anything acceptable in the advanced Chicago work"[35] as Condit describes, bestowed extraordinarily high praise (though with some reservation) on the Rookery. He says:

The office building of the Central Safety Deposit Company, otherwise known as the Rookery, built about 1886, marks another step of progress, with far more adventurous detail. In this we feel the absense of subordination or repose. It was a large field of experiment in Romanesque detail used with an amount of intrepidity which commands respect. Horizontal and vertical divisions have nearly equal value—a fatal error in an architectural composition. There is an immense deal of successful and beautiful invention in these crowded facades, of which much found its way into Root's later, better and more temperate work. The position of this building in the succession shows, I think, into what a state of feverish energy his powers were then stirred, and how large were his resources. Though perhaps the least successful of his more important works, it is one of the most interesting and suggestive... The "Rookery" is not only a noted example of great fertility of design, but there is nothing bolder, more original or more inspiring in modern civic architecture either here or elsewhere than its glass-covered court. Where the work has been committed to such a multitude of new devices in construction and to such a prodigality of invention in ornament, it is not strange that one may find reasonable objection to certain points of detail. One may admire the audacity of the double iron staircase which, supported by ingenious cantilevers, ramps with double curvature out into open space, meeting at a landing in the sky, as it were, from which the straight second run rises soberly backward to the stories above. One may admire this and wonder whether such an obvious TOUR DE FORCE is worth the study which must have been bestowed upon it. Even the imaginative prison visions in the famous etchings of Piranesi, with their aerial ladders and impossible galleries, present nothing more audacious.[36]

Much of the beauty of the glass roof of this interior court that Van Brunt admired, unfortunately, was lost when the owners of the Rookery later covered the outer surface of the skylights with waterproof membranes and painted the inner surfaces of the glass and iron with a uniform gray. Wright designed the present interior ornament of the court which was executed in 1905 at which time hangers were added to the stairway after Van Brunt wrote his description. The original stair-runs originally stood free and literally appeared to meet "at a landing in the sky" as Van Brunt describes.

> The combination of Root's delicate iron-work and Wright's elaborate gold and ivory decorations provides a rich and luxurious but perfectly disciplined effect suggesting a nineteenth-century counterpart of the profusion, magnificence, and delicacy of Baroque architecture. Equally in the spirit of Piranesi—to follow Van Brunt's parallel—is the cast-iron stairway that rises continuously from the second floor to the tenth and is housed in a semicylindrical curtain of glass and bolted cast-iron panels, the whole enclosure projecting entirely beyond the plane of the west court wall.[37]

So reads Condit's verdict.

However, another contemporary scholar—William Jordy, does not seem to be as impressed as Condit by the Rookery. In his *American Buildings and Their Architects* (1972), Jordy writes:

> In truth, the Rookery is a fascinating conglomeration of the rational and the sumptuous. The boldness of the red brick exterior is clumsily composed, with vigorously inventive ornament, beautifully complementing architectural elements, but serving less as a unifying device for the elevations than an emphasis for a scatter of disparate features. The original entrance lobby, before its remodelling by Frank Lloyd Wright in 1905, was a fantasy of ironwork, some of which is still to be seen in a circular stair which projects into the central light court. The view from the stair to the light court, through the pierced "Saracenic" tracery toward the prophetic ribbon windows crisply cut into the flush wall surfaces, and linked by an incised ornamental band in terra cotta, makes the dichotomous nature of Root's esthetic principles clear at a glance. Of all who praised this much praised building at the time, however, it appears that few (if any) remarked on the light court, whereas the entrance lobby was a cynosure of the Loop, and justifiably so despite the brash crudity of its detailing.[38]

Montgomery Schuyler, who in 1891 profusely praised the Rookery seemed to have changed his opinion about it four years later after his second visit to Chicago. Perhaps it was because of his belated discovery in 1895 of the Monadnock Building, a building which he had failed to mention in his first essay even though the building would have been well along towards completion in 1891. Schuyler reflected in 1895:

> The Rookery is not artistically so successful, either in mass or in detail, as some other buildings of the firm, but at the time it was built it was, perhaps, the most impressive of all by dint of the Roman largeness of its plan and of the thoroughness with which this was carried out to the last detail, as a matter not alone or mainly of artistic elaboration, but of practical administration. If it is not so uniquely impressive now, it is because such a project, when it has once been successfully executed, becomes common property, and may be reproduced and varied until, much more than in purely artistic success, the spectator is apt to forget the

original inventor and the fact that the arrangement he takes for granted was not always a commonplace but was originally an individual invention.[39]

He then sought, rather unconvincingly, to identify Burnham's administrative capability with the success of the Rookery:

> One cannot help seeing that the quality of the decorative detail, which in the Rookery is very good, has very little to do with the impressiveness of the interior, which is impressive as so many Roman interiors are of which the detail has either disappeared or is an incongruous application. It is impressive, that is to say, by the faculty of planning that it displays, by the practical satisfaction of the practical requirements, by the administrative faculty.[40]

In the history of Chicago commercial architecture in its formative moments of the 1880s, the Rookery Building of Burnham and Root became linked with Richardson's Marshall Field Store and Adler and Sullivan's Auditorium as the penultimate monuments of the art of masonry architecture; the grand finale was to come at the end of the decade with the Monadnock Block. Three of these four bildings, the Marshall Field Store, the Auditorium and the Monadnock, are particularly good examples of the vernacular tradition in urban architecture, and two of the three are still standing to remind us of it. One of them is the Monadnock Block.

The Monadnock differs radically from the older Rookery in every respect. It represents the ultimate step in construction with stone and brick and stands today, the last great building in the immemorial tradition of masonry architecture. As early as 1885, the first discussion of plans for the Monadnock appeared in a series of letters between Peter and Shepard Brooks and their agent, Owen Aldis. It was not until 1888, however, that the Brooks brothers commissioned Burnham and Root to design the building. The firm completed the working plans by the summer of the following year and the erection of the building was completed two years later in 1891. Located on West Jackson Boulevard, the Monadnock illustrates a number of Root's remarkable technical innovations—floating raft foundation, oriels or projecting bays to provide for maximum admission of natural light, the fifteen-foot piers to carry the great weight of sixteen stories—all of which reveal the designer's creative power in structural engineering. The choice of masonry construction instead of the already-developed skeleton metal frame for the Monadnock was strongly influenced by Root's conservative New England clients who were perhaps understandably hesitant about accepting the more advanced method of building construction. It should be remembered that at that time the new skeleton frame had been untried elsewhere except for a few skeleton buildings that had gone up in Chicago and Bradford Gilbert's Tower Building (1888-89) in New York. However, two years after the completion of the first half of the long block, the same clients commissioned Holabird and Roche to extend the block to take its original size. The addition had a steel frame. That Root's portion was deemed aesthetically superior is apparent in A.N. Rebori's words written in 1915:

> The designer has deliberately renounced colonnades, mouldings and all other customary architectural embellishments, achieving his effect by a frank confession of the structural requirements which conspicuously manifest that need, that in contemplating the bold interpretation one is apt to experience a singular emotion. In spite of this extreme austerity The Monadnock Building is as impressive as it is clearly expressive. The success of it comes from a series of subtle refinements that bring out the latent expressiveness of what without them would in truth be as bald as a bone perforated with square holes. An object lesson to the same effect is most strikingly inculcated in the later extension of the same building, in which the general disposition is followed and the forms repeated but with a result not nearly so impressive. Certainly a comparison of these two buildings is overwhelmingly in favor of the older. In this respect it is only fair to add that the original building is of self-supporting masonry walls, and that the extension is an early example of the developed steel cage construction.[41]

The Monadnock Building, like the other Richardsonian-inspired blocks, is readily perceived as an "entity." The form that the building takes is a tall, thin slab—stripped of every vestige of ornament, because of the long and narrow site (202 feet long and 68 feet wide). It thus appears as a free-standing slab—a shape altogether familiar to modern architecture, softened only by the slight inward curve of the wall at the top of the first story, the outward flare of the parapet, and the progressive rounding of the corners from bottom to top. Like its modern counterparts, the slab carries its burden of functional rationalization and represents in its relentless exactitude the formal beauty latent in the commercial style. This new order of beauty born with tall office buildings was acceptable enough at the time in Chicago where the expression of power and utility seemed wholly appropriate. However, its meaning was not entirely lost in the East. In "The Building and Designing of the Skyscraper" published in the November 1905 issue of *The American Architect and Building News,* the author, Edward S. Hamatt, observes:

> Various other styles of high office, buildings are seen. Few are satisfactory in appearance. Their designs strive for effect by dividing the facades horizontally and vertically. Pretentious details run riot. All our architecture needs restraint, needs a more refined sense of proportion—a more conscientious use of detail. There are a few skyscrapers which are designed in a rational way, their architects realizing that the problem is one of vertical design and treat it accordingly, not even attempting to work out the design in any of its existing architectural styles. The original Monadnock Building in Chicago, designed by Mr. John W. Root, is one of the best examples of good design in skyscrapers. It is a building of the severest plainness. The necessary strength of base is secured by a gentler outward curve above the first story, an effect of batter being secured by champfering up the angles, widening as it rises several stories in height. The superimposed stories have plain, rectangular openings. The expanse of blank wall is broken up by shallow oriels, equally spaced, starting above the

outward curve of base, at top of second story and extending to the story below the frieze line. The cornice is formed by repeating the gentle curve of the base. The proportions of this building are so carefully studied that in spite of its austerity it is one of the most pleasing and satisfactory of skyscrapers. The pleasing effect of the building could have been heightened by using a lighter colored material, the dark-colored brick and terra cotta being almost too somber for such a massive structure.... While we have a few individual examples of fine design the problem of effective treatment of the skyscraper is one still open to solution.[42]

One of the most eloquent and inspired tributes to Root's audacity in connection with the Monadnock that came from the East soon after the building was completed was that of Robert D. Andrews, then president of the Boston Architectural Club. Andrews, in his "The Broadest Use of Precedent," published in the May 1893 issue of *The Architectural Review*, praises Root as follows:

> It was the evident purpose of the designers of this building to simply solve the problem and let the result stand. The integrity of mind through which this decision was made and carried out relates this work to the product of the greatest men everywhere who have advanced the things they stood for and gained the honor of mankind. It took prodigious courage to do this thing. It is an achievement unsurpassed in the architectural history of our country... What I want to dwell upon is the dignity and worth of this simple statement of fact. Most of us seem to apologize for being forced to state the truth. Here were men who rejoiced in it, and, far from apologizing for it, emphasized it... The results arrived at are, therefore, not gotten haphazardly, but with deliberate and conscious intention. This building has no precedent in architecture. It is itself a precedent. Yet it has a precedent outside of architecture; it comes up to an ideal, and by virtue of its correspondence with this ideal it becomes a work of art.[43]

Two years after Andrews wrote his article, Montgomery Schuyler, the only other Eastern critic of the time who appreciated the Monadnock's unique beauty, upon his second visit to Chicago paid a similar tribute to the building. In it, he opened his discussion of the Monadnock with the highest praise for the firm that had built it:

> The business buildings of Burnham and Root were the first tall buildings in which the conditions both of commercial architecture in general and of elevator architecture in particular were recognized and expressed. As soon, however, as the expression was attained it was recognized both by owners and by other architects as the appropriate architectural fulfillment of the new requirement:
>
> > Most can raise the flowers now,
> > For all have got the seed;[44]
>
> and so it comes about that what was at first characteristic of an individual designer has become characteristic of a city. For in no other American city has commercial architecture become so exclusively utilitarian as in Chicago, deserved so exactly the praise that Mr. Bouget bestowed upon it, relied so exclusively upon "the simple force of need" as "a principle of beauty."[45]

It has been mentioned earlier that Schuyler failed to take note of the Monadnock Building when he visited Chicago in 1891 or at least failed to mention it in his 1891 essay even though the building was then underway and possibly just completed. By 1895, the Monadnock had become the favorite building of critics, or at least critics as enlightened as Andrews; and Schuyler now considered Root's masterpiece to be the best in the city and, indeed, among the finest commercial buildings in the country. Time has of course vindicated his judgment. In his 1895 essay, Schuyler declared:

> There is one building in Chicago in which the renunciation is carried so much further than in any other that it bears the same relation to the commercial architecture of the town that the commercial architecture of the town bears to commercial architecture elsewhere; and it happens that this extreme example is the individual design of Mr. Burnham. Of course I mean the Monadnock. Here is a sixteen-story building without an ornament, with one form of opening repeated from top to bottom and from end to end, with no relief to the expanse of blank wall and equal opening except what is furnished by the wide and shallow oriels, equally spaced, five on the long side and two on the short, which run through thirteen stories with only a string course to mark off the plinth and with not even a string course to mark off the cornice, or a single moulding to relieve or to emphasize its outward curve. Nay, the entrance itself, in which some enrichment is allowed even in the severest buildings, is here a rectangular hole in the wall like the rest. Add that the whole, excepting the granite lintels of the basement, is in a monochrome of dark brick and terra cotta. In the description of all this is of no more architectural interest than a box, or rather a honeycomb, and would be dismissed as a mere factory. In fact, although it by no means impresses all beholders alike, it impresses many, including the present writer, as precisely the most effective and successful of the commercial structures to which the elevator has literally "given rise." This, one cannot help seeing, is the thing itself. It may seem easy enough to leave off all ornament from a tall building, and to employ in it but one form and almost one size of opening, and so indeed it is. That is a common scheme in factories which are not works of architecture at all. The point is to produce, by means of or in spite of this extreme austerity, an architectural work which shall be as impressive as it clearly is expressive. This is the rare success that seems to me to have been attained in the Monadnock. Whoever assumes that it must be very easy to do and that it requires no more than merely the omission of architecture makes a great mistake. On the contrary, the success of it comes from a series of subtle refinement and nuances that bring out the latent expressiveness of what without them would in truth be as bald as a factory. An object-lesson to this effect is most strikingly inculcated in the extension to the same building in which the general disposition is followed and the forms repeated, but which it is quite impossible to admire or to regard as a work of art. The square openings are repeated, and the shallow oriels. Only the base is "improved," with the view of giving it more height, of making it more proportionate to the building, and the cornice by giving it more projection. All this seems reasonable enough, but the result of all this is the production of a perfectly commonplace structure in place of a very impressive structure. It is only fair to point out that the original building is not and that the extension is an example of the developed Chicago construction, which has yet to find its developed architectural expression. In the most successful examples of it the designers have felt forced to assume a wall at least as a stylobate, whereas in fact there is no more a continuous wall at the base then there is anywhere else. The original Monadnock has the great advantage over the addition that the walls are real walls that carry themselves and that may properly be thickened at the base. But this thickening at the base, skillfully done in the Monadnock, but it is only one of many refinements. Above the

massive plinth of a single story a whole story becomes virtually a base moulding curving outward with a long and easy sweep that seems to guarantee the stability of what is above, while at the angle begins a chamfer, widening very gradually as it rises, that gives the effect of a batter of the whole wall that it bounds and confirms this sense of stability. Every angel in the openings is slightly and subtly rounded, while at the summit the cornice is the counterpart of the base. With great artistic sensibility, the oriels, as they are begun a clear story above the base are stopped a clear story below the Egyptian cornice, and the intervening story is punctuated with openings, perfectly disposed with reference to the distribution of voids and solids beneath, that give the effect of machicolation. So far from being crude, as the absence of ornament might lead a hasty observer to conclude, the design of the Monadnock, as it revealed by the study of good photographs, or much better of the building itself, is of an extreme refinement, and the impressiveness of it due to the subtlety of the devices that have been employed to mitigate the asperities and bring out the possibilities of expression in a brick box of sixteen stories.[46]

Schuyler was right in quoting Tennyson's "The Flower"—Most can raise the flowers now, For all have got the seed—for even at the present time all still "have got the seed" in the field of high-rise commercial architecture. In Chicago alone, as late as the 1960s, a spate of new office buildings took inspiration from the subtle curvatures and chamfering of the Monadnock that Schuyler describes above such as two buildings designed by Skidmore, Owings and Merrill—The Brunswick Building and the John Hancock Center; and The First National Bank Building designed by C.F. Murphy Associates and the Perkins and Wills Partnership. None of these buildings, however, equal the quality of the Monadnock. All of these three firms are leading Chicago-based architectural offices and at least one of them—Skidmore, Owings and Merrill—is internationally known; and all three still keep the "Chicago spirit" that once governed the commercial structures that Burnham and Root built.

After Root's death Burnham continued the firm alone under the name of D.H. Burnham and Company. Much of the work of design and organization in his prosperous office was entrusted to his chief assistants, Charles B. Atwood, Dwight Perkins and Ernest R. Graham. In the last decade of the century, the firm's commissions grew in number and size to the point where the D.H. Burnham and Company firm was the largest in Chicago. One of its principal commissions was the Reliance Building.

In his classic description of the commercial architecture of Chicago, Paul Bourget, the French visitor, was celebrating the stripped block of masonry construction such as the Monadnock as well as the stripped skeleton. It was the cliff of windows that captured Bourget's enthusiasm. In the wall reduced to skeleton and glass, the Chicago architects "brutally" pushed the aesthetic of the speculator's conditions to a climax. (Boruget used the term "brutalement" which Schuyler translated as "frankly.") In no building of the period is this aesthetic more compelling than in The Reliance whose designing architect was Charles B. Atwood, a member of Burnham's staff. Unlike the Monadnock which is boldly subtle, the Reliance is boldly raw in its magnification of the commercial premise. "One short step further in the design of the Reliance and he (Atwood) would have produced the transparent tower that Mies van der Rohe imagined in his Berlin project of 1919,"[47] so observes Condit. The commission of the Reliance Building to be erected at the southwest corner of State and Washington Streets was awarded to Burnham and Root in 1890. Plans for a sixteen-story building were made by Root shortly afterward. Since leases in the upper stories of the old five-story building at that location ran until 1894, the erection of the Reliance was not begun until them. In the course of design process, plans for the building, originally prepared by Root, were altered and its height was shortened from sixteen stories to fourteen by Atwood who succeeded Root as Burnham's chief designer until his own premature death in 1895, the year in which the Reliance was opened for occupancy. Of this remarkable building, Condit observes:

> The builders performed a remarkable feat of construction in erecting the steel frame of the top ten stories in fifteen days, from July 16 to August 1, 1895. The steel framing system included two unusual provisions for windbracing: 24-inch deep spandrel girders with either solid or trussed webs bolted to the columns through the web depth in rigid connections, and columns of two-story length disposed to provide staggered joints. The street elevations represent the goal that the whole functionalist wing of the Chicago movement was consciously or unconsciously striving to reach, for here the last vestige of a bearing element, or any indication of the hidden presence of one, has disappeared from the elevations.[48]

It can be said with truth that the Reliance was the culmination of the imagination and the architectural achievement of the Chicago School and all it stood for. The architect here developed the modern curtain wall, and thus achieved that very nearly complete dematerialization which is the mark of the best work of the present time. The walls of the Reliance form a thin skin stretched over the skeleton of the building and exhibit an impartial tension in all directions. The appearance of a skin comes partly from the fact that the windows and the opaque portions of the envelope constitute an unbroken plane, the opaque covering being a thin, glazed terra cotta obviously without any bearing property. Sigfried Giedion says that the building is at once the triumph and the "swan song" of the Chicago School In his *Space, Time and Architecture,* Giedion continues:

> Speaking in a broader sense, it might perhaps be said to have grown out of the Chicago soil itself, to be a reflection of the high architectural level that has been reached in that city. The Reliance Building is a glass tower fifteen stories high.[49] The base is formed from some dark and unobtrusive stone, in sharp contrast to the glass and glazed white tile tower which springs up from it. The eaves of the flat roof are only thin slabs, emphasized no more than they must be to serve as protections. There is no overbearing cornice of stone. Ten years' experience lies behind the understanding treatment of the horizontally proportioned "Chicago windows." In earlier office buildings of the Chicago School (the now-destroyed Tacoma Building by Holabird and Roche, for example) the bow windows tend somewhat to

be independent and isolated parts of the design. In the Reliance Building they project no more than they are required to in order to pick up light. They are wholly incorporated into the glass body of the building. This glass tower is still standing, and although its glazed white tiles have become encrusted with dirt, its airiness and pure proportions make it a symbol of the spirit of the Chicago School. It is curious that this building too has been left unnoticed in the history of architecture. It has its place there as a witness to the best of the spirit of the nineteenth century.[50]

The Reliance Building might have been left unnoticed in the history of architecture when Giedion wrote his *Space, Time and Architecture* which was first published in 1941 that for the first time provided the comprehensive treatment of the Chicago School. Since then, the building has been a favorite of historians, scholars and students of American architecture. Actually, the phrase "swan song" that Giedion employed in his description of the Reliance was originally used twenty-six years earlier by another critic. In this essay on Burnham published in *The Architectural Record* for its July 1914 issue, N.A. Rebori writes:

The Reliance Building was the "swan song" to the old traditions, based on independence of design for which were noted the works of Burnham and Root. It stands today a symbol of our inconsistency and an ample proof that no sooner do we approach a common way of working than the promise of a truly expressive style of American architecture is broken by the capricious introduction of a new fashion. Perhaps it is because the design of this building has been rather the statement of a problem than the solution of it, and that the white envelope of terra cotta is confessedly a covering, and does not in the least simulate a structure nor dissemble the real structure, that the same designers fall back in the design of the first Field Annex[51] to the use of an architectural treatment which does simulate a structure of masonry and is meant to be judged as such.[52]

Rebori, in 1915, must have been familiar with Montgomery Schuyler's 1895 discussion on the work of Burnham and Root which was printed in the same periodical in which Rebori's essay was published only nineteen years earlier, for he expressed an opinion on the Reliance almost identical with Schuyler's. In the February 1896 issue of *The Architectural Record,* Schuyler, among the most liberal architectural critics of the day, who is, nevertheless, too often credited with great enthusiasm for skeleton framing than he in fact possessed, echoes this verdict on the Reliance:

As I have intimated, it is probably well for architecture of the Monadnock that it was built before the Chicago construction was developed. In the buildings in which that construction is really followed, and the wall omitted, even at the base, the highest success that has thus far been attained amounts rather to a statement of the problem than to a solution of it. Wherever the steel cage is confessed throughout, the effect is not different in kind, nor very much in degree, from the effect of skeleton itself, which nobody can succeed in admiring, although it is true that the articulation of the skeleton has never been regarded as an architectural but only as a mechanical problem, aesthetic consideration having been devoted only to its envelope. Of the essays in which the skeleton is undraped, and no attempt is made to "do something" with it, the Reliance Building in Chicago, from the office of D.H. Burnham and Co., and from the designs of Mr. Charles B. Atwood, is one of the most typical... Its most obvious peculiarity is that the protecting envelope is of glazed white terra cotta. Practically this is a very eligible material in the atmosphere of Chicago, but the employment of it throughout seems almost like the frank abandonment of architecture, as much as the omission of an attempt to "do something" with the cage. A monument that "will wash" is already pretty nearly a contradiction in terms. The frankness of the treatment is complete. The covering is confessedly a covering and does not at least simulate a structure nor dissemble the real structure. The designer has not allowed himself a base, though he has indulged himself in a pretty and becoming attic. If he says, as he seems to say, that this is the actual sky-scraper, the thing itself and that any attempt to do more than he has done is to deny the essential conditions of the problem, it must be owned that he has a good deal to say for himself. Especially when, as in this case, the designer's other works make it clear that his decision does not proceed from aesthetic insensibility. But on the other hand, it must be owned that if this is the most and best that can be done with the sky-scraper, the sky-scraper is architecturally intractable; and that is a confession one is loath to make about any system of construction that is mechanically sound. Certainly a comparison between the Reliance and the Monadnock is overwhelmingly in favor of the older building.[53]

Reading the praise of progressive-minded observers at the turn of the century like Paul Bourget and Montgomery Schuyler for the Chicago commercial architecture, it is evident that the overwhelming impression that Chicago made on them was one of the stark regularity of relatively heavy buildings meeting the traditional gravitational criterion of coming forcefully to the ground with a considerable feeling for walls. Although Siegfried Giedion in the 1940s could praise the skeleton Reliance as a herald of the aesthetic of airiness and lightness characteristic of the modern movement, none of the observers and critics at the turn of the century expressed such an opinion. To a degree, the Reliance is awkward and Schuyler's criticism was justified in his ranking it below the Monadnock. However, what puzzles us today is that a progressive-minded critic like Schuyler, with an enduring interest in the skyscraper, would remain skeptical of the aesthetic possibilities of the skeleton construction. Here he was less farsighted. While he deplored the Reliance. Schuyler profusely praised the same firm's Monadnock Building which was nearly the last of the tall masonry buildings built for the conservative Boston clients who did not trust the newly developed skeleton construction. The fact that, in the Monadnock, the height of the masonry-bearing walls required six feet of thickness at ground level conclusively demonstrated that further developments in tall building could not be expected from traditional construction. Yet Schuyler was wary of the slightly later Reliance Building, erected for a Chicago client, as a mere terra-cotta-sheathed cage of metal and glass, and nothing more. Schuyler remained ambivalent about the Reliance through his life while he confessed several times that the finest tall buildings were the transitional buildings antedating the full development of metal skeleton construction. As late as 1909, he still would write that the best tall building in Chicago and one of the best in the country was the Monadnock Building. Obviously Schuyler admired the Monadnock which was among the ultimate tributes to Richardsonian Romanesque for the sense of the wall which it displayed. The thick walls, as contrasted to the thin curtains of masonry hung on the outside of the metal frame of the average skyscraper, permitted deep reveals. These in turn provided light and shadow for the wall. Thus the Monadnock possessed a "real wall," with the proportion between wall and window such that the wall maintains its dominance, unlike the transparent Reliance where the expression of interior volume prevailed the sense of exterior mass. In short, Schuyler never wholly escaped the world of Ruskin, Eidlitz, and Richardson, the world of his own aesthetic origins.

D.H. Burnham and Company's works after the Reliance show a steady diverging from its bold transparency. The influence of the Columbian Exposition of 1893 began to make itself felt and seen. This change in architectural point of view was suddenly effected, and the outcome was a skeleton structure profusely covered with rich Renaissance details, abounding in cornices and arches ascending from the sidewalk through story after story to the generous crowning cornice. The first building that came out of the Burnham and Company office in this mode appears to be the Marshall Field Annex (1892-93) and ironically enough it was designed by the same staff designer of the firm who did the Reliance—Charles B. Atwood. The appearance of the Field Annex in Chicago was only the beginning with many more to come.

One of the best designs that issued from the office of Burnham and Company after the turn of the century is the Railway Exchange Building (figure 14), erected from 1903 to 1904 at the northwest corner of Michigan Avenue and Jackson Boulevard. There is in it little dependence on historical forms and fairly consistent exploitation of Chicago construction. The extensive area of glass and the clean, sharp lines form a lively expression of steel framing. The circular openings of the top story, like those of Sullivan's Wainwright Building, are an arbitrary decoration, but they soften the transition to the abrupt horizontal line of the cornice. The Railway Exchange was the subject of a confused and unconsciously ironic, though fundamentally perceptive, article entitled "Rationalizating the Skyscraper" by Harry W. Desmond published in the May 1905 issue of *The Architectural Record.* Desmond, a critic on the staff of the *Record,* regarded Burnham's building as a sound starting point for a rational skyscraper design. His essay begins:

> I was rather surprised the other day to hear an eminent architect, who has himself "committed" many skyscrapers of the prevailing florid type, seriously maintain that we need, more than we need anything else, a period of fasting in architecture. In making this remark, he was innocent of plagiarism, but as a matter of justice, I would like to fix the patent for this proposition upon its veritable author, Mr. Russell Sturgis. The patent will probably not be very much value to its author just at present, but by-and-bye when experience has chastened

the entire profession, there may be little renown in it. For we may recognize later on that there are benefits to be derived from even a very meagre diet. Although the eminent architect, to whom I have referred, is not, I judge, likely ever during his career to profoundly alter his practice to conform with his creed, there are others in his profession, an occasional few here and there, who perhaps as much from necessity as from preference, illustrate what might be derived were the period of fasting actually promulgated... Looking at this Railway Exchange Building, the candid mind can hardly refrain from at least asking whether the theory and practice there exemplified are entirely without merit—whether, indeed, they are not after all very much closer to a thoroughly sound starting point for the design of a skyscraper than the more pretentious methods of our school-men.[54]

Desmond then proceeded to castigate the building:

Of course, it will be said at once: This Railway Exchange Building is monstrously ugly, a tremendous affair of window-sashes, an aggregation of bird cages, lacking structural sufficiency as a matter of design in all its parts, but especially in the basement, in the piers, in the corner abutments, in all horizontal lines, except, possibly, in the crowning story where—mark you!—the architect... has departed from his practical theory and has inserted a row of round windows in a solid wall. It must be admitted one cannot directly shake off this attack... No! The design is not beautiful—it is merely interesting because it is rational, or rather more rational than it would be had the architect been less of a radical. Of course, if we can dispense with the rational in architectural design, and by that means, produce in the course of time an architecture worthy of real consideration, well and good! The verdict then is clean against Mr. Burnham, and all others that shall follow in his foot-steps... One might, possibly ungraciously, perhaps unfairly, ask whether, after all, he had any consistent theory.[55]

Burnham, of course, was not consistent in applying his own theory to the whole building. The lobby of the Railway Exchange, for example, is a work of showy classicism as Desmond was quick to point out:

In the large entrance hall... it may be seen how far he has returned to the conventions, and let us note conventions carried out in white glazed terra-cotta, a material entirely unsuitable to at least some of the forms which he has employed. The piers may pass, but certainly, we cannot forgive fluted columns covered with a glaze which absolutely confounds the flutings and their arrises.[56]

Desmond probably did not realize, when he angrily and unfairly wrote the article out of frustration and as a protest against classicism that was sweeping the country at the time, that some of the good features of the Railway Exchange which he condemned so roundly many of the present generation would admire. In today's judgment the building is not "monstrously ugly" as Desmond emphatically declared it.

Although Daniel Hudson Burnham was almost exclusively pre-occupied with city planning in the last stretch of his career, his office captured an immense volume of major architectural commissions. After 1900, the administration of the office was in the hands of his chief partner, Ernest B.

Graham, who had joined the firm of Burnham and Root in 1888. Burnham's history as an architect epitomizes the trend of the professionals surviving with the tide of public taste in architecture. He knew exactly how to be successful and how to reach the goal of his career, in order to gain what he wanted, was quite prepared to sacrifice the principle, concept and philosophy of a shcool he had helped to develop in its formative moments. Burnham, after Root's death, seemed to ignore what he had learned from his former partner and from his Chicago experience. He willingly opened his arms as wide as he could to the classicism that was to become the order of the day and submitted to the influence of well-educated Beaux-Arts men of the East. All his life, once Burnham said, he felt that lack of mental training at college age. This defect may have been partly responsible for his pliability in the hands of educated Eastern architects. Peter B. Wight, in 1915, bluntly stated that Burnham had swung over into the classical school and taken his cues from New York.[57] However, it must be noted here also that, in spite of what history might have indicated, Burnham was a man of genuine vision and originality, and his presence in Chicago at the turn of the century was altogether critical. It is also true that by the time the First National Bank (1896) of D.H. Burnham and Company was completed, many critics and clients alike had already come to the conviction that the Chicago School of architecture was something of the past. This conviction, indeed, was to last a long time. If one seriously considered Louis Sullivan's celebrated embittered remark—"The damage wrought by the World's Fair will last for half a century from its date,"[58] his phophecy, then, was fulfilled. However, whether or not it was justified is another matter.

8

Conclusion

If one considers the Great Fire of 1871, in the period after which the concepts and techniques of the Chicago School of architecture were formed and implemented, the beginning of the "birth" of the Chicago commercial architecture, then it is not far from truth that the Columbian Exposition of 1893 can be considered the BEGINNING of its "death." In this respect, Louis Sullivan was correct, as history can testify, in saying in his famous so-called "prophecy" that the Columbian Exposition would stop the building progress of the Chicago School for fifty years if not longer. However, it must be noted that Sullivan wrote the "prophecy" in his *Autobiography of an Idea* during the last years of his life when consumed with bitterness. He viewed the whole country through the dark spectacles of his own disintegration and defeat. The *Autobiography* was not published in book form until after his death in 1924. As a result, it caused many people to believe that all fresh design came to a standstill after the Fair when the white cloud of classicism hung threateningly over the whole country while it insured McKim, Mead and White, Graham Anderson Probst and White, D.H. Burnham and Comapny, and Carrere and Hastings, the architectural leadership of the country. That is partially, but not wholly true. In the period from 1895 to 1915, American architecture still at times exhibited fresh vigor. This was the period of Sullivan's own most original work including the celebrated Carson, Pirie and Scott Store; of Frank Lloyd Wright's bold and characteristic development of his Prairie Houses, not to mention his Larkin Building and Midway Gardens. It was also the period of the second generation of the Chicago School whose architects such as Dwight Perkins who still designed educational and park buildings in the spirit of the School in Chicago and George Grant Elmslie who designed the Sullivanesque courthouses for Sioux City, Iowa. The period between 1895 and 1915 was also the period in which the influence of the current periodicals, architectural or popular, was far from being on the side of the new classic movement. *The Architectural Record,* published in New York, *The Western Architect* which was published in Minneapolis from 1902 until 1931, and *The Craftsman,* published in Syracuse, New York from 1902 to 1931, gave modern architecture an impetus by publicizing its good buildings and subjecting them to critical appreciation. As editor of *The Craftsman,* Gustav Stickley presented his American version of the Arts and Crafts Movement. The similarities between the fundamental approach of the Chicago School and the aims of the Arts and Crafts Movement are nowhere better illustrated than in *The Craftsman.* In order to support the Chicago School after the turn of the century. Strickley frequently threw the pages of his magazine open to the architects themselves. In 1906, for example, Sullivan's article, "What is Architecture?" appeared in *The Craftsman.* This article brought him badly needed new clients.[1] *The Western Architect,* as its title suggests, gave almost exclusive treatment to the architectural activities in the Midwest, and through those pages of *The Architectural Record,* Montgomery Schuyler "never hauled down the flag." Even the women's magazines, which came to exert such important influence, were on the side of the innovators. One must remember well the February and July 1900 issues of *The Ladies' Home Journal* in which the plans for "prairie houses" by Wright appeared. All this influence of the periodicals should not be underrated and all took place during the time that Sullivan convinced many people through his *Autobiography* (1924) that the architecture of the Chicago School was suddenly dead after the Columbian Exposition of 1893.

To be fair, it must also be noted here that by the time Sullivan was writing his "prophecy" in the early 1920s, it was then almost thirty years after the conclusion of the Fair and by that time the influence of classicism as a result of the Fair, not only in Chicago but also in other cities all over the country, was quite apparent and almost reached its final phase. By that time, Sullivan's bitterness has taken total possession of the man. He issued several brutal criticisms on the Fair itself, on the late Burnham, and on the classicism of the East. It was not exactly known what Sullivan thought of the Fair immediately after its conclusion. If he had harbored any such negative opinions, his criticisms must have been quite restrained. However, it is known that on August 5, 1893, at the last session of the World's Congress of Architects, Sullivan chose to speak on polychromy, a subject which, in the face of the whitewashed "Court of Honor" of the Fair, posed basic questions. He demonstrated how form could be developed organically from simple geometric shapes. He warned that Americans were not Greeks and that any attempt at such substitution was sheer perversion.

In the days and decades that followed the Columbian Exposition, the world continued to discuss the event and to pass on its merits. Only a few critics, artists, architects and intellectuals voiced reservations. Henry Adams appreciated the sense of unity and direction that the White City demonstrated. Henry Van Brunt, torn between loyalties old and new, cautioned foreign visitors that if they were coming to see the true expression of American architecture, they should expect to find it not at the Fair, but in or near the larger cities. He did not seem to be in agreement with Burnham's claim that the Fair should not be forgotten and should become a model for reforming urban

American. Van Brunt believed that the future relevance of enterprise should not be misunderstood and went on to suggest that the White City should be received chiefly as an educational exercise. No one at the time, not even Burnham, predicted the effect that the Fair would ultimately have on American architectural taste, and most, Adler, for example, thought such "an abuse of the Classic" would only hasten its end. Peter Bonnett Wight, in 1893, wrote a series of articles praising the Columbian Exposition which were published in *The American Architect and Building News* for its numbers from October 7 to December 30. Wight wrote:

> The question has been repeatedly asked that granting the superior excellence of the World's Fair architecture, what will be its influence upon the future of architecture in America? It will undoubtedly have an influence on the grouping of buildings in which its greatest success has been attained, wherever circumstances are such that this is possible. It will evidently result in a greater popular appreciation of the latent ability of the architectural profession in this country. Notwithstanding the great sums that have apparently been lavished on the adornment of Jackson Park—but in fact used very sparingly to produce such grand effect—it must be kept in mind that it is only the cheapness of the material used in finishing merely representative buildings that has enabled the architects to give full vent to the exuberance of their designing powers. With these facilities they have only had the opportunity to show what they could do with permanent materials. This has been the great opportunity which never before existed, to bring the possibilities of architectural art within the view of great masses of people. In this, then, has architecture as an art been greatly benefitted. It is not likely that these buildings will ever be reproduced or copied except by second-rate plagiarists, who will only succeed in caricaturing individual parts of them. There will never be a Grand Court again or any opportunity for one.[2]

In 1897, R.C. McLean recalled how the work of Richardson and Root began to be overshadowed, in the East, by the influence of what he called the "modern French school." In the January issue of that year, he writes in *The Inland Architect* of which he was editor:

> By the time that the World's Columbian Exposition was projected and formulated this influence became most potent, and it is safe to say that in the West it dates from the sudden and unfortunate death of John W. Root, in January 1891. The adoption of a classic treatment for the main buildings of the Exposition gave a stamp of approval from high authority... and the influence exerted by the wonderful object lesson afforded by the aggregation of classic architecture around the Court of Honor, as it was called, has been felt throughout the country ever since.[3]

Burnham, certainly, had no regret. In 1893, he said that if Root had lived, the architecture of the Fair would have been impressed with something of Root's great individuality, but it would not have been better. Burnham thought he was doing very well without his partner.

Montgomery Schuyler, in his "Last Words About the World's Fair," published in the January-March 1894 issues of *The Architectural Record,* also expressed his anticipation of the influence exerted by the Fair:

152 Conclusion

> Doubtless the influence of the most admired group of buildings ever erected in this country, the public buildings at Washington not excepted, must be great. What it is likely to be has been expressed by Mr. Burnham, the Director of Works at the Columbian Exposition, in some remarks, published in a Chicago newspaper, which crystallize into a lucid and specific form a general hazy expectation, and which may well serve us for a text.[4]

Then Schuyler went on to quote Burnham as saying:

> The influence of the exposition on architecture will be to inspire a reversion toward the pure ideal of the ancients. We have been in an inventive period, and have had rather contempt for the classics. Men evolved new ideas and imagined they could start a new school without much reference to the past. But action and reaction are equal, and the exterior and obvious result will be that men will strive to do classic architecture. In this effort there will be many failures. It requires long and fine training to design on classic lines. The simpler the expression of true art the more difficult it is to obtain.[5]

Although Schuyler understood the great depth of the influence of the Fair, he, like other critics, did not expect it to last. He continues:

> The intellectual reflex of the Exposition will be shown in a demand for better architecture, and designers will be obliged to abandon their incoherent originalities and study the ancient masters of building. There is shown so much of fine architecture here that people have seen and appreciated this. It will be unavailing hereafter to say that great classic forms are undesirable. The people have the vision before them here, and words cannot efface it. Doubtless the architecture of the Exposition will inspire a great many classic buildings, which will be better or worse done according to the training of the designers, but it is not likely that any of these will even dimly recall, and quite impossible that they should equal the architectural triumph of the Fair. The influence of the Exposition, so far as it leads to direct imitation, seems to us an unhopeful rather than a hopeful sign, not a promise so much as a threat.[6]

In his "Last Words About the World's Fair" as a whole, however, Schuyler achieved one of his critical masterpieces—a perceptive, far-sighted, balanced, and decisive critique that was the best of all essays written about the Exposition at the time. He praised the classicistic architecture of the Court of Honor in three respects. It achieved unity, magnitude, and illusion, all of which were desirable qualities for a fair. Of the first two respects, Schuyler writes:

> In the first place the success is first of all a success of unity, a triumph of ENSEMBLE. The whole is better than any of its parts and greater than all its parts, and its effect is one and indivisible. We are speaking now of the Court of Honor, which alone it is proposed to preserve, and which forms an architectural whole... Next after unity, as a source and explanation of the unique impression made by the World's Fair buildings, comes magnitude. It may even be questioned whether it should not come first in an endeavor to account for the impression. If it be put to second, it is only because unity, from an artistic point of view, is an achievement, while magnitude from that point of view, is merely an advantage. The buildings are impressive by their size, and this impressiveness is enhanced by their number.[7]

Conclusion 153

Finally, with respect to the quality of illusion, Schuyler made his most telling point about the Fair that it should be frankly enjoyed for what it was. One should value the Fair for itself, as a temporary festive stage set appropriate to its occasion. To laud it as a model for serious architecture or city planning, on the other hand, would be disastrous, since modern architecture and cities must not build illusions or imitations but realities. This is expressed so convincingly by Schuyler as follows;

> There is still another cause for the success of the World's Fair buildings, a cause that contributes more to the effect of them, perhaps, than both causes we have already set down put together. It is this which at once most completely justifies the architects of the Exposition in the course they have developed, and it goes furthest to render the results of that course ineligible for reproduction or for imitation in the solution of the more ordinary problems of the American architect. The success of the architecture at the World's Fair is not only a success of unity, and a success of magnitude. It is also and very eminently a success of illusion... As Mr. Burnham well described it, it is a "vision" of beauty that he and his co-workers have presented to us, and the description implies, what our recollections confirm, that it is an illusion that has been provided for our delight. It was the task of architects to provide the stage-setting for an unexampled spectacle. They have realized in plaster that gives us the illusion of monumental masonry a partner's dream of Roman architecture... The White City is the most integral, the most extensive, the most illusive piece of scenic architecture that has ever been seen. This is praise enough for its builders, without demanding for them the further praise of having made a useful and important contribution to the development of the architecture and of the present, to the preparation of the architecture of the future. This is a praise that is not merely irrelevant to the praise they have won, but incompatible with it. It is essential to the illusion of a fairy city that it should not be an American city of the nineteenth century... Those of us who believe that architecture is the correlation of structure and function, that if it is to be real and living and progressive, its forms must be the results of material and construction, sometimes find ourselves reproached with admiration for these palaces in which this belief is so conspicuously ignored and set at naught.[8]

Most improtant of all, Schuyler concludes his best critical work with the following "last words about the Fair":

> It was a common remark among visitors who saw the Fair for the first time that nothing they had read or seen pictured had given them an idea of it, or prepared them for what they saw. The impression thus expressed is the impression we have been trying to analyze, of which the sources seem to be unity, magnitude and illusion, and the greatest of these is illusion. To reproduce or to imitate the buildings deprived of these irreproducible and inimitable advantages, would be an impossible task, and if it were possible it would not be desirable. For the art of architecture is not to produce illusions or imitations, but REALITIES, ORGANISMS LIKE THOSE OF NATURE. It is in the "naked and open daylight" that our architects must work, and they can only be diverted from their tasks of production by reproduction. It is not theirs to realize the dreams of painters, but to do such work as future painters may delight to dream of and to draw. If they work for their purposes as well as the classic builders wrought for theirs, then they, in their turn, have become remote and mythical and classic, their work may become the material of an illusion, "such stuff as dreams are

made of." But its very fitness for this purpose will depend upon its remoteness from current needs and current ideas, upon its irrelevancy to what will then be contemporary life.[9]

This essay was written in 1894. Indeed, it is astonishing how few architects at the time and in the decades that followed realized the importance of the message that the critic was trying to impart to them. The message representing the core of architectural design: that the art of architecture was not to produce illusions, but realities, organisms like those of nature. It is also astonishing how few architects realized that their task was to "create", not to "imitate" and that they had to work in "broad day light," not in "dreams or illusions." By the end of the first decade of the twentieth century, Peter Wight who did not believe that the influence of the Fair would last, seemed to change his mind as the white cloud of classicism hung lower over the skyline of Chicago. In his article, "Addition to Chicago Skyline: A Few Recent Skyscrapers," published in the July 1910 issue of *The Architectural Record,* Wight expressed his puzzlement:

> The skyscrapers illustrated herewith are the latest "creations" of Chicago architects, some of them just approaching completion, and all erected within the last year. They are not selected with any motive of appreciation, but as historical records of the present-day condition of the art. They show plainly that there has been little or no progress in the development of design applied to commercial high buildings, or buildings for any purpose in the design of which the architect has had occasion to grapple with this serious problem, which is always before us. They seem to suggest that the lessons that have been learned in the Schiller, the Marquette, [and] the Carson, Pirie, Scott stores are forgotten. As a whole, they are mainly "imitations" of the work of Eastern architects.[10]

Wight, by 1910, was too late to recognize this influence of the architects of the East, for by the turn of the century the ideas and principles of the Ecole des Beaux Arts already prevailed throughout the country. The representatives of the Beaux-Arts ideas in America were organized into a society which numbered among its members architects of great ability and prominence in their profession. Several of the leading colleges and universities, also, had Beaux-Arts graduates in charge of their architectural departments, and in the Parisian school itself was then more than ever before the Mecca of American youths as was proved by the fact that there were more than twice as many students from the United States studying classic architecture at the Ecole des Beaux Arts as from any other country except France itself. Wrote Claude Bragdon in the *Architectural Record* in 1904:

> From facts such as these, even more than from the more obvious evidence afforded by those chic and brilliant facades, redolent of the Parisian boulevards, which have lately reared themselves along New York avenues and streets we must conclude that the Beaux-Arts movement is not a purely ephemeral manifestation, since it incarnates not alone in stone and wood and iron, but in the minds of young men destined to create the architecture of the future.[11]

Conclusion   155

In this same article, "Made in France Architecture," published in *The Architectural Record* eleven years after the closing of the Chicago World's Fair, Bragdon made strong comments on the prevailing trend of architecture in America at the time:

> Nowhere in the world are building operations undertaken on so vast a scale as here in America, and nowhere is there so much money spent, and so much popular interest manifested in building. There are sufficient numbers of men of distinguished talent in the profession to render our architecture, under these circumstances, illustrious in the history of the world. False ideals, lack of initiative, and misplaced conservatism, however, delay this consummation... The only American architect of eminence who by precept and example stands for originality—not eccentricity, but invention wedded to reason—is a prophet not without honor save in his own country if we except the small circle of his disciples and admirers. His personality so positive and a talent so unique that I may be pardoned for mentioning him by name. I refer to Mr. Louis Sullivan of Chicago. He stands so uncompromisingly for the democratic, as opposed to the aristocratic idea, for naturalism as opposed to scholasticism, for invention as opposed to imitation, that in his work and in his propaganda he may be said to epitomize and embody the anti-Beaux-Arts spirit, as that spirit comes to be understood from its interpreters in this country.[12]

Bragdon went on to say in his article that at the time there was an apparently irreconcilable antagonism between men of the same country, the same profession, the same training. There was a segregation of forces into two opposite camps, the one represented by what he called the "New York group" in which the Beaux-Arts spirit was dominant, and the other by the "Chicago group," inspired by Sullivan. Bragdon writes:

> Although these two factions are at odds just now, it is to be hoped, and not impossible to be imagined that the coming generation of architects may achieve a larger synthesis in which the two divergent ideals may be reconciled to their mutual enrichment; the devotees of sheer originality learning from the schoolmen that temperance and restraint and refined feeling for beauty which the study of classic architecture indicates and that masterly way of handling a given problem which the solution of many imaginary projects teaches; and the schoolmen being inspired in turn to a more constant effort at creation and invention.[13]

What Bragdon did not appreciate at the time was the fact that it would take more than one generation before his hope was realized.

Meanwhile, as the triumph of the Beaux Arts, scaled by the spectacle of the World's Columbian Exposition, inaugurated an architectural reign in this country, Montgomery Schuyler was duty-bound as a journalistic critic to review some of the Beaux-Arts inspired buildings even though he was fundamentally unsympathetic with them. He made the best of what was presented, with occasional regrets that the best had so little relevance to what he regarded as the good. After the turn of the century, he became increasingly retrospective, writing many pieces on the men, the works, and the ideals of the seventies, eighties, and early nineties, when American architecture had held so much promise for him. What he really felt about the Beaux Arts appeared, covertly and devastatingly, as an anonymous spoof in 1897. In the guise of a letter to the editor, signed "A Classic" published in the September issue of that year of *The Architectural Record* under the title of "A Long-Felt Want," from behind the screen of anonymity Schuyler addressed the profession:

> This is a time of eager competition, and in order that an architect may live it is absolutely necessary that he should spend most of his time in looking out for profitable work. If you will pardon the vulgar expression, he must "hustle for a living." If he stays in his office, in the old-fashioned way, and puts in his time in supervising the work of his draughtsmen, he is sure to fall behind. More than that, if he has any important work on hand, his time is taken up on conversation and correspondence with a host of contractors and material men. If it is a commercial building he is engaged on, he is liable to an almost daily hounding by his client to quicken the rate at which the work is going forward. His professional reputation is at stake in getting the building done at the earliest possible moment, and he has a natural and laudable ambition to beat the record for speed in buildings of the same class and size. For professional purposes every hour that he spends over a drawing-board is lost to him. To a busy architect nothing can be more ridiculous than the clamor of ignorant laymen for an "original style of architecture," as if he had nothing else to think about than design ... If he devoted his time to design he would have nothing to design; and what good would his designs do to anybody?[14]

The satire marked a turning point in Schuyler's criticism. In effect it represented his final gesture of defiance at the triumphant Beaux-Arts aesthetic. He had already bowed to its inevitability. Thereafter, although he sniped at its ideals wherever he could, never again did he attack it substantially.

Finally, after the first decade of the twentieth century concluded and after Peter Wight wrote his "Additions to Chicago Skyline," describing the architectural atmosphere of Chicago, the Beaux-Arts movement, or the "Genteel Reaction" as Lewis Mumford phrased it, proceeded at an uncontrollable pace. The latter offers us, in his *Root of Contemporary American Architecture* the vivid description of the architectural scene in this country at the time:

> After 1910, the Genteel Reaction prevailed unchallenged, for more than a decade, piling up ill-fitting masks of reminiscent beauty that covered the structural reality these architects dared not reveal, and disclosing an enervating emptiness of spirit. Its products ranged from the Roman Baths that became the Pennsylvania Railroad Station in New York to the elongated Guild Hall tower, laced with gold, that was the Woolworth Building. Whether the masks were classic or Gothic made little difference, though occasionally the organic structure itself would be solidly conceived, like the Grand Central Terminal in New York, that it almost nullified, by its own inherent power, the triviality of the architectural detail. With Frank Lloyd Wright preoccupied in Japan with the Imperial Hotel from 1914 onward, with Sullivan passing into joblessness and destitution and some of their weaker breathren gradually fading from originality and conviction into eclecticism and cynicism, American architecture faltered in its development.[15]

Mumford's "classic masks" certainly made some difference. They had brought the Chicago School of architecture to the conclusion of the slow process of its death. Of the four architects chosen to represent the School in this study, only two—Burnham and Sullivan—lived long enough to witness all of these happenings. The years after the turn of the century saw Burnham operating at the head of one of the largest and most prosperous architectural firms in the country. Frequently involved in simultaneous projects on the East and West coasts, Burnham had a Pullman car converted into a traveling drafting office, from which he directed his wide operations. At the time of his death in 1912, Burnham employed a staff of more than one-hundred and fifty in his Chicago office alone, and very possibly an equal number on projects elsewhere in this country and abroad. In 1912 there were two hundred million dollars worth of unfilled contracts in the D.H. Burnham and Company office, and had he lived, it can be assumed that the firm would have grown still larger. In his *Autobiography of an Idea,* Sullivan has the following to say about his one true friend of the early architectural days in Chicago:

> Daniel Burnham was obsessed by the feudal idea of power. Louis Sullivan was obsessed by the beneficient idea of democratic power. Daniel chose the easier way, Louis the harder.[16]

We all know too well what happened to the one who chose the hard way after 1900. Sullivan had one last great building left to him—the Carson, Pirie, Scott Store (1899-1904). A series of smaller works, particularly the country banks throughout the Midwest, were to bring his active architectural practice to a close. Louis Sullivan remains an enigmatic figure today; the story of his life, *The Autobiography of an Idea,* does not cover the period beyond 1893. Toward the end of his career, when his alcoholism became painfully obvious to his friends, Sullivan's relationship with the Chicago School came to be of material importance to him. Often he found himself without funds, he would go to his old friends to seek help. Sometimes, he ate at the Cliff Dwellers Club[16] at the expense of old friends. It was at the Cliff Dwellers Club that Sullivan wrote his *Autobiography of an Idea* which was published in 1924—the year of his death. In that same year, Frank Lloyd Wright wrote an article entitled "Louis Sullivan—His Work" published in the July issue of *The Architectural Record* as a tribute to his "Master." In it, Wright declared:

> Louis Sullivan's great value as an Artist-Architect—alive or dead—lies in his firm grasp of principle. He knew the truths of Architecture as I believe no one before him knew them. And profoundly he realized them. This illumination of his was the more remarkable a vision when all around him cultural mists hung low to obscure or blight every dawning hope of a finer beauty in the matter of this world. As "the name of God has fenced about all crime with holiness" so in the name of Architecture the "classic" perpetually invents skillful lies to hide

> ignorance or impotence and belie creation. But the Master's was true creative activity—not deceived nor deceiving. He was a radical and so one knew, always, where to find him. His sense and thought and spirit were deep-rooted in that high quality of old and new which made them one and thereby he was apprised of the falsity of outward shows that duped his fellows, and that dupe them still. The name, attributes and passions of earth's creatures change, but—that creation changes never; his same and passionate vision leaves testimony here on earth in fragments of his dreams—his work.[17]

Creation may never change as Wright claims in his essay, but most anything else on earth changes in accordance with the passing of time. In looking back to the period around the turn of the century, the demise of the so-called "commercial style" in Chicago coincided with a great divide in American cultural history in general, and with the subtle, but decisive changes of a social and cultural milieu in Chicago after 1890 in particular. The shifts in this milieu encouraged the borrowed finery of the Columbian Exposition for more mundane purposes. Even among those who were as partial to the commercial style as the editors of *Industrial Chicago* or most of the progressive and liberal critics of the time, there remained fatal equivocations about that style: The typical masonry block was too severe; the skeleton frame too spidery. Such equivocation could not withstand the certainties of a High Style, freighted with a Great Tradition, and sponsored by a social and cultural milieu which grew to embrace it. As cultural shifts in Chicago at the turn of the century reflected shifts that were national in scope, Wright's attributing the slow death of the Chicago commercial architecture to the "classic" seems an inversion of causality.

The first ingredient of these social and cultural shifts in Chicago must have been a change in the clientele for architecture, and certainly in its attitudes. As noted at various points throughout this study, the influence exerted by wealthy and powerful clients in Chicago at the time was far too important to be ignored in the forming of the design concepts and philosophy of the Chicago School. Also it must be noted here that, ironically enough, these very same clients were to play a very important role in the fall of the "School" they helped to establish as William Jordy explains:

> The severe style proclaims the self-made capitalists who had founded the big corporations and often stamped them with their personalities, Pullman, Armour, Swift, McCormick, and Field characterize the type, to mention the best-known Chicago names without regard to their actual significance as architectural patrons. The new academic palatial norm for business buildings depended on softer esthetic criteria, less aggressive, more urbane. It provided an ideal setting for the transition from the tycoon of entrepreneurial capitalism to the "organization man" of the emergent finance capitalism. To be sure, the "organization man" at the turn of the century was not quite the equivalent of his counterpart in the middle of the twentieth century. The pioneer "organization man" was a more arrogant breed. He was more overt in the parade of his new-found cultivation, in the columned halls and tapestried offices which echoed the exclusive urban clubs rising in such numbers at the same time, and designed by many of the same architects responsible for the skyscrapers.[18]

Secondly, the new cultivation depended largely on the new cultural establishment. In Chicago, as early as 1865, the Historical Society, the Academy of Science, an art institute and school, and a number of large private libraries had already been established. However, it was not until the period of 1880-1900 that these cultural institutions of Chicago were conspicuously enlarged and the new ones founded. The two decades saw the rise of the foremost works of public building that constituted the initial group of the city's celebrated institutions devoted to the aesthetic and intellectual life. The buildings that house them still stand today. They are monumental structures that reveal at a high level of design the shifting tides of architectural taste near the turn of the century. The need for a big theater to house opera performances, spectacles, public entertainments, and ceremonies led to the construction of the most famous of all these cultural institutions, Adler and Sullivan's Auditorium Building, built in 1887-89 at Michigan Avenue and Congress Street. The Art Institute, founded in 1879, constructed its own museum in 1891-93 on Michigan Avenue at the foot of Adams Street, the Renaissance design of its main block being the work of the Boston architects, Shepley, Rutan and Coolidge. The same Eastern architects also designed the Public Library in the same Renaissance mode in 1896-97. It is located on Michigan Avenue between Randolph and Washington Streets. The establishment of the Chicago Symphony Orchestra in 1891 eventually required an auditorium adequate to the acoustical and spatial demands of the audience. Therefore, the present Orchestra Hall, designed by D.H. Burnham and Company, was completed in 1905 when the literary and artistic Cliff Dwellers Club moved to a penthouse on the roof. It was there that Sullivan wrote many of his late essays on architecture and his *Autobiography of an Idea.* Outside the city's core the most impressive individual work of public building is the Walter L. Newberry Library, a Romanesque masterpiece by Henry Ives Cobb, constructed in 1891-92. So were the John Crerar Library and the Field Museum of Natural History; although they obtained more than makeshift quarters only after the turn of the century, in 1912 and 1920 respectively. The Crerar Library subsequently moved to the campus of The Illinois Institute of Technology. Of all the educational and cultural institutions that were established in Chicago during the marvelously prolific period that centered around the decade of the nineties, none acquired the international influence and prestige of the University of Chicago. With the financial contribution from John D. Rockefeller and the land near the site of the Columbian Exposition given by Marshall Field, the University was established and its construction began in the early 1890s under the design and direction of the talented Henry Ives Cobb. The rate of expansion of the physical plant was probably unmatched in the history of American university: by the end of the century eighteen buildings had been completed; by 1910 another fourteen were added; before the depression year of 1930, thirty-five more were opened for a total of sixty-seven buildings. Cobb designed the

160   Conclusion

first seventeen buildings, and Shepley, Rutan and Coolidge were responsible for the next eight. The best contribution to the university group came from Eero Saarinen, who made distinguished additions to the expansion of the campus after World War II. From all of this educational and cultural establishment in Chicago, and the genteel etiquette of cultivation which it fostered, stemmed other consequences felt in architecture, directly, beneficially or otherwise. Suggests Jordy:

> These cultural institutions encouraged demands for civic embellishment to transform the money-making hive, physically through their need for quarters, propagandistically through their teaching. For this urban monumentality the White City conjured a vision of a marble America from the urban styles of Europe, which increased travel and the coming of the photograph made more available—and more "correct." In its Roman and baroque trappings, moreover, the imperial flavor of the White City accorded with the imperial flavor of American culture at the end of the century. It was not merely, or even principally, the imperialism of foreign affairs which the symbolism of the Exposition made concrete, but the hegemony of the metropolis over the farm.[19]

Finally, the new cosmopolitanism affected the architectural profession itself. The final decades of the nineteenth century witnessed the proliferation of professional organizations in all areas of learned and disciplined endeavor. With these organizations came the concomitants of schools, certificates, and standards together with the professional community's awareness of its special status as an educated and trained elite. Although the American Institute of Architects was founded in 1857 and the Massachusetts Institute of Technology added the first department of architecture in this country to its program in 1868 while other major universities rapidly followed suit. However, not until the eighties and nineties did the A.I.A. and the schools become a dominant influence in architectural practice. Chicago itself was not to feel this influence until after 1890. Jordy continues:

> With professional ideals came an end to catch-as-catch-can training. Gone was the illiteracy of apprentices trained by half-trained practitioners, to be replaced by the informed mediocrity of the average professional. Substantially eroded was the spirit of brash experimentation which could fire on an entire group like that responsible for the plain Chicago buildings simply because it remained unfettered from too great a dependence on precedence, and innocent of the bogey of "correctness."[20]

The impact of cultural developments on Chicago cannot be overlooked in analyzing the demise of its commercial style of architecture. Therefore, it is rather too pat entirely to blame the demise on the Columbian Exposition of 1893 and the subsequent popularity of the Beaux-Arts type of classical mode as did most progressive critics at the turn of the century and, indeed, those of the 1930s and 1940s who reviewed the memories and legends of the Chicago School architects. Only in recent years with the insights of studies and analyses

Conclusion   161

of the School and circumstances surrounding its fate have the attitudes of the present-day critics, historians and scholars changed. William H. Jordy in his *American Buildings and Their Architects: Progressive and Academic Ideals at the Turn of the Twentieth Century* (New York, 1972) offers the best example:

If the vitality of the commercial style depended on its frank acceptance of business requirements, its fate was also linked to this narrow materialism. The commercial style seemed an esthetic dependent on necessity, not a virtue in itself. The negative esthetic of circumstance collapsed before a positive esthetic which promised equivalent efficiency plus the Higher Life of Art. If, as *Industrial Chicago* put it, the "genial sway of associated thought" had banished the excuses of the old palatial style and produced the "commercial style", it might be claimed that the Beaux-Arts-inspired Court of Honor at the Columbian Exposition banished the starkness of the commercial style with a "sway of thought" even more "genial" and more deliberately "associated." Incapable of transcending the materialism which had called it forth, the commercial style collapsed before an esthetic which promised an easy path toward what was believed to be a broader, richer, and more humane architectural philosophy with no sacrifice of the convenience that had motivated earlier design. Convenience AND art: why settle for one where both were available?[21]

But the materialistic side of Chicago was not its only authentic aspect. Chicagoans knew better. So did the occasional visitors who ventured out of the Loop, for the commercial architecture in this central business district was only part, even if a very large part, of the larger picture of the city that had vastly expanded itself during its golden years of the 1880s and 1890s. Concerning the great expansion of the city, the New York journalist Julian Ralph, who earlier vividly described the Chicago commercial buildings in his *Our Great West* (New York, 1893) observes:

One of the foremost business men in the city asserts that he can perceive no reason why the entire business heart of the town—that square half-mile of which I have spoken—should not soon be all built up of cloud-capped towers. There will be a need for them, he says, and the money to defray the cost of them will accompany the demand. The only trouble he foresees will be in the solution of the problem what to do with the people who will then crowd the streets as never streets were clogged before. This prophecy relates to a little block in the city, but the city itself contains 181-1/2 square miles. It has been said of the many annexations by which her present size was attained that Chicago reached out and took herself farms, prairie land, and villages, and that of such material the great city now in part consists. This is true. In suburban trips, such as those I took to Fort Sheridan and Fernwood, for instance, I passed great cabbage farms, groves, houseless but plotted tracts, and long reaches of the former prairie. Even yet Hyde Park is a separated settlement, and a dozen or more villages stand out as distinctly by themselves as ever they did. If it were true, as her rivals insist, that Chicago added all this tract merely to get a high rank in the census reports of population, the folly of the action would be either ludicrous or pitiful, according to the stand-point from which it was viewed. But the true reason for her enormous extension of municipal jurisdiction is quite as peculiar. The enlargement was urged and accomplished in order to anticipate the growth and needs of the city. It was a consequence of extraordinary foresight, which recognized the necessity for a uniform system of boulevards, parks, drainage, and water provision when the city should reach limits that it was even then seen must soon bound a compact aggregation of stores, offices, factories, and dwellings. To us of the East this is surprising. It might seem incredible were there not many other evidences of the same spirit and sagacity not only in Chicago, but in the other cities of the West, especially of the Northwest. What Minneapolis, St. Paul, and Duluth are doing towards a future park system reveals the same enterprise and habit of looking far ahead. And Chicago, in her park system, makes evident her intentions. In all these cities and in a hundred ways the observant traveller notes the same forehandedness, and prepares himself to understand the temper in which the greatest of the Western capitals leaned forth and absorbed the prairie. Chicago expects to become the largest city in America—a city which, in fifty years, shall be larger than the consolidated cities that may form New York of that time.[22]

At the time Julian Ralph expressed his observation on the expansion of Chicago and his admiration of its park system, the city boasted one of the most substantial systems of parks and parkways in the United States. The first step toward that direction was the city's acquisition in 1864 of the North Side shoreland and an adjoining cemetery. These were partially cleared, drained, landscaped, and designated Lake Park. This first lakefront park, extending for a mile from North Avenue to Fullerton Avenue, was renamed Lincoln Park after the assassination of President Abraham Lincoln in April, 1865. It was a modest beginning, but four years later, with the establishment of the park district system of Chicago, the city, by itself and in cooperation with its southern neighbor Hyde Park, initiated what proved for a time to be the foremost program of park and boulevard development in the country. In the cooperative program with Hyde Park, Frederick Law Olmsted was engaged as the chief landscape designer. The ambitious undertaking rapidly achieved results, so that by 1880 Chicago was second only to Philadelphia in the ratio of park area to population. These first parks, however, were mainly landscaped areas lacking recreational facilities for either adults or children. To remedy this deficiency the city council created the Special Park Commission in 1889, appointed Dwight H. Perkins, Chicago's most energetic and effective conservationist, as commissioner, and specified that the body was to develop and act upon a systematic plan for meeting the city's space and recreational needs, with the emphasis on creating play grounds for children, beaches, pools, public baths and parkways. With the zealous and idealistic Perkins in a key administrative position, and with the creative talents of Frederick Law Olmsted, Jens Jensen, and Horace Cleveland available for landscape design, the qualitative results of all these efforts proved considerable. By 1900 the large parks included not only the usual wooded areas, shrubs, meadows, picnic grounds, walks and drives, but a full complement of lagoons for boating, flower gardens, baseball diamonds, golf links, tennis courts, and various indoor recreational facilities as well. The West Park District was the second of the park system to be established. The general plan for the location and size of the big parks in the system was completed shortly after the fire of 1871, and the formal design of the specific parks such as Douglas, Garfield and Humboldt was the work of William Le Baron Jenney, who probably undertook the task shortly after his return from the University of Michigan in 1876. It was not until Jens Jensen was appointed to the dual position of superintendant and chief landscape architect of the entire West Park District in 1905 that the dreams of Chicagoans in this district to have parks of the highest level of the landscape art were fulfilled. Jensen, originally from Denmark, was deeply impressed by the floral beauties of the prairie, which became the basis of his highly personal romantic-naturalistic art. Humboldt was the first park to exhibit the fruit of Jensen's talent, and was succeeded in the fourteen years following his appointment by three more masterpieces, Douglas, Garfield, and Columbus, of which the last is one of Jensen's wholly new creations. The South Park District, established in 1869 like Lincoln Park and West Park, contains the two best-known parks in the Chicago system, Grant and Jackson, the former carefully preserved as the city's showpiece. Jackson was part of the extensive park and boulevard system planned and built cooperatively by Chicago and Hyde Park, with the landscape and boulevard design under the charge of Frederick Law Olmsted and Horace Cleveland. The planning of the system began in 1869, the same year the indefatigable Olmsted laid out the plan for the suburban community of Riverside, and construction on various parts of the program was initiated two years later. The marshy site of Jackson Park involved difficult problems of drainage, impoundment, and dredging of the lagoons, so that although the first operations were undertaken in 1874, the area was little improved by the time of the Columbian Exposition in 1893. The park was not finally completed until about 1905, when this masterpiece of Olmsted's romantic style began to emerge into something like the mature beauty of its lagoons, woodlands, meadows, and islands. Grant Park, symmetrically balanced in its stiff axial formality, is the classical antithesis to the romantic Jackson, but for the first thirty years of its history it was little more than bare fill and grass. The importance of Grant Park to the civic design of Chicago was first fully appreciated by Daniel Burnham, who regarded it as the primary focus of any plan for the urban core as early as 1896. The landscaping came after 1910, much of it dating from the New Deal's public works program of the 1930s.

Outside the Loop, it was not only the parks and parkways of the city, but also the domestic Chicago that impressed visitors such as the New Yorker Julian Ralph who found his way to the city's residential districts, particularly the Prairie Avenue area which then was the most fashionable residential street on Chicago's South Side. Ralph's picture is revealing for its comparisons with the eastern metropoli with which he was familiar. In his *Our Great West*, he writes:

> Once out of the thicket of the business and semibusiness district, the dwellings of the people reach mile upon mile along pleasant boulevards and avenues, or facing noble parks and

parkways, or in a succession of villages green and gay with foliage and flowers. They are not cliff dwellings like [New York] flats and tenements; there are no brownstone canyons like our up-town streets; there are only occasional hesitating hints there of those Philadelphia and Baltimore mills that grind out dwellings all alike, as nature makes peace and man makes pins. There are more miles of detached villas in Chicago than a stranger can easily account for. As they are not only found on Prairie Avenue and the boulevards[23] but in the populous wards and semi-suburbs, where the middle folk are congregated, it is evident that the prosperous moiety of the population enjoys living better than the same function in the Atlantic cities. Land in New York has been too costly to permit these villa-like dwellings, but that does not alter the fact that existence in a home hemmed in by other houses is at best but a crippled living... A sneering critic, who wounded Chicago deeply, intimated that theirs must be a primitive society where the rich sit on their door-steps of an evening. That really is the habit there, and in the finer districts of all the Western cities. To enjoy themselves the more completely, the people bring out the rugs and carpets, always of gay colors, and fling them on the steps—or stoops, as we Dutch legatees should say—that the ladies' dresses may not be soiled... For my part, I think it argues well for any society that indulges in the trick, and proves existence in such a city to be more human and hearty and far less artificial than where there is too much false pride to permit it.[24]

Therefore, as Jordy categorizes it in his *American Buildings and Their Architects*, the complete picture of Chicago at the turn of the century consisted of four images: The commercial buildings of the Loop; the academic Court of Honor at the Columbian Exposition; the vast park and parkway system; and the domestic felicity of the residential districts. Writes Jordy:

No other metropolis at the turn of the century possessed this contrast in urban image on the scale and with the prominence that it had in Chicago. Nor did any city at the time surpass the contribution made in Chicago in all four of these aspects of design and planning. So much was this the case that had the city been fully conscious of the potential in its achievement, and had the disparate elements of its achievement been coordinated to maximum effect, then it is no exaggeration to maintain that a metropolitan ideal could have resulted from this integration of effort different in kind from those that had existed before the "Chicago School"; so the group endeavor in the Loop during the eighties and nineties has been christened. But the relatively unaffected functional approach to commercial buildings, based partly on a consistent realism with respect to the economics of the commercial situation, partly on a committed but inconsistent response to a watershed situation in technology, might perhaps better be specified as the "commercial style." (Even better, it might be considered a "school" rather than a "style," if "school" implies group activity conditioned by a common point of view but applied with some differences of purpose and uncertainty of result.) Then "Chicago School" can encompass those forces, attitudes, and personalities accounting for the totality of the Chicago achievement in architecture and planning around 1900, for its diversity, for those connections that localized the accomplishment for a few decades, and for those tensions that frustrated it. The "commercial style" is only part, even if a very large part, of the larger story.[25]

Julian Ralph's *Our Great West* appeared in 1893, the year of the Columbian Exposition; the year, too, that the architectural principles and concept of the Chicago School began to be overshadowed by the powerful Beaux-Arts-inspired classicism which was rapidly to accelerate influence upon

American architecture around the turn of the century. By that time the final masterpiece of the Chicago School—Sullivan's Carson, Pirie and Scott Store—was completed. It seemed anti-climactic to pursue the course of the School after that since, by then, it has spent its force and could no longer remain untouched by the general shift of taste in architecture which would dominate the first thirty years of the twentieth century. And yet a few isolated buildings serve to maintain a precarious continuity. Sullivan himself, alone and neglected, struggled to uphold his convictions in the little banks that appear here and there in the prairie towns. His great disciple, Frank Lloyd Wright, kept his master's principles alive in domestic architecture. The Carl Schurz High School (1910), designed by Dwight Perkins, represents a kind of transition from Sullivan to Wright; and it provides an illustration of those principles in the architecture of public buildings. The Carson, Pirie and Scott Annex (1917), designed by Hubert and Daniel Burnham, Jr., is a late example of which Sullivan presented in the main store at State and Madison Streets. It reveals the simple, uniform pattern of rectangular cells and wide-windowed horizontality of the older buildings. The sham devices for securing an effect of massiveness at the base and corners have completely disappeared. The compromises are gone, and we realized that a new architecture has been developed. The fact is apparent again in the enormous warehouses designed for Montgomery Ward and Company by Richard E. Schmidt, and erected over a period of years beginning with 1908. These warehouses are unique in the work of the Chicago School because they represent the first use of reinforced concrete for the entire structure. They are gigantic buildings, overwhelming in their vast simplicity and in the emphatic horizontality which is perfectly logical in modern large-scale construction—a building consists essentially of a tier of parallel, horizontal planes on which the disposition of space is determined by plan, and not by elevation. The Montgomery Ward warehouses are a powerful expression of this logic, which is a guiding principle of the work of the contemporary Internationalists. As we all know by now the Chicago School has taken its place in a world movement of which it played the role of pioneer.

In 1939, one of Sullivan's most faithful and long-lived disciples—George Grant Elmslie—read a paper entitled "The Chicago School, Its Inheritance and Bequest"[26] before a meeting of the Illinois Society of Architects:

> Any review of other days, as far back as the late 1880s is naturally a bit empurpled by the mists of time and the manifold changes in human values in our later day. As to the background of our inheritance, which is an open book to all who seek or desire to know, the following may be said, if we are, in a measure, to understand and evaluate the situation as it appeared in that early day. It may, perhaps, deflate our vanity a bit, which in some cases is needed... It was the writer's privilege and honor to be employed by Adler and Sullivan, and later to be associated with Sullivan when that memorable partnership was dissolved, and so has a fair knowledge and understanding of events in the progress of which is called the Chicago School of Architecture. This is as good a name as any, giving it, for the time a local habitation as well as a name... It has been said, of late, that there were only a few grey heads

now alive to carry on the faith, and that nothing by them will live, but will follow shortly to the sharp guillotine of time and pass away forever. This is not true, and is somewhat of an oblique comment clothed in a curious sense of humor; it suggests a protective coloring assumed to cover a manifest failure of the writer to pursue the fair goddess of truth and its involved beauty. Now we are confronted with the Beaux-artisans, and their kind, whose sole idea and ideal is, in some shape or manner, to adapt that obsolete and extensive formulary to the modern way. It cannot be done. The wise thing for them to do is to leave our running brook alone and not, like the cuttlefish, murk its clear and clean waters. The Chicago School within the last few years has many meritorious buildings to show for men's faith and hope, buildings of a public and private nature that will last for many generations to come. Let us hope for the future and believe, even as did the aged Ulysses in Tennyson's poem,

> Push off, and sitting well in order smite
> The sounding furrows; for my purpose holds
> To sail beyond the sunset, and the baths
> Of all the western stars, until I die
> It may be that the gulfs will wash us down:
> It may be we shall touch the Happy Isles,
> And see the great Achilles, whom we knew.
> Tho much is taken, much abides; and tho
> We are not now that strength which in old days
> Moved earth and heaven, that which we are, we are—
> One equal temper of heroic hearts,
> Made weak by time and fate, but strong in will
> To strive, to seek, to find and not to yield.[27]

Elmslie's master—Louis Henry Sullivan—strove, sought, found and never yielded till the end of his life. With the passing of Elmslie in 1952 there was severed one of the few remaining ties with Sullivan and the birth of the Chicago School. As a tribute to its author and as a valedictory message to the architectural profession, Elmslie's paper was published in the July 1952 issue of *The American Institute of Architects Journal*. Written in simple, straightforward language, it represents a characteristic of the architects of the Chicago School in the eighties and nineties who knew exactly what they were doing and why they ought to do it. They strongly believed that they had created a new style of architecture by means of a new kind of thinking about it. Several of them, most notably John Root and Louis Sullivan, wrote extensively about

Conclusion   167

the technical and aesthetic aspects of their art. Architectural journals and societies were founded in Chicago to preserve their words. Among the critics and scholars of the East, a few saw the importance of the architecture that was growing up in the city of the prairies. Montgomery Schuyler and a nucleus of architectural writers revolving around him were the leading exponents of a rational and realistic architecture. They were willing to risk their reputations by making an objective statement of what the Chicago group was doing. One of these Eastern critics was Thomas E. Tallmadge who, in 1908, wrote:

> That Chicago should have a sufficient number of men working in a similar and original manner, and actuated by identical principles, and that such men should have accomplished sufficient work to justify the appellation of a distinct school, is an idea certainly suggestive and worthy of discussion, especially as it has come from the East. As the members of one family can seldom see facial resemblances among their brothers and sisters perfectly apparent to strangers, so, to the architect, the work of his local contemporaries seems as different as can be, and his effort is usually directed toward increasing that difference rather than the reverse. It would be strange, however, seen from a view-point of a thousand miles, if the work of a certain group of Chicago men did not possess within itself a strong family resemblance; as they have a common parentage of architectural principles responsible for its being... In looking back on this period of agitation, the storm center of which was Chicago and its Architectural Club, it is not hard to see that all of the pleading was on one side. Very little interest and no concern was manifested by the East and it is largely on this account that the Chicago men have arrived at their present entirely healthy and proper point of view and position. Divorcing themselves from the idea that they were evangelists of a new dispensation and that their mission in life was to convert the architecturally unregenerate and to fill the land with the glories of a new and American style, they have devoted themselves to the task of justifying their principles by their work... The spirit of architectural unrest is not confirmed to Chicago or even to the West. It is the healthy symptom of the whole nation's approaching manhood. The coming Future certainly will not be able to deny to American genius what has been vouchsafed every people holding the center of the stage in the world drama—a national architecture. The dread hierarchy of the Egyptians, the absolutism of the Assyrians, the glorious democracy of the Athenians, the ecstacy of the early Christians, the soaring faith of the Cathedral builder, the Humanism of the Italians—each has stood forth lustrous in its proper raiment of carven stone, of inlaid marble, of beaten bronze, or mighty timbers. What our destiny materialistic as it may now appear may ultimately prove we know not; and when the time shall come we know not. But we DO know that in that good time we shall not lack a national art to clothe a national spirit. Such is the idealism in the bottom of the hearts of the men of Chicago; it alone is the real basis of the philosophy and of their work.[28]

The vast range of social, economic, and technical forces which gave rise to the "new architecture" in Chciago in the last quarter of the nineteenth century needs no recapitulation here. Yet, overwhelmingly as they were, these forces still required a literature of criticism such as the one just cited to prepare the way for its development and for the acceptance of the new idiom. This critical literature furnished the philosophical substructure upon which the new architecture was erected. And there can be little doubt that the achievement of the Chicago School was in part—a substantial part—due to the critics and editors of varius architectural journals who, for decades, have been basing their arguments on the principles, concept, and philosophy of the School that they believe are purely AMERICAN in nature, as once Montgomery Schuyler proclaimed:

> Any arbitrary restriction upon the freedom of the artist is a hindrance to the life and progress of his art. While it is no doubt more difficult to attain unity by the use of constructions that have been employed and expressed in different ages and countries than by renouncing all but such as have been employed together before, and have been analyzed and classified in the schools, the artist is entitled to be judged by the success of his attempts and not to be prevented from making them. American architects are happy in being freer than the architects of any other country from the pressure of this convention. By the introduction of the elevator, some twenty years ago, an architectural problem absolutely new was imposed upon them, a problem in the solution of which there were no directly available and no directly applicable precedents in the history of the world. That many mistakes should be made, and that much wild work should be done was inevitable. But within these twenty years there has been attained not only a practical but in great part an artistic solution of this problem presented by the modern office building. The efforts of the architects have already resulted in a new architectural type, which in its main outlines imposes itself, by force of merit, upon future designers and upon which future designers can but execute variations. This is really a very considerable achievement, this unique contribution of American architects to their art.[29]

Indeed, "their art" is uniquely American of which every citizen not only of Chicago but also of the whole country should be proud.

Illustrations

Plate 1. Home Insurance Building, 1884-85, by William Le Baron Jenney

Plate 2. First Leiter Building, 1879, by William Le Baron Jenney

Plate 3.   Marshall Field Wholesale Store, 1887, by Henry Hobson Richardson

Plate 4. Auditorium Building, 1887-89, by Adler and Sullivan

Plate 5. Garrick (originally Schiller) Theater, 1891-92, by Adler and Sullivan

Plate 6. Stock Exchange Building, 1893-94, by Adler and Sullivan

Plate 7. Wainwright Building, 1890-91, by Adler and Sullivan

Plate 8. Guaranty (now Prudential) Building, 1894-95, by Adler and Sullivan

Plate 9. Carson, Pirie and Scott (originally Schlesinger and Mayor) Store, 1899, 1903-4, by Sullivan and Company

Plate 10. Montauk Building, 1881-82, by Burnham and Root

Plate 11.   The Rookery, 1884-86, by Burnham and Root

Plate 12. Monadnock Building, 1889-91, by Burnham and Root

Plate 13. Reliance Building, 1894-95, by D.H. Burnham and Company

Plate 14. Railways Exchange Building, 1903-4, by D.H. Burnham and Company

Notes

Chapter 1

1. Montgomery Schuyler, "The Evolution of a Skyscraper," *Achitectural Record* **14** (November 1903), pp. 329-30.
2. Ibid., p. 330.
3. Schuyler wrote almost regularly his architectural criticism in a column of *The Architectural Record* entitled "Architectural Aberrations."
4. Talbot F. Hamlin, "Criticism Might Help Architecture: Let's Try It," *American Architect* **137** (May 1930), p. 41.
5. Ibid., p. 90.
6. The great fire in 1871 in Chicago.
7. Louise B. Pierce, *As Others See Chicago* (Chicago, Ill.: The University of Chicago Press, 1933), pp. 383-84.
8. Paul Bourget was born in Amiens, France on September 2, 1852, the son of a Russian father and an English mother. His early education took place at the Lycean of Clermont-Ferrant, where his father was a professor of mathematics. Later Bourget attended the College of Sainte Barbe, graduating with high honors in 1872. He began his career as a journalist in 1873, and for the next ten years he contributed various articles to different French periodicals and published three volumes of poetry. His first novel, "L'Irreparable," appeared in 1883, by which he was established as a well-known novelist.
9. Montgomery Schuyler also translated Bourget's story and his translation first appeared in his "Architecture in Chicago" series published in *The Architectural Record* in 1895.
10. Montgomery Schuyler, "American Architecture," *Inland Architects and News Record* **17** (February 1891), pp. 5, 6.

Chapter 2

1. Editors' introduction to a new series on architectural criticism in the *American Institute of Architects Journal* **49** (January 1968), p. 46.
2. At the time, Mr. Collins was professor of architecture at McGill University, Montreal, and editor of the *Journal of the Society of Architectural Historians*. A Fellow of the Royal Architectural Institute of Canada, he also is the author of *Changing Ideals in Modern Architecture*, a history of architectural criticism.

Notes for Chapter 3

3. This is published by Farber and Farber Limited, London, 1965.
4. In this respect, it should be noted that J.F. Blondel was not only a practicing architect but also a contributor to the *Encyclopedie*.
5. Lewis Mumford, *Roots of Contemporary American Architecture* (New York: Reinhold Publishing Corporation, 1952), p. 36.
6. Ibid., p. 37.
7. Harold Osborne, *Aesthetics and Criticism* (London: Routledge and Kegan Paul Ltd., 1955), p. 9.
8. Ibid., p. 9.
9. Ibid., p. 9.
10. Jeffrey Guchen, "Proposals for Architectural Criticism," *Connection*, Harvard University Graduate School of Design, Cambridge, Mass. (March 1965), pp. 17, 18.
11. In his *Aesthetics and Criticism*, Harold Osborne quotes Donald Staffer as saying: "The critic has three roles, as an individual responding to the work of art, as interpreter to an audience, and finally as judge"; and Theodore Meyer Green says in his *The Arts and the Art of Criticism* (1940) that criticism has three aspects: the historical, the re-creative, and the judicial.
12. Talbot Hamlin, "What We Should Consider Before We Criticize," *The American Architect* **140** (September 1931), p. 34.
13. It is primarily based on Talbot Hamlin's "What We Should Consider Before We Criticize," pp. 110, 114.
14. Ibid., p. 114.
15. All of the capital letters at the beginning of some words in his article are Desmond's own.
16. Harry W. Desmond, "The Architect and the Critic," *Architectural Record* **19** (April 1906), p. 279.
17. Ibid., p. 279.
18. He probably was referring to the Beaux Arts Society.
19. Desmond, "The Architect and the Critic," p. 280.
20. Peter Bonnett Wight, along with Schuyler and Sturgis, was one of the most tireless and persuasive advocates of the architecture of the Chicago School at the time and was a Chicago-based architect.
21. Herbert D. Croly, "Criticism that Counts," *Architectural Record* **10** (April 1901), p. 398.
22. Ibid., pp. 404, 405.

Chapter 3

1. Theodore L. Shaw, *Hypocrisy About Art* (Boston: Stuart Publications, 1962), p. 114.
2. Ibid.
3. Ibid.
4. Edward R. Smith, "Montgomery Schuyler and the History of American Architecture," *Architectural Record* **36** (September 1914), p. 264.

5. Lewis Mumford, *Roots of Contemporary American Architecture* (New York: Reinhold Publishing Corporation, 1952), p. 15.

6. Ibid., p. 430.

7. Prior to *The New York Sketch-Book,* the only major architectural periodical able to sustain itself was *The American Builder* (Chicago-New York, March 1868 to May, 1895), which became *Builder and Woodmaker* in 1879. This journal was, however, directed at the builder, being specifically hostile to architects. Simultaneous with *The New York Sketch-Book* (1873-1876), but established a year earlier and possibly an influence on it, was the *Architectural Sketch Book* (1873-1876), published in Boston by the Portfolio Club.

8. Schuyler's occasional articles on the architecture of other countries are unimportant such as the story of a trip to Mont Saint-Michel published in Volume 11 (1902), an account of the "Architecture of Mexico City" in Volume 32 (1912), and an article entitled "Les Nouveautés de Paris" in Volume 10 (1900-1901) of the *Architectural Record.*

9. Although much consulted by historians of both American culture and modern architecture, it has been out of print since the sale of its initial edition.

10. Smith, "Montgomery Schuyler and the History of American Architecture", p. 267.

11. William Jordy and Ralph Coe (eds.), *American Architecture and Other Writings* (Cambridge, Mass.: Harvard University Press, 1961), pp. 14, 15.

12. Montgomery Schuyler, "Russell Sturgis", *Architectural Record* **25** (March 1909), p. 146.

13. Ibid., p. 220.

14. Wight moved from New York to practice architecture in Chicago in December, 1891.

15. Peter B. Wight, "Reminiscences of Russell Sturgis," *Architectural Record* **26** (August 1909), p. 123.

16. Ibid., pp. 124, 125.

17. Ibid., p. 123.

18. Ibid., pp. 125, 126.

19. Ibid.

20. Ibid., p. 127.

21. Ibid., p. 124.

22. Jordy and Coe, *American Architecture,* p. 15.

23. Herbert D. Croly, "Criticism That Counts," *Architectural Record* **10** (April 1901), p. 401.

24. Ibid., pp. 401, 402.

25. Ibid.

Chapter 4

1. Anonymous, "Correspondence," *American Architect and Building News* **1** (April, 1876), p. 110.

2. John Wellborn Root, "Architects of Chicago," *Inland Architect and News Record* **16** (January, 1891), p. 91.

188   Notes for Chapter 4

3. The name "Chicago" is a modified spelling of "Chekagou." But this name was applied to a different stream from that of the Chicago River. In the map by Franquelin (1684), the present Chicago River is called "Cheagoumeinan," and "Chekagou" is applied to a small stream heading near the lake and entering the Des Plaines River. Another version of the early spelling of "Chicago" is "Chegakou" which appears in the map believed to be drawn up by Louis Armand de Lom d'Arce in 1703. This map gives a fairly accurate picture of the region at the beginning of the eighteenth century.

4. Bessie Louise Pierce, *As Others See Chicago* (Chicago: Unviersity of Chicago Press, 1933), p. 123.

5. Ibid.

6. Some historians have given this credit to George Washington Snow.

7. Peter Bonnett Wight, "Reminiscences of Chicago in 1859—Architecture and Otherwise, Part I," *Inland Architect and News Record* **20** (September 1892), p. 13.

8. Peter Bonnett Wight, "Reminiscences of Chicago in 1859—Architecture and Otherwise, Part II," *Inland Architect and News Record* **20** (September 1892), p. 13.

9. Ibid.

10. Bessie Louis Pierce, *As Others See Chicago,* pp. 151, 153, 154, 157.

11. Ibid., pp. 183, 184.

12. Ibid., pp. 191, 192, 198.

13. Andrew Shuman, *The Lakeside Memorial of the Burning of Chicago* (Chicago: University Publishing Company, 1872), p. 23.

14. Dankmar Adler, "Some Notes upon the Earlier Chicago Architects," *Inland Architect and News Record* **15** (May, 1892), p. 48.

15. The fires of 1857 and 1871.

16. Dankmar Adler, "Some Notes upon the Earlier Chicago Architects," p. 48.

17. In an earlier footnote, I have mentioned the various early spellings of the term "Chicago." It is also interesting to be noted here a convincing "speculation" of the origin of the term. In an article entitled "A Visit to the States," anonymously published in the October 24, 1887 issue of *The London Times,* the author writes:

> The name of this wonderful city is of Indian origin, a probable corruption of "Cheecagua," said to have been the title of a dynasty of Indian chiefs who ruled the country west and south of Lake Michigan. This was also a word applied in the Indian dialect to the wild onion that grew luxuriantly on the banks of the river; and they also gave a similar name to the thunder, which they believed to be the voice of the Great Spirit, and to the odoriferous animal that abounded in the neighborhood which to the white man was known as the "polecat." These are seeming incongruities of use for the same word, but it has been suggested that all may be harmonized if "Chicago" is to be interpreted as "strong." The Indians were usually not over supplied with words, and they generally selected the most prominent attribute in naming an object. All these various entities in one way or another are undoubtedly "strong," and it is equally evident that a prodigious amount of strength exists in Chicago.

Chapter 5

1. *Industrial Chicago,* Vol. I (Chicago: Goodspeed Publishing Company, 1891), pp. 70, 168.

2. The writings concerned with the development of the commercial architecture of the Chicago School between 1883 and 1893 are for the most part anonymous. The first two volumes of *Industrial Chicago's* six volumes (1891-1896) by the Goodspeed Publishing Company, Chicago, treats the building interests. These two volumes, rarely found in American libraries, are the Vasari of the Chicago School, as Giedion puts it. A set of these (Volumes 1 and 2) used to be stored at the North Campus Annex of the University of Michigan library and Volume 6 is at the University's law library. Across the country, the following institutions have some or all six volumes: The Library of Congress, The Chicago Historical Society Library, Harvard University Library, the University of Virginia library, and the Pennsylvania State University library. However, unfortunately, Volumes 1 and 2 at the University of Michigan have been lost since 1976.

3. In 1891 Schuyler published a volume of his essays under the title *American Architect— Studies* (New York: Harper and Brothers, 1892). Gathered from magazine articles which had appeared earlier, the seven essays in this volume have long been recognized as among the most perceptive and progressive critical writings on certain aspects of nineteenth century American architecture. *American Architecture* has been out of print since the sale of its initial edition. The essay quoted here was one of seven.

4. Lewis Mumford, *Roots of American Contemporary Architecture,* (New York: Dover Publications, Inc., 1972), pp. 223, 224.

5. Ibid., pp. 219, 220.

6. The third Chamber of Commerce Building was designed by Edward Bauman (1838-1889) and Harris W. Huehl (1862-1919) and was erected at the southeast corner of La Salle and Washington Streets between 1888 and 1889. It was demolished in 1928.

7. Bessie Louise Pierce, *As Others See Chicago* (Chicago: University of Chicago Press, 1933), p. 291.

8. Mumford, *Roots of American Contemporary Architecture,* p. 257.

9. Pierce, *As Others See Chicago,* p. 220.

10. *The American Architect and Building News* first appeared in January, 1876 and was then published by J.R. Osgood and Company of Boston until 1904. Since 1908, its title had been changed a few times. It read *The American Architect* from 1909 to 1921, the *American Architect and The Architectural Review* from 1921 to 1924 and again *The American Architect* from 1925 to 1936, *American Architect and Architecture* from 1936 to 1938. It absorbed the *Inland Architect* in 1902 and merged into *The Architectural Record* in 1938.

11. Edwin Erle Sparks, "The Beginning of Chicago," *American Architect and Building News* **81** (September 1903), p. 103.

12. John Mills Van Osdel, the first architect of Chicago, was born in 1811 and began the practice of architecture in Chicago in 1837, the year of incorporation. By the time of his death in 1891, he had designed at least seventy-three commercial and public buildings in the Loop area alone.

13. Mumford, *Roots of American Contemporary Architecture,* pp. 209, 210.

Notes for Chapter 5

14. The volumes of *The Inland Architect*, which first appeared in February, 1883, gave some remarkable insight into the development of the Chicago School. Robert Clark McLean, its editor at the time, was an architectural journalist of exceptional enthusiasm and understanding. His editorial voice generated much of the scene that his journal reported. He was a friend to Root, Burnham, and Sullivan. With his second issue, he began to publish the lectures of Jenney at the University of Chicago and also the reminiscences of Van Osdel, "A History of Chicago Architecture." The title of *The Inland Architect's* first eight volumes reads *The Inland Architect and Builder*. It ceased publication in December, 1908.

15. John Wellborn Root, "Architects of Chicago," *Inland Architect and News Record* **16** (January 1891), pp. 91, 92.

16. Schuyler meant the cast-iron fronts that had been popular among Chicago architects before the fire.

17. Mumford, *Roots of American Contemporary Architecture*, pp. 210, 211.

18. Carl Condit, *The Chicago School of Architecture* (Chicago: University of Chicago Press, 1964), p. 28.

19. Sigfried Giedion, *Space, Time and Architecture* (Cambridge, Mass.: Harvard University Press, 1967), p. 371.

20. Steel was still too expensive for general architectural use until the 1890s, but Jenney experimented with the new material as soon as Carnegie's mills made it available.

21. Pierce, *As Others See Chicago*, pp. 288, 289.

22. Condit, *The Chicago School of Architecture*, p. 26.

23. Carl Condit, *American Building* (Chicago: University of Chicago Press, 1968), p. 121.

24. *The Architectural Review* was first published by Kimball and Guild of Boston in 1891 with eight issues a year and since 1918 the publisher has been The Architectural Review Company, New York. It has become a monthly architectural magazine since 1899. The publication was suspended briefly from May 1910 to December 1911. It supersedes "The Technology Architectural Review."

25. Colin Rowe, "Chicago Frame, Chicago's Place in Modern Movement," *Architectural Review* **120** (November, 1956), pp. 285, 286.

26. *The Architectural Record* first appeared in 1891 and was then published by F.W. Dodge Corporation of New York. It was a quarterly magazine between 1891 and 1902 and since then it has been published monthly.

27. William F. Fryer, Jr., "Skeleton Construction," *Architectural Record* **1** (October-December 1891), pp. 229, 230.

28. Ibid., p. 230.

29. Barr Ferree, "The Modern Office Building," *Inland Architect and News Record* **27** (March 1896), p. 12.

30. Fryer, "Skelton Construction," p. 235. The fire in Boston that Fryer refers to was the fire of 1872 which substantially leveled downtown Boston.

31. Ibid., p. 230.

32. Root, "Architects of Chicago," pp. 91, 92.

33. Ibid.

34. Mumford, *Roots of American Contemporary Architecture*, p. 232.
35. Ibid., p. 233.
36. Ibid., pp. 234, 235.
37. Pierce, *As Others See Chicago*, p. 295.
38. Ibid., p. 239.

Chapter 6

1. Besides the Marshall Field Store, Richardson also designed in Chicago the American Express Company Building (1872-73)—a six-story structure, the Franklin MacVeagh House (1885-87), and the J.J. Glessner House (1885-87) which is still standing at the corner of South Prairie and East Eighteenth Streets and presently serves as the home of the Chicago School of Architecture Foundation.

2. Sullivan's admiration of the Marshall Field Store appeared in his "Kindergarten Chats" series which was first published in the *Interstate Architect and Builder Magazine* from 1901 to 1902. Despite the comparatively small circulation, the fame of these articles spread rapidly and "The Kindergarten Chats" was almost a legend. The reprint of the series, edited by Claude F. Bragdon, was brought out by the Scarab Fraternity in 1934. Since 1936, The Avery Architectural Library of Columbia University has come into possession of the clippings of the complete first publication, originally collected by Lyndon P. Smith who was an architect and a close friend of Sullivan.

3. Sigfried Giedion, *Space, Time and Architecture* (Cambridge, Mass.: Harvard Unviersity Press, 1967), p. 372.

4. Lewis Mumford, *Roots of Contemporary American Architecture*, (New York: Dover Publication Inc., 1972), p. 219.

5. Carl Condit, *The Chicago School of Architecture* (Chicago: University of Chicago Press, 1964), pp. 31, 32.

6. *The Liturgical Arts* is a quarterly journal devoted to the art of the Catholic Church and sponsored by The Liturgical Society, Concord, New Hampshire. Its first volume appeared in 1931 pubslished in Concord, with its editorial office in New York City.

7. Joseph Salerno, "Louis Sullivan—Return to Princple," *Liturgical Arts* **16** (February 1948), p 49.

8. Frank Lloyd Wright, "Louis Sullivan—His Work," *Architectural Record* **56** (July 1924), pp. 28, 29.

9. Condit, *The Chicago School*, p. 141.

10. Chamberlain's article appeared in the December 1956 issue of *The Arts and Architecture*, which was a California-based periodical. It first appeared in 1911 as a monthly magazine and as the official organ of the American Institute of Archtiects, San Francisco Chapter and other chapters. The publication was suspended temporarily between the period of March 1920 and February 1921. Its title varies: 1911-1915, *The Pacific Architect;* 1915-1919, *The Architect;* 1919-1923, *The Builder Review;* 1924-1929, *Pacific Coast Architect;* 1929-1944, *California Arts and Architecture;* and from 1944 on, *Arts and Architecture.* It absorbed *The Inspector* in 1928, *California Southland* and *California Home Owner* in 1929. *Arts and Architecture* is no longer published.

Notes for Chapter 6

11. Betty Chamberlain, "Louis Sullivan," *Arts and Architecture* **73** (December 1956), p. 15.

12. *The Architectural Forum* first appeared in 1892 as a monthly periodical with the title of *The Brick Builder* and was then published by Rogers and Mason Publishing Company of Boston. In 1917, its title was changed to *The Architectural Forum* and since 1923 its editorial and executive offices have been in New York City and published by Time, Inc. It absorbed *The Architectural World* in 1938.

13. Anonymous, "Frank Lloyd Wright on Louis Sullivan," *Architectural Forum* **91** (August 1949), p. 96.

14. John Wellborn Root,"Architects of Chicago," *Inland Architect and News Record* **16** (January 1891), pp. 91, 92.

15. Ibid.

16. Condit, *The Chicago School*, p. 32.

17. Louis H. Sullivan, *The Autobiography of an Idea* (New York: Press of the American Institute of Architects, 1924), p. 313.

18. Talbot Hamlin, "Sullivan Letters at Columbia," *American Architect and Architecture* **149** (November 1936), p. 100.

19. Salerno, "Louis Sullivan—Return to Principle," p. 49.

20. Philip Johnson, "Is Sullivan the Father of Functionalism," *Art News* **55** (December 1956), pp. 45, 46.

21. *The Western Architect* was a monthly journal which first appeared in August 1901 and was published by The Western Architect, Inc., Chicago. Its publication was then terminated in March 1931.

22. Louis Henry Sullivan, "The Tall Building Artistically Considered," *Western Architect* **31** (January 1922), p. 3.

23. The Editor's note, *Western Architect* **31** (January 1922), p. 3.

24. Sidney F. Kimball, "Louis Sullivan: An Old Master," *Architectural Record* **57** (April 1925), pp. 289-304.

25. The American Institute of Architects, "To Louis Sullivan: The Gold Medal of the American Institute of Architects," *A.I.A. Journal* **6** (July 1946), p. 3.

26. Sullivan, *The Autobiography of an Idea*, pp. 304-14.

27. William Jordy and Ralph Coe (eds.), *American Architecture and Other Writings, Volume 2* (Cambridge, Mass.: Harvard University Press, 1961), p. 409.

28. Wright, *Louis Sullivan His Work*, p. 31.

29. Frank Lloyd Wright, *An Autobiography* (New York: Duell, Sloan and Pearce, 1943), p. 101.

30. Louis Henry Sullivan, *Kindergarten Chats* (New York, Wittenborn, Schultz, Inc., 1974), pp. 28-30.

31. James Marston Fitch, *Architecture and the Esthetics of Plenty* (New York: Columbia University Press, 1961), p. 91.

32. John Burchard and Albert Bush-Brown, *The Architecture of America: A Social and Cultural History* (Boston: Little, Brown and Company, 1961), p. 186.

Notes for Chapter 6   193

33. Dankmar Adler, "The Chicago Auditorium," *Architectural Record* 1 (October-December 1891), pp. 415, 433.
34. Anonymous, "The Auditorium Building," *American Architect and Building News* **26** (December 1889), p. 299.
35. Condit, *The Chicago School*, p. 70.
36. Adler, "The Chicago Auditorium," p. 415.
37. Anonymous, "The Auditorium Building," pp. 299, 300.
38. Wright, *Louis Sullivan—His Work*, p. 28.
39. Condit, *The Chicago School*, p. 70.
40. Adler, "The Chicago Auditorium," pp. 415, 417.
41. Schuyler erroneously observed the tower as being square. The fact is that the dimensions of the rectangular tower are 70 feet in width, 40 feet in depth and 240 feet in height.
42. Jordy and Coe, *American Architecture*, pp. 257-59.
43. Ibid.
44. Ibid., pp. 259-61.
45. Ibid., pp. 384, 385.
46. Ibid., pp. 387, 388.
47. *The Craftsman*, edited by Gustav Stickley, was an illustrated monthly magazine "in the interest of the better art, better and more reasonable way of living" as its motto goes. It first appeared in October 1901, and from that time on until December 1916 when it merged into *The Art World*, it was published by the United Crafts, East Wood, New York (1901-1902), Syracuse, New York (1902-1906), and finally by Gustave Strickley, New York City (1906-16).
48. H.A. Caparn, "The Riddle of the Tall Building: Has the Skyscraper a Place in American Architecture," *Craftsman* **10** (April 1906), pp. 477-84.
49. Jordy and Coe, *American Architecture*, pp. 388, 389.
50. Condit, *The Chicago School*, pp. 138, 139.
51. Jordy and Coe, *American Architecture*, pp. 389, 390.
52. Hugh Morrison, *Louis Sullivan: Prophet of Modern Architecture* (New York: W.W. Norton and Company, 1935), pp. 144, 145.
53. Jordy and Coe, *American Architecture*, pp. 390, 391.
54. Johnson, "Is Sullivan the Father of Functionalism," p. 56.
55. This is an unbuilt project by Sullivan which is not mentioned in Hugh Morrison's *Louis Sullivan: Prophet of Modern Architecture*. This project was conceived as a double tower utilizing precisely the same wall treatment as Sullivan's later Bayard Building, even to the cornice, with a lower block between topped by the open loggia which Schuyler mentions.
56. Jordy and Coe, *American Architecture*, pp. 393-96.
57. Lyndon P. Smith, "The Schlesinger and Mayer Building," *Architectural Record* **16** (July 1904), p. 53.

58. Ibid., pp. 53, 59.
59. Caparn, "The Riddle of the Tall Building," pp. 484, 487, 488.
60. Carl Condit, "Sullivan's Skyscrapers as the Expression of Nineteenth Century Technology," *Technology and Culture* **1** (Winter 1959), pp. 92, 93.
61. Fitch, *Architecture and the Esthetics of Plenty,* p. 93.
62. *The American Institute of Architects Journal* first appeared in January 1913 as a monthly journal and during the period between 1913 and 1928 it was published in Harrisburg, Pennsylvania and Washington, D.C. The Journal was discontinued after the number for December 1928. Since then *The Octagon* had been the organ of the Institute until it was superseded by the present version of *The A.I.A. Journal* in 1944. It absorbed *The Institute's Bulletin* in 1957 and is now published in Washington, D.C.
63. Hugh Morrison,"Louis Sullivan Today," *American Institute of Architects Journal* **26** (September 1956), pp. 98, 99.
64. Jordy and Coe, *American Architecture,* p. 404.

Chapter 7

1. Montgomery Schuyler, "Architecture," *Inland Architect and News Record* **17** (February 1891), p. 5.
2. Longfellow, *Divina Commedia,* Sonnet 2.
3. Root was only forty-one years of age at the time of his death.
4. Schuyler, "Architecture," pp. 5, 6.
5. William Jordy and Ralph Coe (eds.), *American Architecture and Other Writings* (Cambridge, Mass.: Harvard University Press, 1961), pp. 269, 271.
6. Carl Condit, *The Chicago School of Architecture* (Chicago: University of Chicago Press, 1964), p. 44.
7. Wight might have written this sentence with prejudices against New York architects, for architectural evidences testify that the influence of Renwick lasted up to Root's death in Gothic details that appeared in some of his buildings.
8. Peter Bonnett Wight, "John W. Root as a Draftsman," *Inland Architect and News Record* **16** (January 1891), p. 88.
9. Harriet Monroe, *John Wellborn Root* (Boston: Houghton Mifflin Company, 1896), pp. 206, 211.
10. John Wellborn Root, "The Value of Type in Art," *Inland Architect and Builder* **2** (November 1883), p. 132.
11. John Wellborn Root, "Architectural Ornamentation," *Inland Architect and Builder* **5** (April 1885), pp. 54, 55.
12. Root, "The Value of Type in Art," p. 132.
13. Root, "Architectural Ornamentation," p. 54.
14. John Wellborn Root, "Broad Art Criticism," *Inland Architect and News Record* **11** (February 1888), pp. 3-5.

15. Condit, *The Chicago School*, p. 42.
16. Peter Bonnett Wight, "Daniel Hudson Burnham: An Appreciation," *Architectural Record* 32 (August 1912), pp. 176, 178.
17. Condit, *The Chicago School*, p. 43.
18. W.A. Starrett, *Skyscrapers and the Men Who Built Them* (New York: Charles Scribner's sons, 1928), pp. 6-7, 10-11.
19. Cass Gilbert, "Daniel Hudson Burnham: An Appreciation," *Architectural Record* 32 (August 1912), p. 175.
20. Burnham's letter, written sometime in March 1894 to the Secretary of the United States Treasury Department, with respect to the qualifications of the Supervising Architect appears in Charles Moore's biography of Burnham, Volume I (Houghton and Mifflin Co., 1921), p. 102.
21. Jordy and Coe, *American Architecture*, pp. 406, 407.
22. A.N. Rebori, "The Work of Burnham and Root," *Architectural Record* 38 (July 1915), pp. 32, 33.
23. It is popularly believed that this sobriquet for downtown Chicago came into being in 1897 when a belt elevated railroad loop went into operation around the downtown district so as to link all radiating transit lines. In fact, the term began to be applied to the area in the early eighties (around 1882-1883) with reference to a trolley that was being operated in the area at the time.
24. John Wellborn Root, "Architects of Chicago," *Inland Architect and News Record* 16 (January 1891), pp. 91, 92.
25. Condit, *The Chicago School*, pp. 51, 52.
26. Ibid.
27. As quoted in Condit's *The Chicago School*, pp. 52, 55.
28. Ibid.
29. Ibid.
30. Wight erroneously recalls Peter Brooks' brother, Shepard, as Brooks' son.
31. Wight, "John W. Root as a Draftsman," p. 179.
32. The Insurance Exchange Building (later the Continental Bank) was completed in 1885 and stood on La Salle Street between Adams and Quincy before its demolition in 1912. Henry Van Brunt praises this building as having had "the most extensive influence over architectural thought in the West," and a "composition of ten stories forced into five for the sake of establishing a harmonic proportion of horizontal division," and also a scheme of design that was "simple, effective and easily understood," in his 1891 essay published in the January 1891 issue of the *Inland*.
33. The Phoenix (later known as the Austin Building) was completed in 1886 at the Southwest corner of Clark and Jackson Streets. It was a tall, narrow structure, eleven stories in height. The building was distinguished by its monumental and highly decorated entrance that Van Brunt, in the same essay as mentioned above, says was of "noble and interesting design." He adds that there was also introduced into this building "a certain amount of richly carved

Notes for Chapter 7

detail, which would never have been invented in America but for the copious suggestions in certain of the babaric topes and Buddhist temples of India." The Phoenix survived longer than most of its contemporaries; it was demolished in 1959 to make way for the Union Tank Car Building (1960-1961).

34. Jordy and Coe, *American Architecture*, pp. 270, 272.
35. Condit, *The Chicago School*, p. 64.
36. Henry Van Brunt, "John Wellborn Root," *Inland Architect and News Record* **16** (January 1891), p. 87.
37. Condit, *The Chicago School*, pp. 64, 65.
38. William H. Jordy, *American Buildings and Their Architects* (New York: Doubleday and Company, 1972), pp. 73, 75.
39. Jordy and Coe, *American Architecture*, pp. 407, 408.
40. Ibid.
41. Rebori, "The Work of Burnham and Root," p. 48.
42. Edward S. Hamatt, "The Building and Designing of the Skyscraper," *American Architecture and Building News* **88** (November 1905), pp. 159, 160.
43. Robert D. Andrews, "The Broad Use of Precedent," *Architectural Review* **2** (May 1893), pp. 34, 35.
44. Tennyson, "The Flower."
45. Jordy and Coe, *American Architecture*, pp. 409-12.
46. Ibid.
47. Condit, *The Chicago School*, p. 110.
48. Ibid.
49. Actually, the Reliance is a fourteen-story building.
50. Sigfried Giedion, *Space, Time and Architecture* (Cambridge, Mass.: Harvard University Press, 1967), pp. 387, 388.
51. Annex to the Marshall Field Store at the southwest corner of Wabash Avenue and East Washington Street (1892-1893) was designed by Charles B. Atwood for D.H. Burnham and Company. This "Annex", inspired by Renaissance palace prototypes, has been absorbed into the main store. The building presently designated as the "Annex" was built in 1914.
52. Rebori, "The Work of Burnham and Root," p. 62.
53. Jordy and Coe, *American Architecture*, p. 62.
54. Harry W. Desmond, "Rationalizing the Skyscraper," *Architectural Record* **17** (May 1905), p. 423.
55. Ibid., pp. 423, 425.
56. Ibid.
57. See Peter Bonnett Wight's "Daniel Hudson Burnham and His Associates," *Architectural Record* **38** (July 1915).

58. Louis Sullivan, *The Autobiography of an Idea* (New York: Press of the American Institute of Architects, 1924), p. 325.

Chapter 8

1. For several years the directors of the National Farmers Bank, Owatonna, Minnesota, had been searching for an architect who could give their new building proper expression. Sullivan's article according to the vice-president of the bank, Carl K. Bennett, resulted in his being chosen as architect for the bank built in 1907 and 1908. This design was the first in a series of banks for small towns throughout the Middle West that were built during the final phase of Sullivan's career.
2. Peter Bonnett Wight, "The Great Exhibition Reviewed," *American Architect and Building News* **42** (October-December 1893), p. 159.
3. R.C. Mclean, "Architects and Architecture in the United States," *Inland Architect and News Record* **28** (January 1897), p. 61.
4. William Jordy and Ralph Coe (eds.), *American Architecture and Other Writings, Volume 2* (Cambridge, Mass.: Harvard University Press, 1961), p. 557.
5. Ibid., p. 558.
6. Ibid., p. 558.
7. Ibid., pp. 559, 568.
8. Ibid., pp. 571, 572, 573.
9. Ibid., p. 574.
10. Peter Bonnett Wight, "Additions to Chicago Skyline: A Few Recent Skyscrapers," *Architectural Record* **38** (July 1910), p. 18.
11. Claude Fayette Bragdon, "Made in France Architecture," *Architectural Record* **16** (December 1904), p. 562.
12. Ibid., p. 566.
13. Ibid., p. 567.
14. Montgomery Schuyler, "A Long-Felt Want," *Architectural Record* **7** (September 1897), pp. 118-20.
15. Lewis Mumford, *Roots of Contemporary American Architecture* (New York: Dover Publication, Inc., 1972), pp. 16, 17.
16. The Cliff Dwellers Club was a popular cultural club of which several members of the Chicago School were regular visitors and which had in its membership a number of architects.
17. Frank Lloyd Wright, "Louis Sullivan—His Work," *The Architectural Record* **56** (July 1924), p. 28.
18. Jordy, William H., *American Buildings and Their Architects* (New York: Doubleday and Company, 1972), p. 78.
19. Ibid., p. 79.
20. Ibid., p. 80.

Notes for Chapter 8

21. Ibid., p. 80.
22. Bessie Louise Pierce, *As Others See Chicago* (Chicago: University of Chicago Press, 1933), pp. 294-95.
23. A network that links Chicago's parks.
24. Jordy, *American Buildings,* pp. 81, 82.
25. Ibid., pp. 81, 82.
26. In 1939, when Leo J. Weissenborn was program chairman of the Illinois Society of Architects, he persuaded Elmslie and a few others to contribute their thoughts and recollections to a symposium on the Chicago School. Elmslie's paper was printed in the July 1952 issue of the *A.I.A. Journal* as a tribute to him upon his death on April 23 of that year.
27. George Grant Elmslie, "The Chicago School, Its Inheritance and Bequest," *The American Institute of Architects Journal* **18** (July 1952), pp. 32-40.
28. Thomas E. Tallmadge, "The Chicago School," *Architectural Review* **15** (April 1908), pp. 69-74.
29. Jordy and Coe, *American Architecture,* pp. 112-13.

Bibliography

Books

Andreas, Alfred T. *History of Chicago,* 3 Volumes. Chicago: A.T. Andreas, 1884-86.
Andrew, Wayne. *Architecture, Ambitions and Americans.* New York: Harper, 1955.
Anonymous. *Industrial Chicago,* Volumes 1 and 2. Chicago: Goodspeed 1891.
Bancroft, Herbert H. *The Book of the Fair.* Chicago: The Bancroft Company, 1893.
Banham, Reyner. *Theory and Design in the First Machine Age.* New York: Praeger, 1960.
_____. *Guide to Modern Architecture.* London: Architectural Press, 1962.
_____. *The Architecture of the Well-Tempered Environment.* Chicago: University of Chicago Press, 1973.
Behrendt, Walter C. *Modern Building.* New York: Harcourt, Brace and Company, 1937.
Bell, Quentin. *The Art Critic and the Art Historian.* London: Cambridge University Press, 1974.
Benevolo, Leonardo. *History of Modern Architecture,* Volumes 1 and 2. Cambridge, Mass.: M.I.T. Press, 1971.
Birkmire, William H. *Architectural Iron and Steel and its Application in the Construction of Buildings.* New York: John Wiley and Sons, 1894.
_____. *Skeleton Construction in Building.* New York: John Wiley and Sons, 1894.
Bishop, Glen A., and Paul T. Gilbert. *Chicago's Accomplishment and Leaders.* Chicago: Bishop Publishing Company, 1932.
Blake, Peter. *Frank Lloyd Wright: Architecture and Space.* Baltimore: Penguin Books. 1964.
Bragdon, Claude F. *Architecture and Democracy.* New York: A.A. Knapp, 1918.
Burchard, John, and Albert Bush-Brown. *The Architecture of America.* Boston: Little Brown, 1961.
Bush-Brown, Albert. *Louis Sullivan.* New York: George Braziller, 1960.
Chambers, Frank P. *The History of Taste.* New York: Columbia University Press, 1932.
Charvat, William. *The Origins of American Critical Thought.* Philadelphia: University of Pennsylvania Press, 1936.
Chicago Plan Commission. *Industrial and Commercial Background for Planning Chicago.* Chicago: Chicago Plan Commission, 1942.
Colbert, Elias, and Everett Chamberlain. *Chicago and the Great Conflagration.* Chicago: J.S. Goodman and Company, 1871.
Coles, Williams A., ed. *Architects and Society: Selected Essays of Henry Van Brunt.* Cambridge, Mass.: Harvard University Press, 1969.
Collins, Peter. *Changing Ideals in Modern Architecture.* London: Farber and Farber, 1965
_____. *Architectural Judgement.* London: Farber and Farber, 1971.
Condit, Carl W. *The Rise of the Skyscraper.* Chicago: University of Chicago Press, 1952.
_____. *American Building Art: The Twentieth Century.* New York: Oxford University Press, 1961.

———. *The Chicago School of Architecture.* Chicago: University of Chicago Press, 1964.
———. *American Building: Materials and Techniques from the First Settlements to the Present.* Chicago: University of Chicago Press, 1968.
———. *Chicago 1910-29: Buildings, Planning, and Urban Technology.* Chicago: University of Chicago Press, 1973.
———. *Chicago 1930-70: Buildings, Planning, and Urban Technology.* Chicago: University of Chicago Press, 1974.
Connelly, Willard. *Louis Sullivan as He Lived: The Shaping of American Architecture.* New York: Horizon Press, 1960.
Conrads, Ulrich. *Programs and Manifestoes on 20th Century Architecture.* Cambridge, Mass.: M.I.T. Press, 1970.
Cromie, Robert. *The Great Chicago Fire.* New York: McGraw-Hill, 1958.
Dedmon, Emmett. *Fabulous Chicago.* New York: Random House, 1953.
De Zurko, Edward R. *Origin of Functionalist Theory.* New York: Columbia University Press, 1957.
Duncan, Hugh D. *Culture and Democracy.* Totowa, N.J.: Bedminster Press, 1965.
Early, James. *Romanticism and American Architecture.* New York: A.S. Barnes, 1965.
Eaton. Leonard K. *Landscape Arttist in America: The Life and Work of Jens Jensen.* Chicago: University of Chicago Press, 1964.
———. *American Architecture Comes of Age.* Cambridge, Mass.: M.I.T. Press, 1972.
English, Maurice. *The Testament of Stone, Themes of Idealism and Indignation from the Writings of Louis Sullivan.* Evanston, Ill.: Northwestern University Press, 1963.
Ericson, Henry, and Lewis Myers. *Sixty Years a Builder.* Chicago: A. Kroch and Son, 1942.
Farbos, Julius G. *Frederick Law Olmsted, Sr.: Founder of Landscape Architecture in America.* Boston: University of Massachusetts Press, 1968.
Farr, Finis. *Chicago.* New Rochelle, N.Y.: Arlington House, 1973.
Fein, Albert. *Frederick Law Olmsted and the American Environmental Tradition.* New York: George Braziller, 1972.
Fitch, James M. *Architecture and the Esthetics of Plenty.* New York: Columbia University Press, 1961.
———. *American Building: The Historical Forces that Shaped It.* Boston: Houghton Mifflin Company, 1966.
Frietag, Joseph K. *Architectural Engineering.* New York: John Wiley and Sons, 1895.
Frye, Northrop. *Anatomy of Criticism.* Princeton, N.J.: Princeton University Press, 1957.
Giedion, Siegfried. *Space, Time and Architecture.* Cambridge, Mass.: Harvard University Press, 1967.
Gifford, Donald, ed. *The Literature of Architecture.* New York: Dutton, 1966.
Gilbert, Paul, and Charles Bryson. *Chicago and Its Makers.* Chicago: Felix Mendelsohn, 1929.
Goodspeed, E.J. *History of the Great Fire in Chicago and the West.* New York: H.S. Goodspeed and Company, 1871.
Gowan, Alan. *Image of American Living.* New York: J.B. Lippincott Company, 1964.
Graham, Anderson, Probst and White. *The Architectural World of Graham, Anderson, Probst and White, Chicago, and their Predecessors, D.H. Burnham and Company, and Graham, Burnham and Company.* London: B.T. Batsford, Ltd., 1933.
Green, Theodore M. *The Arts and the Art of Criticism.* Princeton, N.J.: Princeton University Press, 1940.
Hamlin, Talbot F. *The American Spirit in Architecture.* New Haven, Conn.: Yale University Press, 1926.
———. *The Enjoyment of Architecture.* New York: Charles Scribner's Sons, 1926.
Handy, William J. *Twentieth Century Criticism.* New York: Free Press, 1974.

Bibliography 201

Heyer, Paul. *Architects on Architecture: New Directions in America.* New York: Walter and Company, 1966.
Heyle, Bernard C. *New Bearings on Esthetics and Art Criticism.* New Haven, Conn.: Yale University Press, 1943.
Hines, Thomas. *Burnham of Chicago, Architect and Planner.* New York: Oxford University Press, 1974.
Hitchcock, Henry-Russell. *Modern Architecture, Romanticism and Reintegration.* New York: Payson and Clark, Ltd., 1929.
_____. *Architecture: Nineteenth and Twentieth Centuries.* Baltimore: Penguin Books, 1958.
_____. *The Architecture of H.E. Richardson and His Time.* Hamden, Conn.: Archon Books, 1961.
_____. *Richardson as a Victorian Architect.* Baltimore: Barton-Gillet Company, 1966.
Hitchcock, Henry-Russell and Philip Johnson. *The International Style: Architecture Since 1922.* New York: W.W. Norton and Company, Inc., 1932.
Hoffman, Donald. *The Architecture of John Wellborn Root.* Baltimore: John Hopkins University Press, 1974.
Hoffman, Donald, ed. *The Meanings of Architecture.* New York: Horizon Press, 1967.
Isham, Sammuel. *The Limitations of Verbal Criticism of Works of Art.* Portland, Me.: Southworth Press, 1908.
Jackson, William H. *The White City: The Story of the World's Columbian Exposition.* Chicago: White City Art Company, 1894.
Joedicke, Jurgen. *A History of Modern Architecture.* New York: Praeger, 1959.
Jordan, Elijah. *Essays in Criticism.* Chicago: University of Chicago Press, 1952.
Jordan, Robert F. *Victorian Architecture.* Baltimore: Penguin Books, Inc., 1966.
Jordy, William H., and William H. Pierson. *American Buildings and Their Architects.* Garden City, N.Y.: Doubleday, 1970.
Jordy, William, and Ralph Coe, eds. *American Architecture and Other Writings,* Volume 2. Cambridge, Mass.: Harvard University Press, 1961.
Kaufmann, Edgar, Jr. *Louis Sullivan and the Architecture of Free Enterprise.* Issued by the Chicago Art Institute on Sullivan's Exhibition, Chicago, 1956.
_____. *The Rise of an American Architecture.* New York: Praeger, 1970.
Kaufmann, Edgar, and Ben Raeburn, eds. *Frank Lloyd Wright: Writings and Buildings.* New York: Horizon Press, 1960.
Kidney, Walter C. *The Architecture of Choice: Eclecticism in America 1880-1930.* New York: George Braziller, 1974.
Kimball, Sidney F. *American Architecture.* New York: Robbs-Merrill, 1928.
Kouwenhoven, John A. *The Arts in Modern American Civilzation.* New York: Norton Library, 1967.
Lakeside Memorial. *The Lakeside Memorial of the Burning of Chicago.* Chicago: University Publishing Company, 1872.
Larkin, Oliver W. *Art and Life in America.* New York: Holt, Rinehart and Winston, 1960.
Lewis, Lloyd. *Chicago: The History of Its Reputation.* New York: Harcourt, Brace and Company, 1929.
Lewis, R.W.B. *The American Adam.* Chicago: University of Chicago Press, 1955.
Lowe, David. *Lost Chicago.* Boston: Houghton, Mifflin and Company, 1975.
Lynes, Russell. *The Tastemakers.* New York: Harper, 1954.
Manson, Grant C. *Frank Lloyd Wright to 1910.* New York: Reinhold Publishing Company, Corp., 1958.
Matthiessen, Francis O. *The Responsibilities of the Critics.* New York: Oxford University Press, 1952.

Mendelsohn, Felix. *Chicago—Yesterday and Today.* Chicago: Felix Mendelsohn, 1932.
Monroe, Harriet. *John Wellborn Root.* Boston: Houghton Mifflin Company, 1896.
Moore, Charles H. *The Promise of American Architecture: Address at the Annual Dinner of the A.I.A., 1905.* Washington, D.C.: American Institute of Architects, 1905.
_____. *Plan for Chicago, Prepared by D.H. Burnham and E.H. Bennett, Architects, Chicago, Illinois, 1909.* Chicago: Commercial Club, 1909.
_____. *Daniel H. Burnham, Architect, Planner of Cities,* 2 Volumes. Boston: Houghton Mifflin Company, 1921.
Morrison, Hugh. *Louis Sullivan: Prophet of Modern Architecture.* New York: W.W. Norton and Company, 1935.
Mujica, Francisco. *History of the Skyscraper.* New York: Archaeology and Architecture Press, 1930.
Mumford, Lewis. *Sticks and Stones.* New York: Boni and Liverright, 1924.
_____. *American Taste.* San Francisco: Westgate Press, 1929.
_____. *Roots of Contemporary American Architecture.* New York: Reinhold Publishing Corp., 1952.
_____. *The Brown Decades.* New York: Dover Publications, 1955.
_____. *From the Ground Up.* New York: Harcourt, Brace, 1956.
Museum of Modern Art. *Early Modern Architecture in Chicago, 1870-1910.* New York: Museum of Modern Art, 1940.
Olmsted, Frederick L., Jr., and Theodore Kimball, eds. *Frederick Law Omlsted, Landscape Architect, 1822-1903.* New York: G.P. Putnam's Sons, 1922.
Orear, George W. *Commercial and Architectural Chicago.* Chicago: G.W. Orear, 1887.
Osborne, Harold. *Aesthetics and Criticism.* London: Routledge and Kegan Paul Ltd., 1955.
_____. *The Art of Appreciation.* London: Oxford University Press, 1970.
Owings, Nathaniel A. *The American Aesthetics.* New York: Harper and Row Publishers, 1969.
Paul, Sherman. *Louis Sullivan, An Architect in American Thought.* Englewood Cliffs, N.J.: Prentice Hall, 1962.
Peisch, Mark L. *The Chicago School of Architecture.* New York: Random House, 1964.
Peper, Stephen C. *The Basis of Criticism in the Arts.* Cambridge, Mass.: Harvard University Press, 1949.
Pevsner, Nikolaus. *Pioneers of the Modern Movement from William Morris to Walter Gropius.* London: Farber and Farber, 1936.
_____. *Studies in Art, Architecture and Design,* 2 Volumes. New York: Walker and Company, 1968.
_____. *The Sources of Modern Architecture and Design.* London: Thames and Hudson, 1968.
_____. *Some Architectural Writers of the Nineteenth Century.* Oxford, England: Clarendon Press, 1972.
Pierce, Bessie L. *As Others See Chicago.* Chicago: University of Chicago Press, 1933.
Prak, Niels L. *The Language of Architecture.* Paris: Mouton, 1968.
Pritchard, John P. *Criticism in America.* Norman, Okla.: University of Oklahoma Press, 1956.
Randall, Frank A. *History of the Development of Building Construction in Chicago.* Urbana, Ill.: University of Illinois·Press, 1949.
Rasmussen, Steen E. *Experiencing Architecture.* Cambridge, Mass.: M.I.T. Press, 1962.
Reps, John W. *The Making of Urban America: A History of City Planning in the United States.* Princeton: N.J.: Princeton University Press, 1965.
_____. *Town Planning in Frontier America.* Princeton, N.J.: Princeton University Press, 1969.
Samson, George W. *Elements of Art Criticism.* Philadelphia: J.P. Lippincott and Company, 1874.
Schaefer, Herwin. *Nineteenth Century Design: The Functional Tradition in Victorian Design.* New York: Praeger Publishers, 1970.

Schultz, Earle, and Walker Simmons. *Offices in the Sky.* Indianapolis: Bobbs-Merrill Company, 1959.
Scully, Vincent J., Jr. *The Shingle Style.* New Haven, Conn.: Yale University Press, 1955.
_____. *Frank Lloyd Wright.* New York: George Braziller, 1960.
_____. *Modern Architecture: The Architecture of Democracy.* New York: George Braziller, 1961.
_____. *American Architecture and Urbanism.* New York: Praeger Publishers, 1969.
Shaw, Theordore L. *Hypocrisy About Art.* Boston: Stuart Publications, 1962.
Siegel, Arthur. *Chicago Famous Buildings.* Chicago: University of Chicago Press, 1965.
Smith, Henry J. *Chicago's Great Century, 1833-1933.* Chicago: Consolidated Publishers, 1933.
Smith, Norris K. *Frank Lloyd Wright, A Study in Architectural Contents.* Englewood Cliffs, N.J.: Prentice-Hall, 1966.
Starrett, W.A. *Skyscrapers and the Men Who Made Them.* New York: Scribner's Sons, 1928.
Stolnitz, Jerome. *Aesthetics and Philosophy of Art Criticism.* Boston: Houghton Mifflin, 1960.
Sullivan, Louis H. *Inspiration* (An essay read at the Third Annual Convention of Western Association of Architects at Chicago, November 17, 1886). Chicago: Inland Press, 1886.
_____. *Autobiography of an Idea.* New York: American Institute of Architects Press, 1924.
_____. *A System of Architectural Ornaments with a Philosophy of Man's Power.* New York: American Institute of Architects Press, 1924.
_____. *Kindergarten Chats.* Lawrence, Kan.: Scarab Fraternity Club, 1934.
_____. *Democracy: A Man's Search.* Detroit, Mich.: Wayne State University, 1961.
Summerson, John. *Victorian Architecture.* New York: Columbia Unviersity Press, 1970.
Summerson, John, ed. *Concerning Architecture: Essays on Architectural Writers and Writing Presented to Nikolaus Pevsner.* London: Allen Lane, 1968.
Szarkowski, John. *The Idea of Louis Sullivan.* Minneapolis, Minn.: University of Minnesota Press, 1956.
Talmadge, Thomas E. *Architecture of Old Chicago.* Chicago: Goodspeed Publishing Company, 1891.
_____. *The Story of Architecture in America.* New York: W.W. Norton and Company, 1927.
Therstrom, Stephen. *Nineteenth-Century Cities.* New Haven, Conn.: Yale University Press, 1970.
Tunnard, Christopher. *The City of Man.* New York: Scribner, 1953.
_____. *American Skyline.* New York: New American Library, Inc., 1956.
_____. *Man-Made America: Chaos or Control.* New Haven, Conn.: Yale University Press, 1963.
_____. *The Modern American City.* Princeton, N.J.: Van Nostrand, 1968.
Van Rensselaer, Mariana G. *Henry Hobson Richardson and His Works.* New York: Dover Publications, Inc., 1969.
Wellek, Rene. *A History of Modern Criticism (1750-1950).* New Haven, Conn.: Yale University Press, 1955.
Weisman, Winston. *A New View of Skyscraper History.* New York: Praeger, 1970.
Williams-Ellis, Clough. *The Pleasure of Architecture.* London: Jonathan Cape, 1954.
Wright, Frank L. *Modern Architecture.* Princeton, N.J.: Princeton University Press, 1931.
_____. *An Autobiography.* New York: Duell, Sloan and Pearce, 1943.
_____. *A Testament.* New York: Horizon Press, 1957.
_____. *An Organic Architecture.* Cambridge, Mass.: M.I.T. Press, 1970.
_____. *Genius and Mobocracy.* New York: Horizon Press, 1971.
Ziff, Larzar. *The American 1890's.* New York: Viking Press, 1966.

Periodicals

Anonymous. "Letter to the Editor Concerning the Rebuilding of Chicago after the Great Fire." *American Architect and Building News* **1** (April 1876) : 110-11.

———. "Backwardness of Architecture." *American Architect and Building News* **12** (July 1882): 51.

———. "The Auditorium Building." *American Architect and Building News* **26** (December 1889): 299-300.

———. "The Effect of the Fair Buildings on Chicago." *American Architect and Building News* **38** (November 1892): 100-01.

———. "Official Praise of the World's Fair Buildings." *American Architect and Building News* **42** (October 1893): 51.

———. "The Architecture of Chicago." *American Architect and Building News* **42** (November 1893): 75-76.

———. "New York Life Insurance Company's Building, Chicago." *American Architect and Building News* **42** (November 1893): 78.

———. "Skeleton Construction as Used in the New York Life Building, Chicago." *American Architect and Building News* **43** (February 1894): 70.

———. "The Work of Holabird and Roche, Architects." *American Architect* **118** (August 1920): 165-72, 231-42.

———. "The Chicago Temple Building." *Architecture* **50** (1924): 369-70.

———. "At the Architectural Association, Extracts from Papers on Architectural Criticism and on Ensuing Criticism." *Architect's Journal* **109** (June 1949): 503-05.

———. "Are We to Have Architectural Criticism?" *Architect's World* **1** (February 1938): 1-4.

———. "Architectural Criticism, a Discussion Organized by the Student's Committee." *Architectural Association Journal* **65** (June-July 1949): 9-12.

———. "An Art Critic among the Architects." *Architectural Association Journal* **68** (June 1952): 7-16.

———. "To Louis Henry Sullivan, the Gold Medal of the American Institute of Architect." *American Institute of Architects Journal* **6** (July 1946): 3-6.

———. "Garrick Theater, Chicago," *American Institute of Architects Journal* **37** (March 1962): 51.

———. "Frank Lloyd Wright on Louis Sullivan." *Architectural Forum* **91** (August 1949): 94-97.

———. "Chicago's Sullivan in New Photographs." *Architectural Forum* **101** (October 1954): 128-34.

———. "A Continuing Tradition in Chicago Technology." *Architectural Forum* **116** (May 1962): 89-106, 107, 125-41, 190, 203, 206.

———. "Henry Van Brunt." *Architectural Review* **10** (1903): 44.

———. "Canons of Criticism." *Architectural Review* **109** (March 1951): 135-37.

———. "Wasted Opportunities." *Architectural Record* **3** (July-September 1893): 72-78.

———. "Board of Trade Building." *Architectural Record* **3** (July-September 1893): 96-100.

———. "Some Entrances to the Skyscraper." *Architectural Record* **9** (April 1900): 363-74.

———. "An Amusing Street Front." *Architectural Record* **13** (January 1903): 49-84.

———. "The Sears-Roebuck Building, Chicago." *Architectural Record* **18** (August 1905): 167-69.

———. "The Newest Thing in Sky-Scrapers." *Architectural Record* **19** (May 1905): 398-400.

———. "The Majestic Building." *Architectural Record* **19** (June 1906): 474-76.

———. "Recent Bank Buildings of the United States." *Architectural Record* **25** (January 1909): 4-66.

———. "Russell Sturgis' Architecture." *Architectural Record* **25** (June 1909): 405-10.

———. "The Crowning of the Skyscraper." *Architectural Record* **25** (May 1910): 431-34.

———. "Lessons of the Chicago Fair: An Interview with the Late D.H. Burnham." *Architectural Record* **33** (January 1913): 34-44.

———. "The Apollo Theater, Chicago." *Architectural Record* **53** (April 1923): 533-43.

———. "Was the Home Insurance Building in Chicago the First Skyscraper on Skeleton Construction.?" *Architectural Record* **76** (August 1934): 113-18.

_____. "Montgomery Schuyler Assessed the Requirements of a New Age." *Architectural Record* **119** (January, 1956) : 24, 276, 280, 284, 288.

_____. "Louis Sullivan." *Architectural Record* **120** (October 1956) : 218-20.

_____. "An Assessment of the Success and Failures of the Chicago School." *Architectural Record* **120** (November 1956) : 285-89.

_____. "The Hurst Building, Chicago." *Architectural Building* **31** (April 1912) : 407-12.

_____. "John W. Root." *Inland Architect and News Record* **16** (January 1891) : 85-91.

_____. "Architecture at the World's Columbian Exposition." *Inland Architect and News Record* **21** (July 1893) : 72-73; **22** (August 1893) : 3-4, **22** (September 1893) : 16-18.

_____. "The Organization of the World's Columbian Exposition." *Inland Architect and News Record* **22** (August 1893) : 5-8.

_____. "The New York Life Builidng, Chicago." *Inland Architect and News Record* **24** (October 1894) : 30.

_____. "A Veteran Architect—Mr. W.L.B. Jenney Retires." *Inland Architect and News Record* **45** (May 1905) : 44.

_____. "Architectural Criticism, Students' Evening at the Architectural Association." *Builder* **176** (January 1949) : 678-79.

_____. "New Schlesinger and Mayer Building." *Brick Builder* **12** (1903) : 101-04.

Adler, Dankmar. "Theater-Building for American Cities." *Inland Architect* **11** (November 1867) : 6-10.

_____. "The Chicago Auditorium." *Architectural Record* **1** (October-December, 1891) : 415-35.

_____. "The Right of the Lowest Bidder from the Point of View of the Architect." *Inland Architect and News Record* **18** (January 1892) : 77-78.

_____. "Some Notes upon the Early Chicago Architects." *Inland Architect and News Record* **19** (May 1892) : 47-48.

_____. "The Influence of Steel Construction and Plate Glass upon Style." *Inland Architect and News Record* **28** (November 1896) : 33-37.

Arntzen, Arne. "Will the Prospect Rent?" *American Architect* **137** (March 1930) : 54-55, 95-96, 98.

Boyd, David K. "The Skyscraper and the Street." *American Architect and Building News* **94** (November 1908) : 161-67.

Bragdon, Claude F. "Made in France Architecture." *Architectural Record* **16** (December 1904): 561-68.

_____. "An American Architect: Being an Appreciation of Louis Henry Sullivan." *House and Garden* **7** (January 1905) : 47-55.

_____. "The Use of Ceramic Products in the Embellishment of Building." *Architectural Forum* **26** (July 1917) : 17-19.

_____. "Architecture and Democracy, before and after the War." *Architectural Record* **44** (July 1917) : 75-85.

Bush-Brown, Albert. "Notes toward a Basis of Criticism." *Architectural Record* **126** (October 1959) : 183-94.

Caparn, H.A. "The Riddle of the Tall Building: Has the Skyscraper a Place in American Architecture." *Craftsman* **10** (April 1906) : 477-88.

Chamberlain, Betty. "Louis Sullivan." *Arts and Architecture* **73** (December 1956) : 12-15.

Collins, Peter. "The Philosophy of Architectural Criticism." *American Institute of Architects Journal* **49** (January 1968) : 46-49.

Condit, Carl W. "The Chicago School and the Modern Movement in Architecture." *Art in America* **36** (January 1948): 19-36.

_____. "Sullivan's Skyscrapers as the Expression of Nineteenth Century Technology." *Technology and Culture* **1** (Winter 1959) : 78-93.

Connelly, Willard. "New Chapter in the Life of Louis Sullivan." *American Institute of Architects Journal* **20** (September 1953) : 107-14.

Corbett, Harvey W. "The Birth and Development of the Tall Building." *American Architect* **129** (July-December 1926) : 37-40.

Croly, Herbert D. "Criticism That Counts." *Architectural Record* **10** (April 1910) : 398-405.

David, A.C. "The Building of the First National Bank of Chicago." *Architectural Record* **19** (January 1906) : 48-58.

Desmond, Harry W. "What is Architecture?: A Layman's View." *Architectural Record* **1** (October-December 1891) : 211-18.

_____. "Modern Architecture: A Conversation." *Architectural Record* **1** (January-March 1892) : 276-80.

_____. "The Schlesinger and Mayer Building, an Attempt to Give Functional Expression to a Department Store," *Architectural Record* **16** (July 1904) : 53-67.

_____. "Rationalizing the Skyscraper." *Architectural Record* **17** (May 1905) : 422-25.

_____. "The Architect and the Critic." *Architectural Record* **19** (April 1906) : 279-81.

Duncan, Hugh D. "Legacy of the Chicago School and What Went Wrong." *Inland Architect* **13** (June 1969) : 52-56.

Eidlitz, Leopold. "The Vicissitudes of Architecture." *Architectural Record* **1** (July-September 1891) : 471-84.

_____. "The Architect of Fashion." *Architectural Record* **3** (April-June 1894) : 347-53.

Elmslie, George G. "Sullivan's Ornamentation." *American Institute of Architects Journal* **6** (October 1946) : 155-58.

_____. "The Chicago School: Its Inheritance and Bequest." *American Institute of Architects Journal* **18** (July 1952) : 32-40.

Ferree, Barr. "An 'American Style' of Architecture." *Architectural Record* **1** (July-September 1891) : 39-45.

_____. "What is Architecture." *Architectural Record* **1** (October-December, 1891) : 199-310.

_____. "Architectural Problems in Great Cities." *American Architect and Building News* **38** (December 1892) : 161-65.

_____. "The Modern Office Building." *Inland Architect and News Record* **27** (February 1896) : 4-5; (March 1896) : 12-14; (April 1896) : 23-25; (June 1896) : 43-47.

_____. "The Art of the High Building." *Architectural Record* **15** (May 1904) : 445-66.

Fitch, James M. "The Shifting Basis of Contemporary Criticism." *Progressive Architect* **37** (June 1956) : 143, 192, 194, 197, 202, 208, 210, 212, 218, 222.

Flagg, Ernest. "American Architecture as Opposed to Architecture in America." *Inland Architect and News Record* **35** (June 1900) : 36-37.

Fryer, William F., Jr., "Skeleton Construction." *Architectural Record* **1** (October-December 1891) : 228-35.

Gilbert, Cass. "Daniel H. Burnham, an Appreciation." *Architectural Record* **32** (August 1912) : 175-85.

Gordon, F.C. "The Sky-Scraper." *American Architect and Building News* **46** (December 1894) : 100-01.

Grey, Elmer. "Indigenous and Inventive Architecture in America." *Inland Architect and News Record* **35** (June 1900) : 36-37.

Gutchen, Jeffrey. "Proposals for Architectural Criticism." *Connection* (March 1965) : 12-19.

Hamatt, Edward S. "The Building and Designing of the Skyscraper." *American Architect and Building News* **88** (November 1905) : 158-60.

Hamlin, A.D.F. "The Difficulties of Modern Architecture." *Architectural Record* **1** (October-December 1891) : 137-50.

_____. "The Battle of Styles." *Architectural Record* **1** (January-March 1892) : 265-75; (April-June 1892) : 405-13.

Hamlin, Talbot F. "Criticism Might Help Architect: Let's Try It." *American Architect* **137** (May 1930) : 41, 90.

_____. "What We Should Consider before We Criticise." *American Architect* **140** (September 1931) : 34-35, 110, 114.

_____. "Sullivan's Letters at Columbia." *American Architect* **149** (November 1936) : 100-04.

_____. "Architectural Criticism." *Architect's World* **1** (March 1938) : 73-74.

Hastings, Thomas. "High Building and Good Architecture." *American Architect and Building News* **46** (November 1894) : 67-68.

Herbert, William. "An American Architect." *Architectural Record* **23** (February 1908) : 111-22.

Hitchcock, Henry-Russell. "Richardson's American Express Building, Chicago." *Society of Architectural Historians Journal* **9** (March-May 1950) : 25-30.

_____. "Sullivan and Skyscraper." *Builder* (August 1953) : 197-200.

Hope, Henry R. "Louis Sullivan's Architectural Ornament." *Magazine of Art* **40** (March 1947) : 110-17.

Huxtable, Ada L. "The Home Insurance Building." *Progressive Architecture* **38** (June 1957) : 207-08.

Jenkins, Charles E. "A White Enameled Building." *Architectural Record* **4** (January-March 1895) : 299-306.

_____. "A Review of the Work of W.L.B. Jenney and W.B. Mundie." *Architectural Reviewer* **1** (March 1897) : 1-45.

Jenney, W.L.B. "The Chicago Construction, or Tall Buildings on a Compressible Soil." *Inland Architect and News Record* **18** (November 1891) : 41.

_____. "The Steel Skeleton Is Earthquake Proof." *Western Architect* **9** (May 1906) : 49-51.

Johnson, Philip. "Is Sullivan the Father of Functionalism?" *Art News* **55** (December 1956) : 44-46, 56-57.

Kerr, Robert. "The Problem of National American Architecture." *Architectural Record* **3** (October-December 1893) : 121-32.

Kimball, Sidney F. "The Classic in the Skyscraper." *Architectural Record* **57** (February 1925) : 189-90.

_____. "Louis Sullivan: An Old Master." *Architectural Record* **57** (April 1925) : 289-304.

_____. "The Family Tree of the Skyscraper." *Architectural Forum* **79** (March 1928) : 390-405.

Line, Ralph M. "Art and Architecture—The Past: Louis H. Sullivan." *Craft Horizons* **22** (May-June 1962) : 19-21.

McLean, Robert C. "Dankmar Adler." *Inland Architect and News Record* **35** (May 1900) : 26-27.

_____. "The Passing of the Woman's Temple." *Western Architect* **31** (1922) : 13-14.

McQuade, Walter "Sullivan Survives." *Architectural Forum* **105** (October 1956) : 156-161.

Maginnis, Charles D. "Honoring Louis Sullivan." *American Institute of Architects Journal* **6** (November 1946) : 208-13.

Manson, Grant. "Sullivan and Wright, an Uneasy Union of Celts." *Architectural Review* **118** (November 1955) : 297-300.

Marshall, Henry R. "The Legitimate Design for the Casting of Steel Skeleton Skyscraper." *American Architect and Building News* **66** (December 1899) : 83-84.

Morrison, Hugh. "Louis Sullivan Today." *American Institute of Architects Journal* **26** (September 1956) : 98-100.

Moser, John. "American Architectural Form of the Future." *American Architect and Building News* **13** (June 1883) : 303-05.

Mumford, Lewis. "High Buildings: An American View." *American Architect* **126** (November 1924) : 423-24.

Parson, William E. "Burnham as a Pioneer in City Planning." *Architectural Record* **38** (July 1914) : 13-31.

Purcell, William G. "Sullivan at Work." *Northwest Architect* **8** (January-February 1944) : 11.

_____. "Louis Sullivan, Prophet of Democracy." *American Institute of Architects Journal* **16** (December 1951) : 265-71.

Oakley, David. "Architecture and Criticism." *Building* **212** (June 1967) : 95-96.
Newton, Roger H. "New Evidence on the Evolution of the Skyscraper." *Art Quarterly* **4** (Winter 1941) : 56-70.
Nimmons and Fellows, Architects. "Designing a Great Mercantile Plant." *Architectural Record* **19** (June 1906) : 403-11.
Raetze, Robert A. "Two Stores in Chicago." *Architectural Record* **20** (July 1906) : 71-74.
Rebori, A.N. "The Work of Burnham and Root, D.H. Burnham and Company, and Graham, Burnham and Company." *Architectural Record* **38** (July 1915) : 32-168.
Richards, J.M. "Criticism." *Architect's Journal* **125** (January 1957) : 169.
_____. "The Professional Magazine as Critic." *American Institute of Architects Journal* **49** (May 1968) : 65-68.
Robinson, John B. "Authority in Architectural Design." *Architectural Record* **6** (July-September 1896) : 77-76.
Root, John W. "The Value of Type in Art." *Inland Architect and Builder* **2** (November 1883) : 132.
_____. "Architectural Ornamentation." *Inland Architect and Builder* **5** (April 1885) : 54-55.
_____. "Fire-Insurance and Architecture." *American Architect and Building News* **20** (September 1886): 148-50.
_____. "Architectural Freedom." *Inland Architect and Builder* **8** (December 1886) : 64-65.
_____. "Style." *Inland Architect and Builder* **8** (January 1887) : 99-101.
_____. "What Are the Present Tendencies of Architectural Design in America." *Inland Architect and News Record* **9** (March 1887) : 23-26.
_____. "President's Address to the Western Association of Architects." *Inland Architect and News Record* **10** (December 1887) : 75-76.
_____. "Broad Art Criticism." *Building* **8** (February 1888) : 43-44, 53-55.
_____. "Code for the Guidance of Persons Practicing the Profession of Architecture in the United States." *American Architect and Building News* **26** (November 1889) : 252.
_____. "Individuality in Architectural Design.' *Inland Architect and News Record* **14** (December 1889) : 80-81.
_____. "A Great Architectural Problem." *Inland Architect and News Record* **15** (June 1890) : 67-71.
_____. "Expression in Form." *Inland Architect and News Record* **16** (October 1890) : 30-31.
_____. "Architects of Chicago." *Inland Architect and News Record* **16** (January 1891) : 91-92.
Rowe, Calin. "Chicago Frame, Chicago's Place in Modern Movement." *Architectural Review* **120** (November 1956) : 285-89.
Salero, Joseph. "Louis Sullivan—Return to Principle." *Liturgical Arts* **16** (February 1948): 49-50.
Saltzstein, John W. "Dankmar Adler and The Chicago Fire." *Inland Architect* **11** (October 1967): 8.
Sayler, Henry H. "Make No Little Plan—Daniel H. Burnham Thought It but did He Do It?" *American Institute of Architects Journal* **27** (March 1957) : 95-99.
Schuyler, Montgomery. "Architecture." *Inland Architect and News Record* **17** (February 1891): 5-6.
_____. "Glimpses of Western Architecture: Chicago." *Harper's Magazine* **83** (August 1891) : 395-456; (September 1891) : 554-70.
_____. "State Buildings at the World's Fair." *Architectural Record* **3** (July-September 1893) : 27-301.
_____. "Last Words About the World's Fair." *Architectural Record* **3** (January-March 1894) : 271-301.
_____. "Modern Architecture." *Architectural Record* **4** (July-September 1894) : 1-13.
_____. "Architecture in Chicago: Adler and Sullivan." *Architectural Record*, the Great American Architects Series, No. 2, Part I (February 1896) : 3-48.

———. "Architecture in Chicago: D.H. Burnham and Company." *Architectural Record*, the Great American Architects Series, No. 2, Part II (February 1896) : 49-69.
———. "The Skyscraper Up To Date." *Architectural Record* **8** (January-March 1900) : 231-57.
———. "The Art of City-Making." *Architectural Record* **12** (May 1902) : 1-26.
———. "The Skyscraper Problem." *Scribner's Magazine* **34** (August 1903) : 253-56.
———. "The Evolution of the Skyscraper." *Architectural Record* **14** (November 1903) : 329-43.
———. "A Modern Classic." *Architectural Record* **15** (May 1904) : 431-44.
———. "To Curb the Skyscraper." *Architectural Record* **24** (October 1908) : 300-02.
———. "Russell Sturgis." *Architectural Record* **25** (March 1909) : 146, 220.
Scott, Geoffrey. "A Basis of Architectural Criticism." *Architect's World* **1** (February 1938) : 4-6.
Scully, Vincent, Jr. "Louis Sullivan's Architectural Ornament." *Perspecta* **5** (January 1959) : 73-80.
Sekler, Eduard F. "Thoughts about the Function of Architectural Theory and Criticism," *Connection* **5** (Summer 1968) : 12-19.
Shankland, E.G. "The Construction of the Buildings at the World's Columbian Exposition." *Inland Architect and News Record* **22** (August 1893) : 8-9.
Smith, Edward R. "Montgomery Schuyler and the History of American Architecture." *Architectural Record* **36** (September 1914): 264-68.
Spark, Edwin E. "The Beginning of Chicago." *American Architect and Building News* **81** (September 1903) : 101-04.
Starrett, Theodore. "The Building of a Great Mercantile Plant." *Architectural Record* **19** (April 1906) : 265-74.
———. "Daniel H. Burnham." *Architects' and Builders' Magazine* **13** (1912) : 281-83.
———. "John Wellborn Root." *Architects' and Builders' Magazine* **13** (1912) : 429-31.
———. "The Architecture of Louis H. Sullivan." *Architects' and Builders' Magazine* **13** (1912) : 469-75.
Sturgis, Russell. "The Commonsense Planning." *Architectural Review* **5** (1896) : 44-47.
———. "Good Things in Modern Architecture." *Architectural Record* **8** (July-September 1898) : 92-110.
———. "How to Treat the Classical Order." *Architectural Review* **6** (1899) : 59-62.
———. "An Unscientific Enquiry into Fireproofing Building." *Architectural Record* **9** (January 1900) : 229-53.
———. "The Authorship of Architecture." *Architectural Review* **7** (1900) : 125-27.
———. "Simple Ways of Fireproofing." *Architectural Record* **13** (February 1903) : 119-33.
———. "The Warehouse and Factory in Architecture." *Architectural Record* **15** (January 1904) : 1-17; (February 19040) : 123-33.
———. "The New Thomas Music Hall." *Architectural Record* **16** (August 1904) : 161-64.
———. "The Treatment ot Plain Front." *Architectural Record* **17** (January 1905) : 67-70.
———. "A Chicago Factory—The Kent Building." *Architectural Record* **17** (January 1905) : 66-67.
———. "The Schoonhofen Brewery." *Architectural Recort* **17** (March 1905) : 201-07.
———. "The Whittemore Building." *Architectural Record* **17** (June 1905) : 516-17.
———. "The Whittemore Building Again." *Architectural Record* **18** (October 1905) : 307, 309.
———. "The Paper Mills Building, Chicago." *Architectural Record* **19** (February 1906) : 151-52.
———. "The Chapin and Gore Building, Chicago." *Architectural Record* **19** (February 1906) : 154-57.
———. "Factories and Warehouses." *Architectural Record* **19** (May 1906) : 369-75.
———. "Some Recent Warehouses." *Architectural Record* **23** (May 1908) : 373-86.
Sullivan, Louis H. "American Architecture: Its Characteristic and Tendency." *Building* **4** (January 1886) : 43-44.
———. "Emotional Architecture as Compared with Classical." *Inland Architect and News Record* **24** (November 1894) : 32-34.

———. "The Young Man in Architecture." *Inland Architect and News Record* **35** (January 1900): 38-40.
———. "The Tall Office Building Artistically Considered." *Western Architect* **31** (January 1922): 3-11.
———. "What is Architecture." *American Society of Architectural Historians Journal* **4** (April 1944): 3-22.
Tallmadge, Thomas E. "The Chicago School." *Architectural Review* **15** (April 1908): 69-74.
Tunnard, Christopher. "A City Called Beautiful." *Society of Architectural Historians Journal* **19** (March-May 1950): 31-35.
Weber, Peter B. "A Review of the Works of Holabird and Roche." *Architectural Reviewer* **1** (June 1897): 1-41.
Webster, J. Carson."Richardson's American Express Building." *Society of Architectural Historians Journal* **9** (March-May 1950): 20-24.
———. "The Skyscraper: Logical and Historical Consideration." *Society of Architectural Historians Journal* **18** (December 1959): 126-39.
Weisman, Winston. "Criticism and Commercial Architecture." *College Art Journal* **11** (Fall 1951): 26-29.
Wight, Peter B. "A Millionaire's Architectural Investment." *American Architect and Building News* **1** (May 1876): 147-49.
———. "Reminiscences of Chicago in 1859, Architectural and Otherwise." *Inland Architect and News Record* **20** (August 1892): 3-4; (September 1892): 13-14.
———. "The Great Exhibition Reviewed." *American Architect and Building News* **42** (October 1893): 7-8, 21-23, 32-34, 47-49; (November 1893): 57-59, 86-88, 158-59.
———. "Henry Van Brunt, Writer and Philosopher." *Inland Architect and News Record* **23** (April 1894): 29-30; (May 1894): 41-42; (June 1894): 49-50; (July 1894): 60-61.
———. "The Use of Burned Clay Products in the Fireproof Buildings." *American Architect and Building News* **90** (September 1906): 67-68, 75-78, 84-86.
———. "Reminiscences of Russell Sturgis." *Architectural Record* **26** (August 1909): 123-31.
———. "Utilitarian Architecture at Chicago." *Architectural Record* **26** (February 1910): 189-98, 248-56.
———. "A Transmutation of a Residence Street, Resulting in Another Solution of a Utilitarian Problem by Architects." *Architectural Record* **27** (April 1910): 285-93.
———. "Additions to Chicago Skyline, a Few Recent Skyscrapers." *Architectural Record* **28** (July 1910): 15-24.
———. "Studies of Design without Ornament." *Architectural Record* **29** (February 1911): 167-76.
———. "Daniel Hudson Burnham and His Associates." *Architectural Record* **38** (July 1914): 1-12.
Winkler, F.K. "Some Chicago Buildings Represented by the Work of Holabird and Roche." *Architectural Record* **31** (April 1912): 313-86.
Woltersdorf, Arthur. "The Father of the Skeleton Framing Buildings." *Western Architect* **33** (February 1924): 21-23.
———. "Dankmar Adler." *Western Architect* **33** (July 1924): 75-79.
Wright, Frank L. "Louis Sullivan—His Work." *Architectural Record* **56** (July 1924): 28-32.
———. "Louis Sullivan's Words and Work." *Architectural Record* **77** (March 1935): 116-17.
———. "Chicago Dynamic." *American Institute of Architects Journal* **29** (January 1958): 18-23.
Van Brunt, Henry. "Architecture of the West." *Inland Architect and News Record* **14** (December 1889): 78-80.
———. "Historic Style and Modern Architecture." *Architectural Review* **1** (August 1892): 59-61; **2** (January 1893): 1-4.

Index

Adams, Henry, 150
Adler and Sullivan, 8, 27, 87-120, 137, 159
  Auditorium, 88, 90, 99, 101, 101-3, 104-9, 115, 120, 137, 159
  development of the firm, 88, 98, 114, 119
  influence of clients, 104
  influence of Richardson, 98, 101
  Stock Exchange building, 112-13
  Walker Warehouse, 101
Adler, Dankmar, 26, 58-59, 81, 82, 87-120
  and Sullivan, 88, 97
  architect, 81, 90, 91, 105
  as architectural critic, 26
  biography, 91-92
  Central Music Hall, 92
  on the Chicago fire, 58-59
Architectural criticism, 1-8, 9-23, 42, 45, 110
  and influence on architectural development, 43-45, 110
  as historian, 45
  change in, 9
  defined in terms of function, 12
  description, 14
  evaluation, 16
  format for, 16-18
  general analysis, 1-8, 9-23, 42, 45
  history of, 9-11
  interpretation, 14
Architectural professionalism, 160
Architectural Record, 1, 3, 18, 20, 26, 27, 29, 30, 33, 38, 40, 41, 42, 81, 97, 99, 102, 104, 105, 116, 128, 129-30, 143, 149, 150, 151, 154, 155, 156, 157
  beginnings of, 26, 29, 40
  citations, 1, 3, 18, 20, 26, 27, 28, 29, 30, 33, 38, 40, 42, 81, 97, 99, 102, 104, 105, 106, 116, 128, 129-130, 143, 149, 150, 151, 154, 155, 156, 157
  critical appreciation found in, 149-50
Armour, Philip, 85-86, 158
  biography, 85-86

Arts and Crafts Movement, 150
  and Gustav Stickley, 150

Baudelaire, Charles, 11
  as architectural critic, 11
Beaux Arts, 154, 155, 160, 161, 164
Beman, S.S., 80, 81, 86, 90, 105
Bernini, 10
  critic of architecture, 10
Bourget, Paul, 6, 7, 69, 82, 141, 144
Boyington, W.W., 74, 80
  Insurance Exchange Building, 74
Burnham and Root, 8, 74, 77, 79, 81, 88, 90, 98, 104, 106, 121-47, 157
  as leaders of Chicago School, 120, 123, 128
  Calumet Building, 74
  Carson Pirie Scott, 117-18
  Chicago School of Architecture, 81, 90, 142, 143
  Commerce Building, 130
  Counselman Building, 90
  influence of clients, 104, 131, 144
  influence of Richardson, 98, 99, 120, 137, 138, 145
  Insurance Exchange Building, 122, 134
  Montauk Building, 79, 83, 90, 131-33
  Monadnock Building, 74, 83, 88, 104, 130, 134, 136, 137-41, 144, 145
  partnership, 123, 127, 130, 131
  Phoenix Building, 122, 134
  Reliance Building, 74, 77, 114, 141, 142, 143-45
  Rookery, 74, 84, 122, 130, 134, 135-37
Burnham and Sullivan, 157
  leaders of the Chicago School, 157
Burnham Co., D.H., 145, 149, 157, 159, 163
  Orchestra Hall, 159
  Park space, 163
Burnham Daniel H., 38, 68, 80, 93, 127-29, 130, 141, 145-47, 150, 151, 157

212   Index

and World's Columbian Exposition, 129, 131, 145, 150, 151, 152
architect, 81, 90
biography, 80, 93, 127-30, 141, 157
Chicago as training ground, 38, 68
city planning, 146
First National Bank, 147
partnership with Root, 123, 130, 141, 147
Railway Exchange Building, 145-46
Reliance Building, 74, 77, 141, 142
Burnham, Hubert and Daniel Jr., 165
Carson Pirie Scott Annex, 165

Carrere and Hastings, 149
Carter, Asher, 80, 128
Centennial Exposition, (1876), 29
Chicago, 47-59, 63, 68-71, 84, 85, 122, 130, 149, 150-51, 158-61, 162, 163, 164, 165
architectural advancements, 47
architectural phases, 48
city growth, 163
cultural shifts, 158-62
fire, 48, 149, 162
history, 47, 48-53, 55, 56, 69-71, 84, 159, 161
park space, 162, 163, 164
railroads, 50-51, 55, 70
World's Columbian Exposition, 47, 48, 149, 150-51, 158, 163, 164
Chicago construction, 2, 38, 47, 52-54, 63, 66, 68, 71-79, 83, 109, 142
balloon construction of frame buildings, 47, 53-54
cast iron facades/columns, 65, 66, 68
Chicago caisson, 47, 48, 74, 75
Chicago windows, 77
elevators, 66, 68, 72
fireproof construction, 38, 47, 63-65, 66, 72, 78-80
foundation, 72-75, 83
grill foundation, 38, 47
isolated footings, 47, 48, 73, 75
reinforced concrete construction, 47, 48
skeletal construction, 47, 48, 68, 71-72, 75-76, 109
wind bracing, 47, 77, 142
Chicago Fire of 1871, 2, 8, 48, 51, 54, 57-59, 63, 84, 123, 130, 149, 162
Chicago School of Architecture, 2, 7, 9, 27, 61-86, 106, 109, 120, 131, 144, 149, 164, 165, 167-68
American school, 164-65, 168
and Arts and Crafts Movement, 150
and clients, 83, 104, 131
and William Le Baron Jenney, 68
Burnham and Root as leaders of the school, 120

Commercial style, 2, 7, 8, 9, 36, 61-86, 109, 133, 134, 141, 142
dates, 2, 147, 149
demise of, 164, 165
description, 3, 7, 61-62, 144, 165, 167-68
ideals of, 27, 149, 154
second generation of, 149
skyscrapers, 95, 96, 106, 132, 133, 144, 154
Louis Sullivan representing, 28, 63, 99, 149, 150
Cleveland, Horace, 162, 163
Cobb, Henry Ives, 80, 159
Newberry Library, 159
University of Chicago, 159
Commercial Style, 2, 5, 7, 8, 9, 22, 36, 61-86, 109, 126, 131, 134, 141, 142, 154, 155, 158, 159, 160, 161
clients and change, 158-59
critics of, 36
demise of, 158, 160
elevator buildings, 66
foundations, 73, 133
fireproofing of, 39, 64-65, 66, 133
indigenous American architectural style, 61, 72-86, 126, 134, 153, 154
skyscrapers, 158
structural system of, 65-66, 132, 137, 141, 142, 143
The Craftsman, 149, 150
Croly, Herbert David, 8, 20-21, 26, 40-42
architectural critic, 8, 20-21
biography, 40-42
criticism that counts, 20-21
found of *Architectural Record,* 26, 40, 41
Davis, Alexander, 55
Desmond, Harry, 18-19, 28, 145-46
architect and the critic, 18-19, 28
Diderot, Denis, 10, 11, 12
first architectural critic, 11, 12
Downing, Andrew Jackson, 56

Eidlitz, Leopold, 30, 31, 35, 39, 121, 124, 145
biography, 39
writings of, 40, 121, 124
Eliot, T.S., 12-13
Function of Criticism, 12-14
Elmslie, George Grant, 149, 165-66
disciple of Louis Henry Sullivan, 165-66
Ferree, Barr, 26, 40
founder of the *Architectural Record,* 26, 40
Field, Marshall, 74, 85, 87, 158, 159
biography, 85
warehouse, 87
Fletcher, Sir Banister, 9
historical styles defined by, 9
Frost, Charles S., 80

Giedion, Sigfried, 3, 7, 87, 142, 143, 144
    architectural critic, 7, 144
    Space, Time and Architecture, 3, 87, 142
Graham, Anderson, Probst and White, 149
Greenough, Horatio, 11-12, 31, 124
    architectural critic, 11-12, 31, 124
Grimm, 10
    architectural critic, 10

Hamlin, Talbot Faulkner, 3-4, 7, 18
    architect, 7
    critic, 3-4, 18
Hitchcock, 7
    critic, 7
Holabird, William, 68, 80, 90, 109, 128, 137

Jenney, William Le Baron, 67-68, 76, 77, 80, 81, 87, 109, 127, 163
    architect, 81, 127
    biography, 67-68, 80, 163
    Home Insurance Bulding, 68, 76, 87, 109
    LaSalle-Monroe Building, 67
    Leiter Buildings, 68, 77, 88
    Manhattan Building, 74, 77
Jennings Building, 51
Jensen, Jens, 162, 63
Johnson, Philip, 26, 95, 114
    as architectural critic, 26, 95, 114, 119

Kinzie, John Harris, 50

Le Corbusier, 7, 94
    architect, 94
    architectural critic, 7
Loos, Adolf, 7
    architectural critic, 7

Marshall Field Warehouse, 62, 87-88, 98, 99, 101, 105, 106, 115, 120, 137
Matz, Otto H., 66, 78
    Nixon Building, 66, 78
McCormick, 158
McKim, Mead and White, 35, 37, 42, 97
Morrison Hugh, 3
Mumford, Lewis, 2, 7, 27, 28, 157
    architectural critic, 7, 28
    The Brown Decades, 2, 27
    genteel reaction, 156
Mundie, William B., 76, 80
Murphy Assoc., C.F., 141
    First National Bank Building, 141

New Path, 32
Nixon Building, 67

Ogden, William B., 50, 54

Olmstead, Frederick Law, 162, 163,
    park space development, 162-63
    World's Columbian Exposition, 163
Osdel, John Mills van, 54, 56, 64, 65, 78, 79, 85
    Court House, 64
    fireproofing, 78
    introduces cast iron columns, 64
    Kendall Building, 79

Palmer, Potter, 84-85
Perkins, Dwight, 149, 162, 165
Perkins and Wills partnership, 141
Peusner, Sir Nikolaus, 9
Pugin, 9, 35, 124
Pullman, George M., 51, 80, 81, 86, 158

Richardson, Henry Hobson, 30, 37, 39, 62, 88, 95, 98, 99, 105, 106, 114, 120, 122, 137, 145
    Glessner House, 99
    influence on Chicago architects, 98, 100, 105, 145
    Marshall Field Warehouse, 62, 87, 98, 99, 105, 106, 114, 120, 122, 137, 145
Rockefeller, 159
Root, John Wellborn, 2, 26, 38, 49, 65, 80, 81, 83, 91, 96, 121, 122-24, 125-26, 130-31, 141, 151, 167
    and clients, 83
    architect, 81, 83, 96, 121, 122, 128, 138
    as architectural critic, 26, 48, 65, 91, 123-24
    author, 166
    biography, 121, 122-23, 141
    Chicago School of Architecture, 2, 38, 98, 137, 138, 151
    organic-functional architectural metaphor, 124, 125-26
    partnership with Burnham, 123, 127, 130, 131
Ruskin, John, 9, 11, 12, 27, 29, 32, 35, 36, 37, 124
    architectural critic, 9, 11, 12, 27, 29, 37, 124
    Seven Lamps of Architecture, 11, 28, 36
    Stones of Venice, 11, 32, 36, 38

Saarinen, Eero, 160
Schmidt, Richard E., 165
    Montgomery Ward Warehouse, 165
Schuyler, Montgomery, 1, 2, 4, 7, 9, 26, 27, 28-31, 40, 41, 42, 61, 88, 98, 106-8, 112, 114, 115, 119, 120, 121, 122, 129, 134, 136, 140-41, 143, 144, 150, 151-53, 155-56, 167-68
    and World's Columbian Exposition, 152, 155
    architect, 9
    Architectural Record, 28, 29, 30, 40, 81
    biography, 28-31, 41

214   Index

critic, 1, 2, 4, 7, 8, 27, 28, 42, 61, 67, 88, 98, 106-8, 112, 114, 115, 119, 120, 121, 122, 129, 134, 136, 140-41, 143, 144, 150, 151-53, 155-56, 167-68
  Evolution of a Skyscraper, 1, 38
  influenced by Ruskin, 28, 29, 145
Scott, Geoffrey, 9
Sears Tower, 23, 47
Shaw, Theodore L., 25
  Hypocrisy About Art, 25
Shepley, Rutan and Coolidge, 159-60
  Art Institute, 159
  Public Library, 159
Skidmore, Owings and Merrill, 141
  Brunswick Building, 141
  John Hancock Center, 141
Skyscraper, 1-2, 22, 68, 93, 106, 110, 113, 117, 119, 130, 132, 144, 145, 154, 156, 158
  criticism of as office space, 22
  Evolution of a Skyscraper, 1
  Home Insurance Building, 68
Smith, William S., 75
Social function of architecture, 4-5, 10, 11, 12, 42
Stickley, Gustav, 150
  editor of *The Craftsman,* 150
Sturgis, Russell, 2, 7, 9, 26, 28, 29, 31-36, 40, 41, 55
  and *Architectural Record,* 29, 40
  architect, 9, 55
  biography, 31-36, 41
  critic, 2, 7, 9, 26, 28
  influenced by Ruskin, 28, 32, 35
Sullivan, Louis Henry, 2, 6, 9, 12, 26, 27, 28, 31, 63, 81, 88-91, 92-98, 111, 112, 114, 115, 116-18, 149, 155, 156, 157, 159, 165, 166
  AIA Gold medal, 97
  an analysis as architect, 157
  and Adler, 88, 97
  and World's Columbian Exposition, 145, 149, 150
  architect, 81, 93, 94, 156
  architectural critic, 27, 31, 87, 88, 89, 93, 149
  author, 166
  Autobiography of An Idea, 157, 159
  biography, 89-91, 92-93
  Carson Pirie Scott, 117, 119, 149, 154, 157, 165
  Chicago School of Architecture, 2, 9, 27, 28, 63, 113-14, 122, 147, 155-56
  disciples of, 165
  friends with Burnham, 157

form out of function, 6, 11, 94, 114-15, 155
Garrick Building, 111, 112
Guaranty Building, 95, 96, 113, 114, 115
influence of Richardson, 98-101
organic philosophy, 97, 155
Prudential Building, 96
relation to Chicago School, 157
social function, 6, 11
Tall Commercial, 95, 96, 113, 118, 119
Transportation Building, 95
Wainwright Building, 95, 97, 113-14, 115, 119
writings, 94-96, 150
Swift, 158

Upjohn, Richard, 55

Van der Rohe, Mies, 142
Van Brunt, Henry, 26, 135, 136, 151
  architectural critic, 26
Vaux, Calver, 56

The Western Architect, 149, 150
Wheelock, Otis, 80
Whitehouse, Francis, 80
Wight, Peter Bonnett, 8, 20, 26, 27, 29, 32, 34, 35, 40, 41, 42, 54, 80, 123, 127, 128, 133, 147, 151, 154, 156
  and World Columbian Exposition, 151, 153-54
  architect, 79, 80, 128
  architectural critic, 8, 20, 26, 27, 29, 32, 36, 38, 42, 54, 123, 133, 147, 151, 156
  Architectural Record, 40
  biography, 36-38
  influenced by Ruskin, 32, 36
Wilde, Oscar, 11
  The Critic as Artist, 11
World's Columbian Exposition, 35, 41, 48, 94, 95, 121, 129, 131, 145, 147, 149, 150-55, 158, 159, 160, 163, 164
Wright, Frank Lloyd, 7, 9, 26, 27, 91, 93, 95, 99, 122, 134, 135, 136, 149, 150, 156, 165
  architect, 7, 9, 93, 122, 134, 136, 156, 165
  architectural critic, 26, 89, 99
  author, 157
  influenced by Ruskin, 27
  Larkin Building, 149
  Midway Gardens, 149
  Prairie House, 149
  student of Sullivan, 95, 99